THE
BLACK
HAND

BOOKS BY STEPHAN TALTY

Nonfiction

Agent Garbo

Escape from the Land of Snows

The Illustrious Dead

Empire of Blue Water

Mulatto America

The Secret Agent

Fiction

Hangman

Black Irish

THE BLACK HAND

The gripping true story of
the origins of the mafia in America,
a deadly secret society and a detective
who gave his life to stop them

STEPHAN TALTY

EBURY
PRESS

1 3 5 7 9 10 8 6 4 2

Ebury Press, an imprint of Ebury Publishing
20 Vauxhall Bridge Road
London SW1V 2SA

Ebury Press is part of the Penguin Random House group of companies whose addresses
can be found at global.penguinrandomhouse.com

Penguin
Random House
UK

First published by Houghton Mifflin Harcourt in the United States in 2017
This edition published by Ebury Press in 2017

www.penguin.co.uk

A CIP catalogue record for this book is available from the British Library

ISBN 9781785037122

Printed and bound in Great Britain by Clays Ltd, St Ives PLC

MIX
Paper from
responsible sources
FSC® C018179

Penguin Random House is committed to a sustainable
future for our business, our readers and our planet.
This book is made from Forest Stewardship Council®
certified paper.

To the memory of my father,
the immigrant

CONTENTS

Prologue: "A Great and Consuming Terror"   xi

1. "This Capital of Half a World"   1

2. Hunter of Men   15

3. "In Mortal Dread"   29

4. The Mysterious Six   44

5. A General Rebellion   54

6. Explosion   67

7. Wave   80

8. The General   96

9. "The Terror of Hurtful People"   109

10. Once to Be Born, Once to Die   127

11. "War Without Quarter"   138

12. Backlash   150

13. A Secret Service   165

14. The Gentleman   178

15. In Sicily   189

16. Black Horses   201

17. Goatville   217

18. A Return   231

Acknowledgments   249

A Note on Sources   250

Notes   251

Select Bibliography   278

Index   281

Non so come si può vivere in questo fuoco!
(I don't know how it's possible to live in this fire!)

— AN ITALIAN IMMIGRANT ON FIRST
SEEING NEW YORK CITY

PROLOGUE:
"A GREAT AND CONSUMING TERROR"

O N THE AFTERNOON OF SEPTEMBER 21, 1906, A HIGH-SPIRITED boy named Willie Labarbera was playing in front of his family's fruit store, two blocks from the glint of the East River in New York City. Five-year-old Willie and his friends ran after one another shouting at the top of their lungs as they trundled hoops down the sidewalk, laughing when the wooden rings finally toppled onto the cobblestone street. They ducked behind the bankers and laborers and young women wearing ostrich feather hats, making their way home or to one of the neighborhood's Italian restaurants. With each wave of pedestrians, Willie and the other children would vanish from one another's sight for a second or two, then snap back into view once the walkers passed by. This happened dozens of times that afternoon.

More people passed, hundreds of them. Then, as the silvery river light began to dim, Willie turned and dashed down the street once more, disappearing behind yet another group of workmen. But this time, after the pedestrians had strolled past, he failed to reappear. The spot on the pavement where he should have stood was empty in the fading sunlight.

His friends didn't notice right away. Only when they felt the first pangs of hunger did they slowly turn and examine the small expanse of sidewalk where they'd spent their afternoon. Then they began to look for Willie more earnestly in the lengthening shadows. Nothing.

Willie was headstrong and once boasted that he'd run away from his parents as a lark, so perhaps the other boys hesitated a few moments before entering the store and reporting that something was wrong. But eventually they had to let the adults know, and so they went inside. After a few seconds, the boy's parents, William and Caterina, dashed from the shop and began searching the surrounding streets for some sign of the child, calling out to ask the proprietors of candy stands and small grocery stores if they'd seen the boy. They hadn't. Willie was gone.

It was at this moment that something odd and almost telepathic occurred. Even before the police had been called or a single clue was gathered, Willie's family and friends simultaneously arrived at a revelation about what had happened to the boy, without speaking a single word to one another. And strangely enough, people in Chicago or St. Louis or New Orleans or Pittsburgh or the tiny unheralded towns strung between them, the mothers and fathers of missing children, of whom there were more than usual in the fall of 1906, would have come to the same conclusion. Who had their child? *La Mano Nera*, as the Italians called it. The Society of the Black Hand.

The Black Hand was an infamous crime organization — "that fiendish, devilish and sinister band" — that engaged in extortion, assassination, child kidnapping, and bombings on a grand scale. It had become nationally famous two years before with a letter dropped into a mailbox in an obscure neighborhood in Brooklyn, at the home of a contractor who'd struck it rich in America. Since then, the Society's threatening notes, adorned with drawings of coffins and crosses and daggers, had appeared in every part of the city, followed by a series of gruesome acts that created, according to one observer, "a record of crime here during the last ten years that is unparalleled in the history of a civilized country in time of peace." Only the Ku Klux Klan would surpass the Black Hand for the production of mass terror in the early part of the century. "From the bottom of their hearts," one reporter said of Italian immigrants, "they do fear them with a great and consuming terror." The same could have been said for many Americans in the fall of 1906.

When the letters began arriving for the Labarberas several days later, their fears proved correct. The kidnappers demanded $5,000 for Willie's return, an astronomical sum to the family. The exact words the criminals used haven't been passed down, but such letters often contained phrases like "Your son is among us" and "Do not give this letter to the police for if you do, by the Madonna, your child will be killed." The message was reinforced by drawings at the bottom of the page: three crude black crosses had been inked onto the paper, along with a skull and crossbones. These were the marks of the Black Hand.

Some claimed that the group and others like it not only were creating an entirely new level of murder and extortion in America, a dark age of spectacular violence, but also were at that moment acting as a fifth column, corrupting the government to their aims. This idea had plagued the new immigrants from Italy for at least a decade. "There was a popular belief," said Massachusetts senator Henry Cabot Lodge about a supposed Italian secret society, "that it was extending its operations, that it was controlling juries by terror, and that it would gradually bring the government of the city and State under its control." Skeptics, including the Italian ambassador, who bristled at the mere mention of the Society, countered that the group didn't exist, that it was a myth created by Americans to curse Italians, whom the "whites" hated and wished to drive from their shores. One Italian wit said about the Society, "Its sole existence is, in fact, confined to a literary phrase."

But if the Society was a fiction, then who had Willie?

The Labarberas reported the kidnapping to the police, and soon a detective knocked on their door at 837 Second Avenue. Joseph Petrosino was the head of the famous Italian Squad, a short, stout, barrel-chested man, built like a stevedore. His eyes — which some described as dark gray, others as coal-black — were cool and appraising. He had broad shoulders and "muscles like steel cords." But he wasn't a brute; in fact, far from it. He was fond of discussing aesthetics, loved opera, especially the Italian composers, and played the violin well. "Joe Petrosino," said the *New York Sun,* "could make a fiddle talk." But his true vocation was solving crimes. Petrosino was "the greatest Italian detective in the world," declared the *New York Times,* the "Italian Sherlock Holmes," according to popular legend back in the old country. At forty-six, he'd already had "a career as thrilling as any Javert in the mazes of the Paris underworld or of an inspector in Scotland Yard — a life as full of adventure and achievement as ever thrilled the imagination of Conan Doyle." He was shy with strangers, incorruptible, quiet-voiced, brave to an almost reckless degree, violent if provoked, and was so adept with disguises that his own friends often passed him by on the street when he was wearing one. He had only a sixth-grade education but possessed a photographic memory and could instantly recall the information printed on a piece of paper he'd glanced at years before. He had no wife or children; he'd dedicated his life to ridding America of the Society of the Black Hand, which he felt threatened the republic he loved. He hummed operettas as he walked.

Petrosino was dressed in his customary black suit, black shoes, and black derby hat when William Labarbera opened the door of his apartment and escorted him in. The father of the missing boy brought out the letters he'd received but could tell the detective little else about the case. The Black Hand was everywhere and nowhere; it was almost occult in its all-knowingness, and it was cruel. This both men knew. Petrosino could see that Willie's parents were "nearly crazed with grief."

The detective emerged back onto the streets and immediately went to work, pumping his informers and contacts for clues. He had a vast network of spies and informants — *nfami* — spread across the metropolis: bartenders, doctors, peddlers, lawyers, opera singers, street cleaners (known as "white wingers"), bankers, musicians, scar-faced Sicilian thugs. Willie's description soon appeared in many of the city's dozens of newspapers.

But no one had seen or heard from the boy. A fourth letter arrived, demanding the family sell their modest home to raise the ransom. The building was the Labarberas' only asset in America, something they'd spent their lives saving for. Selling it would doom the parents and their children to grinding poverty, a poverty they'd left the Mezzogiorno to escape. It would snuff out their American dream for at least a generation.

Somehow, the Society had anticipated the family's reaction. Included in the fourth letter was an incentive, perhaps directed at Mrs. Labarbera. When the paper was unfolded, something fell out and tumbled to the floor. A dark lock of Willie's hair.

· · ·

THE DAYS PASSED. NOTHING. THE BOY HAD BEEN ATOMIZED.

Then, in the third week, a tip from an *nfame*. This man had heard a curious story from Kenilworth, New Jersey. A woman had been out strolling in a working-class neighborhood when she passed a man carrying a large bundle. Just as the woman walked past, something inside the bundle had emitted a piercing cry. The man hurried into a nearby house, so crude and ramshackle that it was described as a "hut," and closed the door. But the woman, startled by what she'd heard, remained outside, watching the door intently. A few minutes later, the same man emerged from the house, still carrying the package—which was silent now—and placed it in a covered wagon. Then he drove away.

On hearing the story, Petrosino immediately hurried to the foot of West 23rd Street and stepped aboard one of the steamship ferries to New Jersey. As he watched the docks of the West Side recede, with the lamps that hung from peddlers' pushcarts glowing in the dusk like distant campfires, the detective leaned over the railing and listened to the waters of the Hudson *whoosh* and sigh against the ferry's prow. His mind was whirring with possibilities, names and faces of suspects, stored in his memory months and years earlier and now called to account. Perhaps he sipped a glass of buttermilk bought from one of the vendors (two cents for the unsterilized version, three cents for the sterilized). The trip would take about a quarter of an hour, so Petrosino had a few minutes to think.

The Black Hand was growing more daring and ruthless with every passing month. The scale of what was happening in New York was difficult to comprehend. In the Italian colonies, as the immigrant neighborhoods were known, the men patrolled in front of their homes with loaded shotguns; children were locked inside barricaded rooms, forbidden to go to school; buildings stood open to the weather, their fronts ripped off by bombs the organization had planted. Certain quarters of New York, one of the most prosperous and cosmopolitan cities in the world, were being bombarded as though the metropolis were under siege from a dreadnought anchored in Upper Bay. "The society of darkness" had killed dozens of men, mutilated and maimed others, and now held tens, perhaps hundreds, of thousands of citizens under its spell. The panic had grown to such proportions that a family had only to return home and spot a black hand imprinted on their door in coal dust — a sign that the Society had paid a visit — for them to hurriedly pack up their belongings and board the next ship back to Italy.

And it wasn't happening just in New York. As Petrosino had long predicted, the fear had spread from city to city, blazing across the country like a prairie fire. The Black Hand had materialized in Cleveland, Chicago, Los Angeles, Detroit, New Orleans, San Francisco, Newport, Boston, and in hundreds of smaller cities, midsized towns, mining camps, quarries, and company villages in between. It had murdered men and women in many of those places, blown up buildings, triggered lynching parties, and deepened the mistrust of Americans for their Italian neighbors. Countless Americans — not just Italian immigrants — were in the thrall of the Society, and more would soon fall victim: millionaires, judges, governors, mayors, Rockefellers, lawyers, members of the Chicago Cubs, sheriffs, district attorneys, society matrons, gangster kingpins. That January, members of Congress had been threatened by a series of Society letters, and although their story had a unique and rather bizarre ending, several of the representatives from various states had fallen victim to "nervous prostration" as a result.

There were towns in the coal belt of Pennsylvania that had been taken over by the Society as if by armed coup; its leaders held the power of life and death over their citizens. After a shocking Black Hand murder, the residents of Buckingham County would send a message to the Pennsylvania governor that resembled those from settlers in the early West surrounded by Apache: "Conditions here intolerable; a gang of assassins strongly entrenched three miles away; one citizen shot in back, others threatened; county authorities appear powerless." The petitioners asked for "detectives and bloodhounds." New laws were being written and passed to slow a wave of terror that seemed incapable of being stopped. The South was in revolt against Italian immigrants, largely because of the Society's outrages. President Teddy Roosevelt, a friend of Petrosino's from his days as New York police commissioner, was said to be closely following developments from the White House. Even the diminutive king of Italy, Victor Emmanuel III, had taken time away from the vast coin collection that obsessed him to write Petrosino about the issue, which was close to his heart, enclosing an expensive gold watch along with the letter. Citizens of nations from India to France and England were enthralled by this contest between the forces of civilization and those of anarchy, and perhaps touched with *Schadenfreude* at the difficulties the young upstart of a country was having with its dark-eyed immigrants.

Petrosino was well aware of this attention, with good reason. He wasn't just a salaried employee of the New York Police Department; he was famous, perhaps the most famous Italian American in the country. And with fame, at least in Petrosino's eyes, came responsibility. Along with a small vanguard of his compatriots — a lawyer, a district attorney, the founder of a fraternal society — the detective had set out to spark a movement that would lift Italians out of their precarious situation. They were accused of being a savage people unfit for American citizenship; Petrosino furiously disagreed. "The Italian has a natural love of liberty," he argued to the *New York Times*. "He has had to fight bitterly for enlightenment in his own country and what Italy is today has been attained by heroic struggling." But *his* struggle, to make Italians into full-fledged Americans, was faltering in the face of the ongoing war against the Society; even the *Times* had joined the calls for an end to immigration from southern Italy. How could you redeem your race when the "vampires" of the Black Hand were bombing, maiming, and killing their way across the entire country?

As Petrosino had learned, you couldn't. The struggles were too intimately connected. The writer H. P. Lovecraft would later provide an example of the animosity Americans felt toward the newcomers in a letter to a friend in which he described immigrants from Italy crowded into the Lower East Side as creatures who "could not by any stretch of the imagination be call'd human." Instead, "they were monstrous and nebulous adumbrations of the pithecanthropoid and amoebal; vaguely moulded from some stinking viscous slime of earth's corruption, and slithering and oozing in and on the filthy streets or in and out of doorways in a fashion suggestive of nothing but infesting worms or deep-sea unnamabilities."

If Petrosino had been winning the battle against the Black Hand, his crusade would have proceeded more smoothly. But 1906 had gone badly; blood, allies, and territory had been lost. The shadow of the Society now extended over the whole of Petrosino's adopted homeland, from the stone mansions of Long Island to the craggy inlets of Seattle. Petrosino was filled with foreboding.

But tonight he would put aside his worries. He needed to find Willie Labarbera.

Petrosino reached the far shore and disembarked. He hired a carriage, and the driver hissed at the horses and sped off toward Kenilworth, about twenty miles due west, with the detective aboard. The pier cleared of its passengers, and a horse cart filled with coal trundled aboard the ferry to supply its engine room with fresh fuel, then departed, after which the ferry pulled out for the return trip to Manhattan. The dock grew quiet. A few hours later, a carriage reappeared at the dock and Petrosino climbed out. He waited for the ferry to arrive, then stepped aboard. The vessel pulled away from the New Jersey pier and slipped across the dark, rippling water toward the gas lamps glittering in the low-slung city across the Hudson. He was alone. The boy had been nowhere to be found.

When Petrosino was worried over a particularly difficult case, it was his habit to take refuge in the operas of Verdi, his favorite composer. He'd pick up his violin and bow and play one song in particular, "Di Provenza il mar," Germont's aria from *La Traviata*. In it, a father consoles his son over the loss of his beloved by reminding the young man of his childhood home in Provence, its dazzling sun and sweet memories:

> *Oh, rammenta pur nel duol*
> *ch'ivi gioia a te brillò;*
> *e che pace colà sol*
> *su te splendere ancor può.*
>
> *(Oh, remember in your pain*
> *that joy shone on you,*
> *and that peace only there*
> *can yet glow upon you.)*

Sitting in his bachelor apartment, Petrosino would play the aria "incessantly," his powerful hands moving the bow slowly through the lyrical opening notes before progressing into the difficult portions. It's a lovely piece, but a mournful one; it expresses a longing for things that are past and will probably never return.

We can imagine that Petrosino's neighbors heard the aria many times that night.

THE
BLACK HAND

1

"THIS CAPITAL OF HALF A WORLD"

O N JANUARY 3, 1855, A DEAD MAN LAY ON AN EMBANKMENT OF THE Mississippi River not far from New Orleans as the water just a few feet from his out-flung hand rolled southward toward the Gulf of Mexico. Even from a distance, it would have become clear to any observer that the man's passing had been a violent one. His shirt was covered in blood and pierced at several points; he'd been stabbed over a dozen times. In addition, his throat was cut from ear to ear, and the blood from the wound was caking thickly in the heat. The man's name was Fransisco Domingo, and he was the first known victim of the Black Hand in America.

Joseph Petrosino wouldn't be born for another five years. The Society had preceded him to the continent by almost two decades.

Unlike Domingo, unlike the majority of his future enemies, Petrosino wasn't Sicilian. He came from the province of Salerno in the Campania region, near the front of the ankle in the boot of Italy. Giuseppe Michael Pasquale Petrosino was born in the village of Padula, home to a famous Carthusian monastery, on August 30, 1860. His father, Prospero, was a tailor, his mother, Maria, a housewife. It was a small family by Italian standards; Petrosino had one younger brother and one younger sister in the tailor's humble house, which was struck by twin tragedies when Giuseppe was young. His mother died during his boyhood—of what was never recorded—and Giuseppe came down with a case of small-pox, an often fatal illness, in the 1860s. He survived but bore the scars on his skin for the rest of his life.

The first crisis was likely the one that affected the young child most deeply. Petrosino never spoke of his mother—he rarely spoke of per-sonal matters at all—but he would become notorious for his silences, for an inwardness that many would remark upon and give their theories for: his lack of a good education and the difficulties of his job were two popular explanations. "He never smiled" was a stock description in the newspaper profiles that proliferated in the early 1900s as Petrosino rose to national fame. It was untrue. Petrosino was capable of strong emotion, of joy and tenderness as well as great rage; a few intimates even swore he could be persuaded to do impersonations at parties. But certainly the loss of his mother left a deep and mournful mark on his personality.

His boyhood years were formative ones for Italy. Giuseppe Garibaldi was leading the war to unify the states of the peninsula, including the Kingdom of the Two Sicilies and the Papal States, to create the modern nation of Italy. But poverty and misrule persisted, especially in the southern regions, and in 1873, when Petrosino was thirteen years old, his father decided to try his luck in America. Prospero bought tickets for the family on a steam-assisted sailing ship headed for New York City.

Thirteen is considered an important age in the Mezzogiorno: it marks the time when a boy leaves his childish cares behind and learns the shape of the world and how one is expected to act in it. It's widely considered to be the age when manhood begins. By that point Petrosino would have absorbed many of the rules of Italian life and honor, the most important being the *ordine della famiglia* (order of the family), the essential values and customs that dictated all behavior in the towns of southern Italy. One of the most important tenets of the *ordine* said that you never placed yourself before the family, never allowed your ambitions to overrule your duty. The harsh Mezzogiorno, where life was a battle, demanded obedience to your loved ones.

Twenty-five days later, the Petrosinos arrived in New York, part of an early wave of Italian migration made up mostly of skilled workers and the educated. They settled in Manhattan and Petrosino enrolled in public school, where he began to learn English. (As an Italian speaker, he would have been held back from his natural grade.) The age of mass Italian immigration to America hadn't yet begun. There were only 25,000 immigrants from the old country by 1875, and they'd assimilated into the fabric of cities like New York and Chicago with relative ease. It wasn't until the 1880s that huge numbers of desperately poor migrants from Italy would begin to pour into the Eastern Seaboard. This often caused simmering tensions with the native population. In 1888 a series of cartoons in a New Orleans newspaper ran under the title "Regarding the Italian Population." One panel depicted a cage crowded with Italians being lowered into a river. The caption read, "The Way to Dispose of Them." But even in 1873, the young Joseph met hatred in the streets of lower Manhattan.

Italians were moving into neighborhoods that had belonged to the Irish for at least two generations. The new arrivals, with the strange, flowing music of their language, their riotous festivals, their olive skin and bewildering foods, were outnumbered and bitterly despised. When an Italian family moved into a tenement, the Irish often moved out. At one flashpoint, policemen lined the streets every day as the last bell rang at the local school. When the Italian kids emerged from the front door, a howl rose up from the nearby tenements, echoing off the cobblestones as one Irish mother after another pulled up the sashes on their windows, leaned out, and shouted at their sons below to *"kill the dagos!"* The fair-skinned boys heard them, picked up rocks, and sent them spinning at the heads of the Italian boys and girls, who fled the school in packs. Small gangs charged at the dark-haired children and attempted to cut off the stragglers. If they cornered one, they beat him until his blood flowed. "It used to be simply bedlam," recalled one man who had endured the daily ritual when he was a boy.

Fearing shattered teeth and cracked bones, one group of Italian students turned to a newcomer who seemed to radiate strength. Young Joe Petrosino never avoided a battle with the Irish; in fact, he seemed to relish them. When the dismissal bell rang, Joe would lead his fellow immigrants out into the streets, his eyes alert for enemies. If an Irish kid managed to slip by a cop and aim a rock at one of the Italian children huddled behind him, Joe would turn and charge. He would begin by raining haymakers on the assailant's head and then attempt to crack the Irish boy's skull on the cobblestones. Petrosino often returned home with his shirt covered in blood. Over time, a small legend began to grow up around his name.

Despite his often brutal initiation into Manhattan life, Petrosino showed signs of being a typical American immigrant: he began looking for a way up. He and another Italian boy, Anthony Marria, opened a newspaper business and shoeshine stand directly in front of 300 Mulberry Street in what would soon be known as Little Italy. The building happened to be the headquarters of the New York Police Department, and while Petrosino hawked copies of the *World* and the *Herald,* he polished the shoes of the beat cops in their dark blue wool uniforms with shining gold buttons. Some of the officers treated the boys with kindness, but others called them "dago," "wop" (short for "without papers"), or "guinea," a particularly hated slur that linked the Italians directly to slavery, as the term originally referred to the people stolen from Guinea, on the west coast of Africa.

The abuse didn't deter the young teenager. "Petrosino was a big, strapping boy," his friend Anthony remembered, "and he was very ambitious." Most Italian kids abandoned their schooling early on and went to work in the garment sweatshops that sprang up all over Little Italy, or they picked rags or were apprenticed to junk dealers or pushcart men. Joe held on longer at school than most other immigrant boys while holding down what amounted to a full-time job shining shoes. But his education eventually lost out to his need for money. Petrosino quit his classes at Public School 24 at the corner of Bayard and Mulberry after the sixth grade.

With his school days over, Joe joined the thousands of other Italian boys, some of them barefoot even in the freezing New York winters, who swarmed the streets as bootblacks, crying out "Shine your shoes?" Once hired, Petrosino would throw down an old piece of carpet to cushion his knees and take a brush from his box, knocking away the muck from workingmen's brogans and the ankle-high lace-ups of the lawyers and journalists who clustered around police headquarters, before bringing the leather to a high shine with his cloth.

Bootblacks, who might make twenty-five cents a day, dwelled at the bottom of the economic ladder in 1870s Manhattan. The job introduced the young Italian to the raw side of New York capitalism — that is, to Tammany Hall. Under the Irish politicians who ruled the city, Italian bootblacks were forced to pay cash for the privilege of working a certain corner, and were even required to shine policemen's shoes for free, as a bonus. Any boy who rebelled invited a visit from a head-cracking son of Galway.

There was an urgency to Petrosino's drive; his father's tailoring business had failed, and the only other male in the family, Joe's younger brother, Vincenzo, had proved himself to be a complete no-account. "He was irresponsible," says their grandnephew Vincent Petrosino. "One profession after another. He never found his feet in America." In fact, Joe's entire family lacked his burning ambition; they were, according to grandnephew Vincent, "a bunch of bums" who soon began to depend on the teenager's earnings just to survive. Joe's father, Prospero, dreamt only of returning to Italy, buying a plot of land, and living out his last years amid the citrus groves of Campania. But Joseph was different. "He was bent, bound, and determined to make it in New York," remembered his friend Anthony Marria.

Along with determination and brute strength, Joe as a teenager began to display signs of what the Italians call *pazienza*. The literal translation is "patience," but the term had a special meaning in south-ern Italian culture. It meant to keep one's innermost feelings close, awaiting the proper time for their release. It was part of the masculine code of life in the Mezzogiorno, a defense against oppression and *mise-ria*. "*Pazienza* does not involve a repression of the forces of life," writes Richard Gambino. "The code of reserve, of patience, of waiting for the moment, of planning for the event, and then of decisive impassioned action, serves life . . . Impetuous, ill-controlled behavior meant disas-ter." One way to show *pazienza* was to remain cool, almost detached, until the need for action arose. Then, nothing less than violent passion was called for.

One day Anthony and Joseph were shining shoes in front of a saloon at the corner of Broome and Crosby streets. Petrosino knelt on his old carpet, buffed the leather boots of a customer, then stood up to collect his pennies. Part of his earnings would go toward paying his family's rent, another for their food, coal, and clothing. This left little, if anything, for himself and his dreams of breaking out of the Italian colony.

That afternoon, something in Petrosino rebelled. As Anthony watched in astonishment, Joseph picked his heavy shoeshine box off the pavement, hoisted it over his head, his thick arms bulging with the effort, then brought the box down and smashed it onto the sidewalk. The box cracked apart and split into pieces. Anthony stared up at his partner as passersby stepped around the shards of wood and walked on. "Tony," Petrosino told him calmly, "I won't shine shoes anymore. I'm going to be somebody."

The story is so iconic in its Americanness that one suspects Anthony lifted it from a Horatio Alger novel, which often featured starry-eyed bootblacks. But Anthony swore it really happened. Young Joe had drunk deeply of the American ideal. With his box broken beyond repair, Petrosino had to find another way to make a living. He never shined another shoe, in New York or elsewhere, again.

His outburst told Anthony something. Behind his friend's quiet exterior, strong emotions churned.

• • •

PETROSINO WENT LOOKING FOR A BETTER JOB, ROAMING ALL OVER Manhattan inquiring in stores and shops. He tried a succession of tasks: butcher's assistant, railroad crew timekeeper, hat store associate, stockbrokerage runner. He even toured the country as an itinerant musician, playing his violin as far away as the Deep South before returning to Manhattan. But none of the assignments offered Petrosino a way up and out of the humiliating poverty he saw all around him.

Finally, when he was seventeen or eighteen, Petrosino landed a position as a "white winger," or street cleaner, for the City of New York. It didn't sound like much of an advancement, but at the time, the city's sanitation department was run by the New York Police Department. For the right kind of immigrant, it could be a stepping-stone to greater things.

Petrosino had the good fortune to come under the protection of the tough and fabulously corrupt inspector Aleck "Clubber" Williams, known as the "Tsar of the Tenderloin." Williams was Irish to the marrow, gregarious and physically intimidating, a figure instantly recognizable to New Yorkers as he strode down Seventh Avenue, patrolling his precinct. (And it was very much *his* precinct: no saloon could operate, and no criminal could long survive, without Williams's permission.) "I am so well known here in New York," he once boasted, "that car horses nod to me mornings." One day, wanting to impress some newspapermen who'd come to interview him, he hung his watch and chain on a lamppost at 35th Street and Third Avenue, in the heart of the wild, crime-ridden Gas House district, then took a leisurely stroll around the block with the reporters. When the group returned to the lamppost, Williams's watch was still hanging where he'd left it. None of the hundreds of gangsters who populated the neighborhood had dared to touch his valuables.

Williams's talent for corruption was another envy of the department. He owned a sprawling seventeen-room mansion in Cos Cob, Connecticut, and a fifty-three-foot yacht, all ostensibly on the modest salary of an NYPD inspector. When asked how he'd come by his fortune, he had a splendidly nonsensical answer: "Japanese real estate."

In his new position, Petrosino worked hard. New York was infamous for its grime; the city was far dirtier than London or Paris. It was Petrosino's job to push his three-wheeled cart through the streets and sweep the cobblestones clean of the incredible array of filth that had collected there overnight. Horse manure was a particular challenge. The 150,000 horses living and working in New York and Brooklyn (an independent city until 1898) produced 3 to 4 million pounds of manure each and every day, and the animals themselves lasted only an average of two and a half years before dropping dead from overwork. The carcasses weighed over a thousand pounds, too heavy for the white wingers to lift, so they had to wait until the corpses had partially decomposed before they could hoist the various body parts onto their carts. Petrosino spent his days sweeping up heaping piles of ash, fruit rinds, newspapers, and broken furniture, as well as dead pigs, goats, and horses.

He advanced. Petrosino was soon commanding the scow that towed the city's garbage far out into the Atlantic, where he would dump the malodorous stuff among the breakers. Every day, Petrosino would steer the scow into the waves, the water smacking the front of the vessel and sending bursts of salt spray back over the pilothouse. If he looked to his left or right, he might have caught a glimpse of the trim runabouts commanded by rich Madison Avenue swells as they swept by him. Perhaps he was even passed by the robber baron Jay Gould as he commuted from his home in Tarrytown in his magnificent 230-foot yacht, the *Atalanta,* the "most magnificent private craft afloat," whose interiors were decorated as sumptuously as any rajah's palace. A man less secure in himself might have felt a bit ridiculous in the company of these glamorous ships, commanding a vessel filled to the gunwales with rotting horse heads and banana peels. A sparkling dream ship for the son of Campania! But Petrosino was undeterred. He never lacked for confidence.

As the young Italian advanced, the city around him was growing higher, brighter, and faster. The first elevated subway had opened along Ninth Avenue in 1868. Electric light began to replace the old gas lanterns in 1880; steam heat pulsed out from underground mains beginning in 1882; the Brooklyn Bridge, completed in 1883, stretched its gorgeous and improbable frame across the East River. The country was hungry for new labor; its industries were growing at a rapid clip, and they needed strong backs to mine, quarry, forge, build, and dig. New York was at the center of this transformation. Eighty of the nation's one hundred largest companies had their headquarters in Manhattan. "Wall Street supplied the country with capital," wrote the historian Mike Dash. "Ellis Island channeled its labor. Fifth Avenue set its social trends. Broadway (along with Times Square and Coney Island) entertained it." Every four years, the city added to its numbers the equivalent of the population of Boston; it was already the largest Jewish city and the largest Italian city in the world. (One writer fondly called Manhattan "this capital of half a world.") And many of its new citizens were newcomers from southern Italy, *contadini,* poor peasants of the Mezzogiorno. The number of Italians living in the city swelled from 833 individuals in 1850 to half a million by 1910.

For many Americans, the swarming mobs, the dark faces and unfamiliar languages, were a sign not of progress but of anarchy. Henry Adams was one:

> The outline of the city became frantic in its effort to explain something that defied meaning. Power seemed to have outgrown its servitude and to have asserted its freedom. The cylinder had exploded, and thrown great masses of stone and steam against the sky. The city had the air and movement of hysteria, and the citizens were crying, in every accent of anger and alarm, that the new forces must at any cost be brought under control. Prosperity never before imagined, power

never yet wielded by man, speed never reached by anything but a meteor, had made the world irritable, nervous, querulous, unreasonable, and afraid . . .

A traveller in the highways of history looked out of the club window on the turmoil of Fifth Avenue, and felt himself in Rome, under Diocletian, witnessing the anarchy, conscious of the compulsion, eager for the solution, but unable to conceive whence the next impulse was to come or how it was to act.

But to others, the changes were an opportunity to make money and secure their hold on power. Tammany Hall, which was reaping millions from the new wealth pouring into Manhattan, took notice of the immigrants who were blasting out the subway tunnels and manning the garment factories. The Irish needed men who could make their way among the Sicilians and Calabrians and bring them to the polls on election day. So when Clubber Williams saw a scow maneuvering gracefully along the waterfront, with a young Italian calling orders in a commanding voice, he paid attention. There was something in Petrosino's manner —a calmness across his brow—that drew the inspector's eye.

Williams called out across the waves, "Why don't you join the police force?" Petrosino eyed the inspector, steered the vessel to shore, hopped out, and walked over. Williams could immediately see there was a problem. At five feet three inches, the young Italian was too short to qualify as a police recruit; the minimum standard was four inches taller. But the Irish cop had solved far thornier problems than a lack of height, and he began lobbying to get Petrosino on the force. Soon after, on October 19, 1883, the twenty-three-year-old was sworn in as a policeman.

It was a coup for the former bootblack. Petrosino became one of the first Italian policemen hired by the NYPD, which in 1883 was an overwhelmingly Irish force, filled out with a sprinkling of German and Jewish cops. His hiring was also a milestone for Italian Americans, who'd managed to gain only tiny footholds in the power structure of their new country. But if Petrosino thought his breakthrough would be hailed among his own people, if he thought shield number 285 would earn him the cheers of Neapolitans and Sicilians out on Mulberry Street, he was to be deeply disappointed. On his first day on the job, the new policeman walked out of the building in Little Italy where he rented an apartment, dressed in his woolen blues and a domed felt helmet, a locust-wood nightstick slotted into a leather loop at his side. The new clothes were the outward signs of his reinvention as an American. From his first steps, Italians began calling out to him — not words of congratulation, however, but "insults and obscenities." Street peddlers, when they saw him coming, yelled, "Fresh parsley for sale!" (in Sicilian dialect, *petrosino* means "parsley"), warning the neighborhood criminals that a cop was approaching. Not long after, Petrosino received his first death threats in the mail.

In the sun-withered places that southern Italians came from, as Petrosino surely knew, any man wearing a uniform was considered an enemy. "The government is a huge personified monster," wrote an official in the Sicilian town of Partinico in 1885, "from the office servant all the way up to that privileged being who calls himself King. It desires everything, steals undisguisedly, disposes over property and person for the benefit of a few because it is supported by henchmen and bayonets." Even the church despised the people who enforced the law. In the *Taxae cancellariae et poenitentiarieae romanae,* published between 1477 and 1533, the archbishop of Palermo absolved those who perjured themselves in court, including those who bribed judges or obstructed justice in other ways, provided the defendant went free. In the church's view, criminals could redeem themselves by paying alms to their local parish; they were even allowed, under this special interpretation of church law, to keep the stolen goods. But the *birro,* the policeman? He was a rotting piece of carrion.

In an Irish or a German neighborhood, a newly minted cop was often a cause for celebration, but this wasn't the case in Little Italy. Petrosino, many believed, had joined the oppressors in the new land. He "was *contadino*-born," one Sicilian American said later. To join up with the foreigners and volunteer to police your own kind was "an extreme and deliberate affront" that wasn't easily forgotten. "Petrosino's behavior constituted a very offensive immorality, nothing less than an *infamia* that demanded punishment. As [Sicilians] saw it, Petrosino [had] violated a kind of extended *ordine della famiglia* by publicly taking the side of strangers against his own kind and thus advancing his own individual position in life." In the minds of some southern Italians, Petrosino had sold his honor to the whites.

If Italians had entered America as the last and poorest of the western Europeans, they didn't lack confidence in or love for their homeland. In many ways, they believed that the culture they carried in their blood was superior to that of the Americans. It was the duty of every Italian to honor it.

But Petrosino had completed a voyage that many southern Italians found difficult to make: he'd wholeheartedly embraced the promise of his new country. He'd accepted its values as his values. The looks of hatred from his own must have been a shock. To be called an *nfame,* an informant and a spy, on the streets of Little Italy would forever remain painful to him. "Parsley will make the American police taste better" went one witticism about the new cop, "but indigestible it will always be."

There were many Italians who felt differently, who knew that Italian policemen were badly needed in the colony and were proud of Petrosino's achievement. But others sent him a constant stream of menacing letters, letters that became so alarming Petrosino was forced to look for another place to live. He found a small apartment in an Irish neighborhood and moved his meager possessions there. In Italian American culture, it was almost unthinkable for a single man to leave the colony and live alone among foreign people. It marked Petrosino as a *straniero,* a foreigner, living among the pale and inscrutable Irish. To be alone without one's family was to almost cease to exist, to become what the Sicilians called *un saccu vacante* (an empty sack), *un nùddu miscàto cu nènti* (a nobody mixed with nothing). But early in his career, Petrosino signaled his willingness to break with the traditions that had ruled life in the Mezzogiorno for centuries. In order to rise, he would leave.

. . .

FOR HIS FIRST ASSIGNMENT, PETROSINO WAS SENT TO THE Tenderloin, between 23rd and 42nd streets, from Fifth to Seventh avenues, the most fractious precinct in the city. His first arrest to make the *New York Times* was of an overzealous actor who'd been so eager to practice his craft that he'd broken the ban on Sunday theatricals. As he gained more experience, he was assigned to other beats as well. One evening he'd ventured as far as the piers at the foot of Canal Street, a festering hellhole filled with sailors' bars and bordellos. As he strode along at his usual energetic pace, Petrosino heard urgent cries. Ahead of him he spotted a commotion. A group of white men were bent over a figure on the pavement, viciously attacking a black man named William Farraday.

The reputation of African Americans among the officers of the NYPD wasn't a favorable one. Many cops were thoroughgoing racists. Even the man who would soon be police commissioner expressed a low opinion of the city's black citizens. "The Tenderloin Negro," said William McAdoo, "is an overdressed, bejeweled loafer and in many instances a general criminal." But, hearing Farraday's cries, Officer Petrosino didn't hesitate. He dashed forward, pulling his club from its leather ring as he ran and, on coming up on the scrum, slammed the locust-wood stick into the head of the first white man he encountered. After a few more blows, the attackers ran off. "Four men were trying to kill me," recalled Farraday. "Joe came along and saved me in the nick of time." Farraday would remember the incident for the rest of his life.

Petrosino proved to be a natural policeman. He was a wizard at languages: he'd mastered not only the regional dialect of his native Campania but also most of the regional tongues spoken by New York's Italians: Abruzzese, Neapolitan, Sicilian, and Pugliese. He was incorruptible: not once would he even be accused of taking a bribe. And he was exceptionally tough. If he lost a single street fight in his long career, no one ever reported it. But his excellence went mostly unnoticed in the early years of his career. Petrosino had joined an Irish fraternity composed of the same kind of men who had tried to separate his head from his neck in street brawls when he was a schoolboy. There was little hope of advancement for an Italian in the New York City police department. Only the Irish and the Germans seemed to be chosen for the homicide unit or the detective bureau, considered the elites of the department. There wasn't a single Italian detective sergeant in the entire department in the late 1800s — in the entire *country*, for that matter. The Irish looked at a spot within the NYPD as their birthright; veteran cops often gave their young sons toy nightsticks as birthday gifts, to tide them over until they were old enough to join the department. Wrote one Irishman: "You couldn't walk two city blocks without running into a bluecoat named O'Brien, Sullivan, Byrnes, O'Reilly, Murphy, or McDermott . . . Deep down my father's desire to make me a policeman was ruled by the Irish blood in his veins, even when I lay in my cradle."

Even with a mentor like Clubber Williams, Petrosino was an outsider. The police reserve stations where he often slept that first winter, his uniform steaming on a line hung against one wall and a potbellied stove blazing in the center of the room, were cold places for any son of Italy, where Irish cops regarded him with disgust or thinly veiled hatred. Some refused to speak to him or, when they did, addressed him as "guinea" to his face. "Every hand in the department was turned against him," a journalist wrote about this time in Petrosino's life. "Silently, and with dignity, he withstood the taunts, slurs, and insults that were heaped upon him by those of different nationalities." As the rate of Italian immigration increased year by year, and prejudice bubbled up from the streets, silence was expected of any immigrant wishing "to be somebody." But it wasn't the full price, as Petrosino would soon learn.

2

HUNTER OF MEN

In the early days of 1895, teddy roosevelt, at loose ends after his wife forbade him to run for mayor of New York City, was ensconced at his Sagamore Hill estate in Cove Neck, Long Island. He was depressed and tetchy, feeling he'd missed "the one golden chance which never returns." One afternoon, he opened a book of photographs by the social reformer Jacob Riis. *How the Other Half Lives: Studies Among the Tenements of New York* exposed the desperation that had sprung up in the shadows of the new Manhattan: poverty, hopelessness, and alcoholism were Riis's subjects. The new technology of flash photography enabled him to go inside tenements on Mulberry Street and other areas of lower Manhattan and bring back images of barefoot children sleeping on grates and men and women packed into tiny rooms like grimy rabbits.

The photos shocked Roosevelt, as they did many upper-class New

Yorkers, who rarely set foot below 14th Street, the dividing line between modernizing New York and the world of the immigrants. Teddy sprang into action. "No man ever helped as he did," Riis remembered. "For two years, we were brothers in Mulberry Street." Roosevelt became head of the New York Board of Police Commissioners and threw himself into reforming the NYPD, which was notorious for its corruption. "Sing, heavenly muse, the sad dejection of our policemen," crowed the *New York World,* the flagship of Joseph Pulitzer's newspaper empire. "We have a real police commissioner. His name is Theodore Roosevelt . . . His teeth are very white and almost as big as a colt's. They seem to say, 'Tell the truth to your commissioner, or he'll bite your head off!'" Roosevelt hired cops on the basis of ability instead of party affiliation, installed phones in precinct station houses, ordered yearly physical exams and firearm inspections, and walked from precinct to precinct making sure his men were taking their duties seriously. Detectives were reassigned and even fired. Positions opened up, and Roosevelt, who knew that the immigrant colonies needed to be policed, went looking for an Italian to champion. He found Joseph Petrosino. On July 20, 1895, after only two years on the job, he became the first Italian detective sergeant in the nation.

Meeting T.R. was like being touched on the shoulder by a prince of the blood. The two men, so similar in their bulldog tenacity, became friends of a sort. "He didn't know the name of fear," Roosevelt would later say about Petrosino, in words that could have described his own character. For his part, Petrosino quickly grasped how important a patron like Roosevelt could be to his career. He praised the commissioner to reporters and fellow cops every chance he got.

In his new role as a detective, Petrosino blossomed; he barely seemed to sleep. He innovated. He used disguises in ways that other detectives scoffed at. It was said that the closet at his bachelor apartment looked like something from the backstage warrens of the Metropolitan Opera. His dizzying array of costumes could transform him into any one of a dozen identities: a dollar-a-day laborer, a gangster, an Orthodox Jew, a blind beggar, a Board of Health bureaucrat, a Catholic priest. Petrosino would walk into the apartment as himself and leave as someone else. He would don torn work clothes, carry a pickaxe, and get a job working the streets, where he looked like every other Sicilian workman. He'd return to headquarters after weeks on these undercover assignments with his hands covered with calluses — Petrosino didn't portray a laborer, he *became* one — and his notebook would be full of new leads. He even inhabited the ultimate Italian stereotype: the organ grinder with his monkey.

Even though his education had ended in the sixth grade, the young detective was hungry for knowledge. "It was one of his chief pleasures to discuss aesthetic subjects with intellectual men," wrote one journalist. "He was sensitive and emotional. He loved friendships, too, and social pleasures." He could *look* stupid, but only because it served his work. He'd learned to imitate the stock *grignono,* or greenhorn, who'd just arrived on a steamship from Genoa. It was something Petrosino actually practiced. "He is a master in the art of feigning a timid naiveté," said one Italian writer. "But more than one robber and killer have learned to their cost how quick is his mind and how nimble is his arm." It was, in a way, a commentary on the low esteem in which most Americans held Italians: What better way to become invisible than to slip behind the mask of the dumb guinea? More than one Irish cop passed by the detective in disguise and never even noticed.

In his new position, Petrosino's brilliance shone. Instead of using files, as was customary among detectives, he carried his cases "in his hat"; that is, he memorized every detail, along with the names of thousands of Italian criminals, their faces, vital statistics, regional background, habits, and the crimes they were charged with. One evening he was climbing the stairs to see some friends who lived on the top floor of a building at 2428 First Avenue. As Petrosino ascended, he glanced to his right into the open doorway of an apartment where a man sat at a kitchen table. Petrosino climbed a few more stairs, stopped, stood still for a moment, then reversed course. He turned at the open door and walked toward the man, telling him to stand up, then informed him that his name was Sineni, that he'd been accused of killing Oscar

Quarnstrom with a razor four years before in Chicago, and that he was wanted by the police for capital murder. Forty-eight months before, Petrosino had glanced briefly at a circular sent by the Chicago police, and something in this man's face — seen for a split second — had chimed with that memory. Sineni confessed and was sent to Chicago to be prosecuted.

Petrosino was soon outpacing his peers. He tracked and broke up the "resurrection insurance" ring, whose members were buying policies, getting themselves pronounced dead, and then living off the proceeds. He uncovered a scheme in which innocent Italians were being murdered by gangsters who pretended to have known them in the old country, then took out insurance policies in their victims' names before administering a lethal dose of poison. In one year Petrosino won seventeen murder convictions, an NYPD record; by the end of his career, he would send one hundred killers to the electric chair or to long terms at Sing Sing.

Manhattanites, not just Italians, began to talk about this new whirling dervish of a detective. Petrosino became so famous that criminals arriving from southern Italy asked to be taken to see him. They would gather across the street from 300 Mulberry, watching in silence as blue-coats and detectives in overcoats emerged and congregated on the steps or headed off to their assignment. The criminals would sometimes wait hours, until a friend leaned over and said, "It's him." There was Petrosino, bull-necked, dark-eyed, dressed all in black, with his distinctive derby hat. They would memorize the lines of his face, his height (he sometimes wore lifts to alter how tall he looked), his striding gait. There was a practical reason for this inspection: the men wanted to know what Petrosino looked like so they could avoid him during their criminal activities. But they were also, surely, a bit starstruck. *An Italian by birth who knows Teddy Roosevelt!* They were thieves and killers, yes, but they were immigrants, too. "Petrosino seemed to epitomize the American success story," wrote crime historian Humbert Nelli, "for many within and outside the Italian colony."

Some of these men would become the early members of the Society of the Black Hand, which was, in the last days of the century, beginning to spread like typhus in the tenement hallways of Mulberry Street.

It's telling that the most famous Italian American in the country in the late 1800s was the one deputized by the powerful to track down and imprison his fellow countrymen. There were artists and intellectuals among the migrants from the Old World — classics professors, writers, opera singers, stonemasons who created great civic artworks — but the country largely ignored them. It was Petrosino, the "hunter of men," who fascinated the old American stock of Knickerbockers and WASPs, and they embraced him like no other Italian American of his time. It was as if the nation's idea of the Italian was so narrow and constricted that it could take in only two figures among the thousands entering through the gates of Ellis Island: the killer, who terrified Americans, and his opposite. The lawman. The savior.

• • •

THERE WAS A SPECIFIC QUALITY THAT EXPLAINED WHY THE DETEC-tive was respected, even idolized, on Mott Street, at least by those who didn't loathe him. It was amply demonstrated in the Angelo Carbone affair.

The young Italian was drinking at a café called the Trinarcia one night in 1897 when he got into an argument with a forty-two-year-old man named Natale Brogno. During the scuffle, Brogno ended up with a knife in his back. Carbone swore he was innocent, but after an eight-hour trial (one of the fastest in New York history up to that time), a Manhattan jury convicted him of murder. The Irish judge, who also happened to be the Grand Sachem of Tammany Hall, sentenced Carbone to death, telling him that the conviction was a warning to all Italians, "who were too prone to commit crimes of that sort." The bewildered defendant was asked if he had anything to say. "Your honor," Carbone said, "why should I, who am innocent, be obliged to die as an example to others?" The young man was taken to Sing Sing to await his date with Old Sparky, the wooden electric chair built by a dentist who'd received his inspiration from the account of a drunkard electrocuted after touching a power line.

Petrosino wasn't involved in the case, but soon after the conviction he began to hear whispers on Mott Street that Carbone was a hard-working man, respectful, different from the *marmaglia,* or riffraff, who were usually involved in stabbings. Evidence pointed toward another man. There was no particular reason for Petrosino to care about Angelo Carbone; there had been no outcry in the press, no calls for a retrial, and the NYPD was confident it had the right man. Reopening the case would stir up resentment among his fellow cops. Still, Carbone's story nagged at the detective throughout the last days of 1897. Finally, he decided to take a look at it.

The detective took the train upstate to Sing Sing (the notorious prison that got its name from a local Native American tribe, the Sinck Sinck, meaning "stone upon stone"), on the east bank of the Hudson River, thirty miles north of the city. He entered the prison, carved out of native gray marble and watched over by armed sharpshooters who studied the yard from their conical watchtowers. Guards ushered Petrosino to the Death House, where the condemned men were kept, then to Carbone's damp and freezing three-foot-by-eight-foot cell. There the inmate told the detective the whole story in Italian. *"Io non l'ho ucciso,"* he said at the end. "I didn't kill him." Petrosino agreed to investigate the murder.

The detective first looked into the life of the victim, Brogno, and found he'd had several known enemies. One in particular stood out: Salvatore Ceramello, sixty-two, who had a record of violence and had been in the café the night Brogno died. One fact Petrosino found especially interesting: Ceramello had disappeared the day after the murder and hadn't been seen in Little Italy since.

Petrosino set out to locate Ceramello, chasing leads first to Jersey City and Philadelphia. Finding nothing, he went farther, to the Italian neighborhoods of Montreal, where his search again came up empty. The detective then boarded a ship for Nova Scotia. In his suitcase he carried a variety of disguises that he alternated regularly: laborer, health worker, businessman. The Nova Scotia lead, however, turned out to be yet another dead end. Ceramello was nowhere to be found. Discouraged, Petrosino returned to New York and began pressing his *nfami* for new intelligence. Carbone's date with the electric chair, when he would be brought to the death chamber by seven guards and a chaplain at the traditional time of eleven o'clock on a Thursday night, was drawing closer.

Several days after his return, Petrosino received a tip that Ceramello was living in a house in the Baltimore suburbs. Petrosino immediately boarded a train south and made his way to the street where Ceramello had been spotted. He set up surveillance in the neighborhood, watching the house day and night. He observed men and women entering and leaving the residence, but no one who fit Ceramello's description.

Time was running out. Petrosino had to get back to his caseload in Manhattan, and, more pressing still, Carbone's execution was now only a few days away. The detective couldn't wait any longer.

Donning a fake beard, Petrosino knocked on the door of the house. A woman answered and peered at Petrosino, clearly suspicious. "I'm from the Board of Health," the detective informed her. "I was told there was a case of smallpox here." The woman took this in. Suddenly, she grabbed the door and tried to slam it in Petrosino's face. He stepped forward and shoved the door roughly before she could close it. The woman stumbled back, cursing Petrosino as he entered the apartment. The detective turned to study the room he found himself in, and his gaze fell on an old man who was sitting in a chair, holding an axe in his hand. The man had been cutting lengths of firewood so they would fit into the stove. Petrosino asked him his name.

"My name is Fioni."

Petrosino shook his head. "You mean your name is Ceramello."

The old man stared at this stranger and asked who he was.

The detective replied, "My name is Petrosino."

Ceramello was armed. But at the sound of the detective's name, the life seemed to go out of him. He gave up without a fight. Petrosino led the man out of the house, and the two headed to the nearest telegraph office. Minutes later, a dispatch arrived at 300 Mulberry: "BALTIMORE — ALLESANDRO CIAROMELLO ARRESTED. GOT FULL CONFESSION. HAVE THE KNIFE WITH WHICH HE KILLED NATTALI BROGNO. COMING TODAY. PETROSINO."

That evening, Angelo Carbone was sitting in his cell at Sing Sing when a guard approached and slipped a piece of paper through the bars. The prisoner unfolded it. A telegram. Carbone looked at it blankly; the message was in English, which he couldn't read. A translator was called in, and he told Carbone that the telegram was from his brother Nicolo. "Be at ease," the interpreter read. "Ciaramello has been arrested." Carbone stood in stunned silence, then broke into tears and cried out, "I'm saved!"

Less than a week before his scheduled execution, Angelo Carbone walked out of Sing Sing a free man and into the arms of his family. Ceramello took his place on Death Row and was eventually executed.

Carbone never fully enjoyed his miraculous freedom. In the months after his release, he began to behave erratically and showed signs of extreme nervousness. Exactly what he did or said was never recorded, but it was disturbing enough for his family to take him to be examined by a series of doctors, who eventually came up with a diagnosis of insanity. Carbone had become obsessed with the idea that he would be taken back to Sing Sing and die in the electric chair. The thought had unbalanced his mind.

Many Italians sympathized with Carbone's fear. Uncounted Italian men languished in New York prisons, convicted because they'd happened to be near the scene of a crime or because they were considered violent by their very nature. "In every crime, of whatever kind," wrote Arthur Train, who worked in the New York D.A.'s office, the public judged Italians "capable of nothing but acts of brigandage."

To be Italian in America was to be half-guilty.

This was the secret reason why Petrosino was beloved in the colony. In the absence of Italian elected officials, he was a brother, a shield. If he believed you to be guilty, he would pursue you to the very ends of the earth. If he thought you were innocent, he wouldn't rest until you were free.

• • •

THE DETECTIVE BEGAN TO MAKE FRIENDS AMONG THE POWERFUL: prosecutors, defense lawyers, judges, and journalists. These men found that underneath Petrosino's stern exterior lay a vein of sociability, like a spring bubbling beneath a hard limestone landscape. "Petrosino was no nervous temperamental Latin," wrote a journalist for the *Evening World*. "He was a sympathetic friend, a gay entertainer with songs, stories and imitations." One Harvard-educated blueblood invited Petrosino over to talk about a case he was going to prosecute the next day, a murder in the Bronx's Van Cortland Park that Petrosino had solved in brilliant fashion. It was a business invitation of sorts, but it turned into something else entirely: "the most thrilling evening of my life," recalled the prosecutor. Petrosino sat bolt upright in an armchair, "his great, ugly moon-face expressionless save for an occasional flash from his black eyes," the prosecutor and his wife listening next to a crackling fire as Petrosino unspooled his narrative. "So vivid was Petrosino's account of his labors," said the prosecutor, "that in opening the case next day to the jury I had but to repeat the story I heard the night before." The murderer was promptly convicted.

Journalists sought him out, feeling he held a key to the mystical core of the Italians. They found him a surprisingly charming dinner companion. "A big, strapping man with flashing coal black eyes and a melodious voice" was how one newsman remembered him, "quick-witted and resourceful." When Petrosino walked through Little Italy, children followed him as he made his rounds, "his dark restless eyes studying the faces of everyone he passed." Often, when he went to arrest a man in one of the city's cellar taverns, he wouldn't even present a badge or pull out his service weapon, a .38 Smith & Wesson. He would simply say, "My name is Petrosino," and the criminal would, almost always, stand up and come along. It was as if that one word — "Petrosino" — outweighed the prestige of the entire ten-thousand-man New York Police Department.

The detective spent his days with policemen, journalists, and judges; he lived in a largely male world. Unlike many of his colleagues, he had no girlfriend or wife, and he claimed that this was by design. "The police department is the only wife I have a right to have," he once said. "There's so much sudden death in this business. A man hasn't the right to bring a woman into it." But he did have friends all across the city, and these relationships were often built around his first love: opera. "If he talked music to you," wrote a journalist from the *New York Sun,* "he would tell you that 'Lucia' was his favorite, that 'Rigoletto' held second place and that he thought well of 'Ernani' and 'Aida.' Wagner, he would admit, wasn't so pleasing to his ear, although he liked 'Tannhauser' very much." Michael Fiaschetti remembered the detective coming over to his family's apartment on Sundays to chat and to listen while Fiaschetti's father played their favorite pieces on the piano. Even then Fiaschetti knew who Petrosino was. "His reputation was all over the city," Fiaschetti recalled. "Walking in on him was like taking a bow before a king." Between arias, the young man would ask the detective about this or that arrest, and Petrosino would humor him with an account of his latest adventures. The eighteen-year-old was thrilled to be in the presence of this demigod, but surprised to find Petrosino different from what he'd imagined: "middle-aged and quiet of manner . . . You would scarcely have taken him for the hero whose risky ventures and hand-to-hand encounters . . . were a legend." Fiaschetti, a muscular youth with gleaming black hair, measured himself against Petrosino and found, to his surprise, that "I looked more like a tough detective than he did." But when Fiaschetti spoke with Petrosino on those long Sunday afternoons, and heard of his pursuit of men who had killed ten or fifteen times in Italy, and how he'd arrested this or that gangster without backup, his impression began to alter. "There was something about his quiet and rather deadly manner," he recalled, "that kept a man from talking too loud."

As Petrosino's fame spread, a myth began to grow up around him. The precise source of the story is untraceable, but it remains part of his legend today. It was said that, as a young boy, Petrosino had emigrated ahead of the rest of his family to live with his grandfather in Manhattan. In this version of the story, the grandfather was killed in a streetcar accident and Petrosino and his young cousin Antonio were left on their own. Eventually they ended up in Orphans Court. A kindly Irish judge took pity on the two boys and, instead of sending them to an orphanage, brought the pair home and cared for them until members of Petrosino's family arrived in America. "In consequence," the legend recounts, "Joseph Petrosino and his cousin Anthony Puppolo lived with a 'politically connected' Irish household for some time, and this opened up educational and employment avenues not always available to more recent immigrants, especially Italian immigrants."

The story is a fiction. There was no grandfather in America, no streetcar accident, no Irish judge. Petrosino was raised in an Italian household and learned everything he knew about integrity from his fellow immigrants. He was entirely a product of his own culture and his rough education in American life.

The tale was an insult to poor Italians, who were judged incapable of producing a Joseph Petrosino. It was another, subtler taste of the prejudice that awaited the detective in his career, a prejudice that most Italians faced at the turn of the century and that would shadow every step of the war Petrosino was soon to begin.

• • •

PETROSINO HAD ALREADY BEEN DUBBED "THE ITALIAN SHERLOCK Holmes," but he hadn't yet met anyone approximating his Moriarty. That would change with the events that began on the morning of April 14, 1903.

Soon after daybreak, Frances Connors, a cleaning woman, was walking down 11th Street as it approached Avenue D when she came across a barrel sitting in the middle of the sidewalk, an overcoat draped over the top. Curious, she lifted the wool coat and looked inside. And then she screamed. For what the cleaning woman had seen inside was the face of a dead man, his head shoved down between his knees. The corpse was completely naked, and his head had been nearly severed by a savage knife thrust across the throat. When the victim turned out to be a Sicilian, the lead investigator called for help. "Send for the dago," he told his men. He meant Petrosino.

The detective, along with agents of the Secret Service, who believed the murder was connected to a counterfeiting ring, chased down the suspected killers: a gang led by Giuseppe Morello, a Sicilian from the town of Corleone known around Little Italy as "Clutch Hand" or "the Old Fox." The first nickname was the result of his deformed right hand, which resembled a lobster claw, and which he supported with a white string tied around his neck. Black-eyed and cunning, Morello carried a .45-caliber pistol in his waistband and a knife tied to his left leg, the tip plunged into a small cork to avoid stabbing him when he walked. He was arrested along with a towering brute named Tomasso "the Ox" Petto, "an oval-faced hulk of muscle and menace" who was known for both his great strength and his paltry intellect. Petrosino suspected it was Petto who'd cut the throat of the man in the barrel. Each member of the Morello gang was rounded up and brought into court for his arraignment — all except one: a tall, piercing-eyed Sicilian named Vito Cascio Ferro, who apparently had better sources of information than his compatriots and had fled town before the cops swept down.

In court, the judge was proceeding with the case when the man booked as Tomasso Petto angrily called out from the dock. Something in Italian. The judge tried to move on, but the suspect refused to quiet down. Finally, an interpreter spelled out what he was saying to the judge: "I am not Tomasso Petto."

Onlookers began to whisper and laugh. The man looked exactly like Petto. What game was he playing?

"Then who are you?" asked the judge.

"My name is Giovanni Pecoraro," the suspect called out. "I can prove it."

With that, the man produced several pieces of identification, all with the same name: Giovanni Pecoraro. The district attorney had no choice but to drop the charges against Pecoraro. It was a disaster for the prosecution and a public embarrassment for the police. How had this happened? The suspect, especially to non-Italian eyes, looked exactly like the Ox.

It turned out that the missing suspect, Vito Cascio Ferro, had come up with an ingenious plan to beat the charges: have the real killer disappear and put a double in his place. The scheme worked to perfection. The prosecutors, unable to find the murderer, were forced to release all the suspects. Pecoraro and the others walked free, much to the delight of Little Italy's underworld, and the killers of the man in the barrel were never prosecuted.

Petrosino had outwitted the Italian underworld for years, but here for the first time was evidence of a man who thought at his level. The substitution of a look-alike was wonderfully neat — not to mention brazen. "Something was changing in the world of American crime," wrote one author.

In 1903, Petrosino had no idea of Vito Cascio Ferro's importance. The Sicilian was a kind of organizational genius, soon to be a super-boss of the Palermo Mafia, the man who some believed had reinvented crime for the urban age. He was a master strategist held "in unlimited esteem" by more ordinary criminals, even gang bosses such as Morello. But after his spectacular trick in the Manhattan courtroom, the American adventure of Vito Cascio Ferro was over. The suspect fled to Italy via New Orleans, and Petrosino, swamped with other cases and criminals, filed Cascio Ferro's name away in his memory and moved on. The Sicilian, however, didn't return the favor.

When he got back to Italy, Cascio Ferro began reshaping the Mafia from small groups of bandits and extortionists into something far more visionary and profitable. He had vast ambitions and a keen mind with which to work. It was said that it was he who had invented the "protection" schemes that would soon spread from Little Italy across the country. But his great years were all in the future. For now, he was a poor man returning unwillingly to the country of his birth, nursing a deep and lasting animus toward Joseph Petrosino. In the port of New Orleans, Cascio Ferro walked up the gangplank to the steamship bound for Italy, carrying a suitcase with his clothes and meager belongings inside. To his mind, he'd been turned back by the man in the derby hat, that *straniero,* that infamous person. In his pocket Cascio Ferro carried a picture of Petrosino, which he would keep with him always. It was said that, back in Italy, he would take out the picture and study it, remarking to his friends, "I who have never been tainted by a crime, I swear that I will kill this man with my own hands." The story may have been an underworld legend invented after Cascio Ferro's death, but there's little doubt that he maintained an unhealthy fixation on the detective.

Petrosino would hear the name Cascio Ferro again, would in fact write it one day six years later in the leather notebook he carried with him at all times; he may even have met the *capo* face-to-face, this time in a foreign land, under enigmatic circumstances, where the advantage rested entirely with the Sicilian. But that encounter lay at the end of a long and obsessive journey that the detective was just about to embark on: the war, which began as *his* war, with what some Americans called "the Sicilian wolves" and others considered "that mysterious and weirdly elusive organization," but which was formally known as the Society of the Black Hand.

3

"IN MORTAL DREAD"

PETROSINO HEARD ABOUT THE SOCIETY BEFORE HE ACTUALLY
encountered it. Sometime in the early years of the century — we
cannot be sure when — he was given information about a shadowy
group that was lurking in the Italian colony. It was at first mostly whispers, about how *La Mano Nera* was striking terror in the hearts of immigrants by threatening them with death if money wasn't paid. They were
taking children, blowing up homes, burning homes; they were meeting reluctant victims on the streets with knives and guns. Few in the
Italian colony were willing to say what the Black Hand was or what it
did; women crossed themselves when they spoke the words. The fear
Petrosino's friends and informants exhibited was startling. There were
stories of dead bodies, *headless* bodies, children stuffed in chimneys
and left to decompose. But what was this Society? Where had it come
from? How did it operate? Was it even real?

In the early years of the century, Petrosino took up his diary and first recorded his thoughts on the Society. "Scores of Italian murderers are lurking in the lower part of the city and plying their trade of Black Hand extortion. Unless checked at once, they will so extend their operations that the police will be sorely tried in running them down." Something —a corpse? a letter?—had made it clear to him that the Society was quite real.

America hadn't yet awakened to the threat incubating in its cities. There had been scattered reports of the Black Hand's operations since before the turn of the century, but no panic. That would change beginning one sultry morning in August 1903. It was then that the Society broke out into the open. Nothing would ever be quite the same for Italian Americans, for their new country, or for Petrosino again.

It began in Brooklyn. A letter was dropped into the mailbox of a contractor named Nicolo Cappiello in the thriving but largely nondescript Italian neighborhood of Bay Ridge. Inside the envelope was a set of instructions: "If you don't meet us at 72nd Street and 13th Avenue, Brooklyn, tomorrow afternoon, your house will be dynamited and your family killed. The same fate awaits you in the event of your betraying our purposes to the police." It was signed "*La Mano Nera*" and illustrated with black crosses and daggers.

Cappiello was from Naples and he'd never heard of the Black Hand, a name taken from a group of anarchists and protesters that had flourished in the late 1800s in rural Spain. He dismissed the letter. Two days later another arrived: "You did not meet us as ordered in our first letter. If you still refuse to accede to our terms, but wish to preserve the lives of your family, you may do so by sacrificing your own life. Walk in Sixteenth Street, near Seventh Avenue, between the hours of four and five tonight." Cappiello again did nothing, and after a few days, men began showing up at his house, some of them friends and others claiming to be representatives of this "Black Hand" organization. They informed him that a price of $10,000 had been put on his head, but if he handed over $1,000, they would make the problem disappear. With his friends, some of whom he'd known for a dozen years, was a "mysterious stranger," Cappiello said, who left him "filled . . . with a nameless horror."

He now believed that the Black Hand would kill him if he didn't obey. He paid the $1,000.

The letters stopped. But a few days later the men were back, asking for $3,000 more, their threats more insistent and ugly. His family stopped going out in the street, afraid of being assassinated. When a reporter called at Cappiello's home, the door opened and a revolver was pointed at his head. The reporter stuttered out his name and was told to enter. Once he was inside, Cappiello's wife apologized. "We are in mortal dread of our lives," she told him, "and for more than a month we have been living in constant expectation of death. We knew not whom to trust."

Cappiello had had enough and went to the police. They arrested five men, who were convicted and sent to jail.

The Black Hand might have remained an obscure crime fad contained to the Italian neighborhoods of a few American cities, except for one thing: the fierce competition among the New York City tabloids. A reporter from the *Herald Tribune,* which was known for its sensationalist crime stories, heard about the letter and the extortion attempt and wrote it up. The editors gave it serious play, and other newspapers soon ran stories about this terrifying new phenomenon. "COWERS IN FEAR OF BLACK HAND," cried a headline from the *Evening World.* "THE BLACK HAND AT WORK HERE," the *Tribune* warned. The Society, which had been familiar only to its Italian victims and their friends, suddenly became known in millions of households across America in a matter of days.

And then the children began disappearing.

On August 2, eight-year-old Antonio Mannino, son of a prosperous contractor, walked into a confectionery store at the corner of Amity and Emmett streets in Brooklyn. He eyed the selection of candy and soda water and chose several of his favorites for his friends. He paid with "a shining fifty-cent piece." Outside the shop, eighteen-year-old Angelo Cucozza, who worked for the boy's father, was waiting on the sidewalk.

When the boy emerged, Cucozza called to him, "Come along, Tony, it is time we were off." The boy and his friend "disappeared down the street in the darkness, and that was the last seen of him."

When Tony's father, Vincenzo, began receiving letters signed by the Black Hand, the kidnapping became a sensation. Papers in Newark and Baltimore picked up the story and splashed it across their front pages, then Chicago, Los Angeles, and other cities followed. "ALL NEW YORK STIRRED BY THE LATEST OUTLAWRY," cried a headline from the *St. Louis Dispatch*. When a newspaperman tried to take a picture of Vincenzo Mannino near his home, the man exploded in anger. "My picture must not be printed," he shouted at the photographer. "I would be a marked man. They would all know me and any of them could kill me." Afterwards Mannino took to his bed and remained there for a week, nursed by his wife. The family's fear and the larger community's growing terror seemed to feed off each other. When the police went before an Irish American magistrate named Tighe to ask for warrants for the arrest of two suspects, the judge not only granted the request but also told the policemen, "Go out and make arrests—alive if you can, dead if you must."

As in almost every crime involving Italians, the call went out: "Send for the dago." Petrosino was assigned the case. He immediately began chasing down reports of two suspicious men on the ferry to New Jersey, and searched several towns there without finding anything. Sightings poured in from points farther west and south. "Evidently," wrote one journalist, "there are scores of pairs of Italians wandering around the country, each pair accompanied by a boy who looks like Tony Mannino." A rumor of a secret cave in Manhattan popped up, and detectives were sent to inspect it. The piers were watched. When a boy matching Tony's description was spotted walking in Astoria, Queens, cops poured into the neighborhood at midnight and began knocking on doors, "pulling little Italian boys out of bed wherever they found them." A photograph of Tony was held up to the boys' faces for comparison, and their parents were questioned. But the child was nowhere to be found.

The Black Hand responded to the police pressure by sending a letter to a Brooklyn station. It was addressed to the captain in charge of the investigation. "Stop chasing us," it read, "or be killed." Papers across the country played up each new development, and readers woke up every morning anxious to know if Tony had been found. Americans looked at their immigrant neighbors with a newfound distrust. "The Mannino kidnapping case," reported one newspaper, "gave the public so distinct a feeling of the danger from the Italian population that the wildest stories of blackmailing, kidnapping, and similar criminal brotherhoods were circulated, and none seemed too wild to receive credence."

Manhattan was on the edge of panic. In October, a rumor went around East Harlem that the Black Hand was threatening to blow up Public School 172 unless a ransom was paid. Parents of children who attended classes there streamed out of nearby tenements and raced toward the building. "Five hundred frenzied men and women clamored at the doors," wrote one journalist, "demanding that the pupils be immediately released." The heavy wooden doors began to buckle as the mob pushed forward, screaming for their children. The school's principal emerged from his office at the last moment and managed to calm the crowd before a riot could break out.

A reporter for the *Times* sought out Petrosino and asked him about this new secret society that had seemingly appeared out of nowhere. "The 'Black Hand' gang is undoubtedly at work in this city," Petrosino acknowledged, before trying to pour oil on the waters. "One man claims to have received four such letters and did not give up any money. He is still alive and in no danger of dying." The detective encouraged any Italian who'd received a Black Hand letter to keep his money and report the matter to the police. If people like Tony's father were brave, Petrosino announced, the scourge of the Black Hand could be ended before it truly began.

The Society wasn't impressed. It sent another letter to Mannino. "We will not kill the boy, having behaved himself quietly," it read. But they announced that they were thinking of selling him. "A childless family promised us by letter $2,000 if we sent them the boy. Be sure we will if Mr. Mannino does not come upon an agreement with us. We are not ignorant nor criminals, but gentlemen like you, only this big land of America disappointed our expectations, and we need money to go back to our beautiful, picturesque Italy." It was signed, "Very respectfully yours, Capitano of" with the outline of a black hand.

Then, on August 19, a week after the disappearance, a breakthrough. Mannino's cousin was out walking at midnight when he saw a small figure approaching from the other end of the street. The cousin ran toward the boy and saw that it was Tony. He embraced him and took him home. The Mannino family refused to say if they'd paid a ransom to have the boy freed, then cut off all contact with Petrosino and the police. It was clear to the detective that money had been exchanged. Mannino had not listened to him. He had judged that the Society of the Black Hand was stronger than the NYPD.

It was Petrosino's first public defeat by the Society, and it was a dispiriting one. Every ransom that was paid strengthened the group, burnished its growing legend, and attracted new members to its ranks. The detective believed that there were already thousands of Black Hand criminals in New York, formed into small gangs of a handful or a few dozen men, who used common tactics and cooperated with one another.

The number of Society cases started rising. Men — it was always the men who came to see Petrosino — began showing up at 300 Mulberry and shoving letters into his hands, letters that threatened the very existence of their families. Some days he received as many as thirty-five. There were, he knew, too many cases for him to investigate them all.

The tension rose all through the summer, fed by stark headlines. The Black Hand burned down a candy stand in Brooklyn and immolated the shop's owner, Ernest Curci, inside. A bomb exploded on 151st Street, sending glass and wood splinters through the air, injuring twenty people. Five girls in East Harlem were kidnapped, but their families were too terrified even to report the crimes. There were rumors — though it couldn't be confirmed — that one of their bodies was found stuffed inside a chimney. The girls' parents never came forward, so Petrosino had no way of knowing the truth.

But something else, too, must have haunted Petrosino: the stories told by recovered children. When one six-year-old boy named Nicolo Tomoso was taken from the streets near his home on East Houston, the kidnappers kept him for two months. Finally, after a ransom was paid, the boy returned home, pale and shaken. He told Petrosino that he'd been lured away by a man who gave him a penny and a stick of candy. When the boy had refused to go with the stranger, he'd picked him up and carried him to his car. The child was driven to a house in Brooklyn and kept there.

During his imprisonment, little Nicolo was treated fairly well; his captors fed him steak and macaroni, but he wasn't allowed to take off his shoes even when he slept. If he cried, one of the kidnappers would threaten to cut his tongue out. When his family finally scraped together enough money to pay the ransom, Nicolo was taken from his bed, carried to the steps of a school near his family's home, and left there.

But the most disturbing thing was that Nicolo hadn't been alone in his little prison. After he was safely back home, he told Petrosino that a small boy named Tony (not Tony Mannino) and two little girls were kept in the same room with him, and they'd remained behind even when he was freed. The girls were mostly silent during the long days, but Tony "cried most of the time and said he wanted to go home."

Even with his network of informers, Petrosino had no record of another boy named Tony being kidnapped, or of two missing girls. Now when Petrosino walked the streets, he was forced to imagine the interiors of the buildings he passed, to see through the brick and mortar to the scenes inside. Were there children languishing in the airless attics, their hands bound and their skin striped with welts? Were their corpses buried under the trash heaped in basement corners? For Petrosino, Manhattan must have become, in that season of kidnappings, a haunted city.

• • •

OVER THE COURSE OF THE ENSUING YEAR, SOCIETY ACTIVITY smoldered quietly in the Italian ghettoes of the Northeast, forcing

Petrosino to work on one case after another. Then, in the summer of 1904, "Black Hand fever," as it had come to be called, burst into flame. On August 22, Joseph Graffi was murdered in a New Rochelle tenement, his heart cut in two by a knife thrust. A bomb blew up Poggroriale Ciro's grocery store on Elizabeth Street in Manhattan, injuring his wife. And a wealthy Bronx contractor, Antonio Barroncini, entered his home at 81 Van Buren Street to find that Mrs. Barroncini had vanished from the house. He searched every room and then went out on the streets, calling on friends and relatives. Barroncini walked the city nonstop for six days before returning exhausted and brokenhearted to Van Buren Street. Then, at midnight one evening, he heard a knock at his front door. When he rushed down and turned the doorknob, he found two Italians standing on his porch; the pair told Barroncini they were holding his wife and he would have to pay a ransom to get her back. Barroncini quickly found the money and handed it over to the two. When the traumatized woman was returned home, she told her husband that the Black Handers had knocked on their door one afternoon and rushed into the house before she could react. They bound and gagged her, then dragged her from her home.

The first hints of a Black Hand–inspired backlash emerged. The *Brooklyn Eagle,* the *Washington Times,* the *New York Times,* and other papers went on the record supporting curbing the number of Sicilians allowed into the country. One newspaper even cautioned Italians "to remember the fate of their countrymen in New Orleans some years ago," a reference to the 1891 lynchings of eleven Italians after the murder of the city's police chief, an event seared into the memory of many Italian Americans. The Society received so much press, and the anger at Italian immigrants escalated to such a pitch, that Italy's representative was forced to issue a public statement. "The kidnapping of young Mannino is certainly a serious matter," said the ambassador, Baron Edmondo Mayor des Planches, "but it is nothing that concerns the Italian government . . . When Italians leave Italy and come to this country we expect them to be good citizens . . . I condemn the fact that Italians have been engaged in kidnapping or other crimes . . . and I hope they will receive full punishment." The government in Rome, headed by the ineffectual King Victor Emmanuel III, had effectively washed its hands of this Black Hand business.

A number of Americans came to the defense of the country's new residents. The *New York Mail* listed the virtues of the immigrants and called for "the sound American doctrine" of "equal treatment." The *New York Evening Journal,* owned by William Randolph Hearst, published a strongly worded editorial on October 14, 1904, that stood foursquare against the simmering hatred: "To say that the Italians are a criminal race is utterly false. They have their criminals among them, as have other races. A great majority of them . . . are law-abiding, honest, hard-working, devoted to their families."

The *Nashville American,* one of the rare southern voices that came out in support of Italians, chastised publishers who allowed their papers to issue blanket condemnations. "Newspapers," it declared, "especially such as are owned and edited by men that were immigrants themselves, should refrain from appealing to the stupid race prejudice of the crowd by false and stupid charges of race criminality." The opening dig was most likely aimed at Hearst's main competitor in New York, Joseph Pulitzer, the most powerful newspaperman in the country, who'd emigrated from Hungary in 1864, his journey financed by military recruiters who were gathering men to fight on the side of the Union in the Civil War. The *American* also opined that, even if Sicily was uncontrollably violent, Kentucky was worse.

Despite the panic and the headlines, Petrosino found that his superiors, to his surprise and consternation, appeared largely indifferent to Black Hand crime. Time after time, Petrosino implored the NYPD to go after the Society and mount serious prosecutions. "He was laughed at," reported the *Washington Post,* "and told that 'Black Hand' was but a term coined by some sensational writer and alarmist. 'Run along and tend to your work on the waterfront,' was the advice given." It was as if the Italians, with their *omertà* and their stilettos, weren't worth protecting.

Petrosino himself opposed any cutoff in immigration from southern

Italy, knowing that every time passage was denied to an Italian family, it snapped a lifeline for men and women desperate for dignity and bread. But he also knew that each sensational Black Hand crime tilted the balance of American sentiment closer and closer toward raw hate. Defeating the Society wasn't just a matter of stopping a few murders. It was tightly bound up with the destiny of his people in the new land.

• • •

IN THE SUMMER OF 1904, PETROSINO BEGAN TO FORMULATE A PLAN for stopping the Black Hand. Once he had worked out the details, he called a journalist friend and the two met for an interview. When the resulting piece was published, it became clear that the detective's opinion of the Society had changed and grown more somber. "The ramifications of this confederation of outlawry," he told the reporter, "reach the uttermost parts of the earth." The explosion of violence and kidnapping had shaken him. But he believed he'd arrived at a solution. Petrosino was calling on the NYPD to create a special bureau of detectives, to be called "the Italian Squad," to take on and destroy the Society. "Give me twenty active and ambitious men of my own people to drill in the detective service," he said, "and within a few months at most, I shall root out every vestige of the accursed guilds from this free country." Petrosino lost no time in presenting the idea to Commissioner William McAdoo at 300 Mulberry Street.

The urbane McAdoo was an immigrant himself, having been born in County Donegal, Ireland, and brought to America during the height of the Civil War as a twelve-year-old boy. Balding, vigorous, and ruggedly handsome, he was a former Democratic congressman from New Jersey who'd worked his way through law school by taking a job as a reporter in Jersey City. It showed; he was a marvelous writer. His description of running a police department in wide-open Manhattan in the early 1900s could hardly be improved upon: "Imagine the captain of a steamer in mid-ocean on the bridge, his vessel struggling with a hurricane, fierce and cruel winds, mountainous seas, blasts of thunder, shafts of lightning; the bulwarks have gone, the anchors torn from their fastenings;

the engines are plunging and racing; the whole fabric is rending and groaning." His view of the commissionership, in which he was asked to please Tammany Hall while preventing New Yorkers from killing one another, was even darker: "His official life is a plaything of the moment. He is a king on sufferance . . . The more original, radical, honest, and earnest he is, the less likely he is to remain in office."

McAdoo was by all accounts an honest man; he was never touched by the corruption scandals that regularly rocked the department. But he didn't want an Italian Squad: in this matter, he had no desire to be either "original" or "radical." There was no German or Irish Squad, so why should there be an Italian one? As a native-born Irishman, McAdoo knew how unpopular the idea would be with his Celtic rank and file. A new squad would create a powerful bureau led by a deeply maligned group that maintained the merest fingerhold within the NYPD; only Italian speakers would be eligible to staff it, shutting out the Irish from jobs and promotions. Furthermore, every detective assigned to the Italian colonies was one who wasn't protecting other New Yorkers. When he weighed the matter, McAdoo saw no reason to risk his position for an incorrigible lot of violent men.

From the point of view of the men who controlled the NYPD — that is, the Irish grandees of Tammany — protecting Italians was a losing proposition. New York cops were meant to protect voters, who in their turn kept Tammany in power. And the Italians were notorious for not voting, for clinging to the memories of their orchards and their town squares at the expense of integrating into their new country. At the turn of the century, 90 percent of Irish immigrants were American citizens, but by 1912, fewer than half of their Italian peers were naturalized. If one scanned the list of state legislators supported by Tammany around 1900, one would see how successful the organization was in absorbing the waves of new immigrants into its fold: here was a Dolan and a McManus, yes, but also a Litthauer, a Goldsmith, and a Rosen from the very same streets where the Italians lived. But where were the Zangaras, the Tomasinos, the Fendis? There were none. In Tammany's cosmos, the Italians were residents of a distant planet.

So when Petrosino brought the commissioner his idea, an argument broke out. When the detective pointed out the obvious — that Italians didn't trust Irish cops, for excellent reasons — McAdoo had an answer waiting. The police in Sicily often dealt with Italians who didn't trust them and still managed to make cases. Why couldn't he? The problem wasn't with the department. "The trouble now is that an Italian criminal at once seeks refuge behind racial and national sympathy," he told the press. "Police work with the Italians, even at its best, will not get the results desired, unless it is followed up by a moral movement on the part of the better class of Italians." The translation: the cancer lay within the Italian soul.

This was a common response to "the Italian problem" in 1904. It was considered as impossible to separate an Italian from violence as it was to cleave an Irishman from the love of his mother or a German from his hard-earned money. And if the Italians were indeed incorrigible, what was the point in policing them? The fact was that Sicilians reacted especially badly when approached by a cop. "The sight of a uniform," commented a magazine writer of the time, "means to them either a tax-gatherer, a compulsory enlistment in the army, or an arrest, and at its appearance the men will run and the women and children will turn to stone."

Petrosino refused to accept this argument. He told McAdoo that this wasn't a question of genetics or culture but rather one of money, tactics, attention, the *seriousness* with which Americans confronted the Black Hand problem. "Do you know what my compatriots say when they talk about America?" he told the commissioner. "They say, 'An Italian discovered it and the Jews and the Irish run it.' Try giving the Italians a little power, too, and maybe there will be some change."

It must be pointed out that this quote, which comes from Petrosino's Italian biographer Arrigo Pettaco, cannot be confirmed. Pettaco provides no source for the wonderful line, and it can't be located in any newspaper of the time. It might easily be an example of wishful thinking on the part of an Italian writer outraged over the treatment of his people. But even if Pettaco couldn't resist making up the quote out of whole cloth, the spirit of his account is accurate. This was an argument about power in New York City, about who wielded it and whether Italian Americans deserved a share of it, if only to save themselves from violent death.

McAdoo stood firm. He vetoed the idea of an Italian Squad. The city's Board of Aldermen backed the decision.

Petrosino was in despair. His people were being abducted and killed, and the rulers of Manhattan didn't care a whit. And it wasn't just the NYPD. The courts, Petrosino believed, rarely took Black Hand crime seriously. The maximum sentence for attempted extortion was two and a half years; first offenders received even lighter sentences. In Franklin Park, New Jersey, a prolific extortionist who had signed his letters "President of the Black Hand" received just eight months in the workhouse after his conviction. "Of other crimes than murder on the part of Italian malefactors," wrote the journalist Frank Marshall White, who was the sharpest observer of the Black Hand in New York, "few ever reach the courts or are heard of outside the Italian colonies."

With Roosevelt now occupying the White House, Petrosino was alone within the department. There are no mentions in the many hundreds of articles on his career of his first mentor, Clubber Williams, intervening on his behalf. There were no Italian politicians to look to for support; the Italians were the fastest-growing segment of the city's population but were barely represented in city or state government. It wasn't just that Petrosino chose not to complain but that, had he done so, he would probably have lost the only support he had: the support of the public. "Petrosino could expect no favors," wrote a journalist, "and in consequence he asked for none."

What he had, too, was the press. Petrosino the path breaker, the incorruptible one, had become a favorite theme of the metropolitan dailies. Pulitzer's *World* and Hearst's *Journal* as well as Adolph Ochs's *New York Times* found in the burly, intellectual detective a champion. "When murder and blackmail are in the air," declared the *Times*, "and the menfolk are white-faced and the womenfolk are saying litanies to the Blessed Mother . . . all Little Italy looks to the Italian detective to protect it and guard it." If the press couldn't quite love the Italians, it was bound and determined to love Petrosino.

The detective pressed his case. Without an Italian Squad, he feared the Society would become even more powerful and cruel; it would spread across the country and cripple any chance his people had of being accepted as true Americans. Already the knife-wielding Italian was a stock figure on the stages of Broadway and Chicago. As long as the Black Hand ruled the headlines, the Italian would always be a thing apart. A monster.

Petrosino reasoned with the bureaucracy at 300 Mulberry. "He endeavored to impress upon them," wrote one journalist, "the urgent need of drastic measures to crush the ever-growing peril." On occasion, Petrosino was granted a meeting. "At other times, he was dismissed with scant courtesy, although even the highest in authority well knew that this policeman's record was flawless, and that in no essential was he an alarmist." The detective buttonholed journalists and repeated his warnings about the Society. He even managed to enlist a powerful ally, Elliott Norton, the president of the Society for the Protection of Italian Immigrants, who called on McAdoo and urged him to approve the Italian Squad. But McAdoo rebuffed Petrosino again, and the detective fell into a depression.

His mind turned to the people he was trying to protect. He felt betrayed by the many hundreds of Black Hand victims who'd failed to testify against the Society and who'd funded its outrages, breathed life into it. "The problem with my people," he told one journalist, "is that . . . they are timid, and will not give information about their fellow-countrymen. If they would form a Vigilance League that would drive into the hands of the police Italian malefactors, they would be as safe as any one else and not have as the penalty of their industry and prosperity the payment of large sums to the idle and worthless." This was his public stance; it was one of quiet regret. But there were moments when Petrosino lost patience with his own people and hated the victims of the Black Hand more than he hated the criminals themselves. He "called the victims sheep," said the Italian journalist and author Luigi Barzini, "and threw on them fierce invective." Petrosino was at a low point, filled with despair. Why did his people refuse to unite against these barbarians?

And yet the city he was so enamored with, the city that Italians were building with their exhausting labor, had also failed to live up to its duty. It was freeing Black Handers to kill and kidnap again. "The endless frustration," wrote his Italian biographer, "of seeing the courts promptly release men he had arduously hunted down made him hard and pitiless." In the face of the city's indifference, Petrosino issued a warning. The Society, he told reporters, was just beginning its work. If it wasn't stopped, the pestilence would spread. "At present," he said, "the Black Hand desperadoes attack only their own countrymen, but unless they are checked, they will get bolder and attack Americans." It wasn't just a tactic; Petrosino really believed this to be true and repeated the statement often.

The detective could sense the future for Italian Americans darkening; he foresaw catastrophe. The belief in himself and his country that had propelled him to smash his shoeshine box that afternoon years before was nearing exhaustion. "He felt abandoned," said Barzini, "left alone in the huge fight."

4

THE MYSTERIOUS SIX

THE BATTLE WENT ON ALL THROUGH THE SUMMER OF 1904. Petrosino continued to lobby for an Italian Squad; McAdoo issued rejection after rejection. Then a series of grisly Black Hand crimes tipped the balance. It became clear that the Society, rather than disappearing, was growing in power and that the journalists on Park Row would continue to play up the stories. Headlines trumpeted the Society's rise.

On September 14, McAdoo called Petrosino into his office. "They finally granted your request," he told the detective grudgingly. "You are now authorized to set up an Italian Squad. You yourself will select its members." It was an unexpected coup. Petrosino's would be the first such bureau in the nation's history. But McAdoo was being sly. Petrosino had asked for "a little power" for the Italians and that's exactly what the commissioner gave him — a *little* power. Petrosino had requested twenty men but got five instead, and no budget to speak of.

When McAdoo announced the new squad to the press, he gave it a benign mission. "The honest Italian," McAdoo said, "must be made to understand that the police are not his enemies, but his friends." Petrosino knew that this was only half the story: first he had to stun the Black Hand into submission; only then could he win the confidence of his people.

The detective began to look around Manhattan's squad rooms for his five men. In selecting his team, the detective didn't have a large pool to choose from. The NYPD had around ten thousand policemen in 1904, but fewer than twenty could speak Italian, and perhaps only four or five could converse in Sicilian. The first members of the Italian Squad were detectives whom Petrosino pulled from various precincts in the city, men he'd worked with or knew by reputation.

His first choice was Maurice Bonnoil, son of French-Irish parents who'd grown up in Little Italy. Bonnoil was known for his fluency: his Sicilian was actually better than his English. He'd worked with Petrosino for years and was in the middle of a highly colorful career, in which he'd done everything from saving a young woman from being forced into an opium den to arresting "the Beautiful Twins," transvestite brothers who were fond of strolling down Broadway in "rustling skirts and picture hats." Next came Peter Dondero, a well-spoken twenty-seven-year-old who'd been on the force for three years and had proved himself a bit of an aesthete. "This is the prettiest decorated city I have ever had the pleasure to visit," he told the *Los Angeles Herald* while on a visit to pick up a prisoner. "The bright sunshine with the cool breeze makes this an ideal city." Despite his fine eye for urban planning, Dondero was tough; he would later wear a jagged scar across his face from a battle with a vagrant named Harry "Pussy" Meyers. During another collar, an Italian criminal pressed a revolver to Dondero's mouth and pulled back the hammer. Dondero managed to snatch the gun away from his face just before it fired.

George Silva, John Lagomarsini, and Ugo Cassidi rounded out the squad. The last recruit asked his new partners to call him "Hugh Cassidy," in tribute to his favorite Wild West gunfighter, Butch Cassidy.

His most famous case before joining the squad was retrieving $6,000 stolen from a chiffonier owned by the son of the favorite masseur of the king of Belgium by thieves who'd lowered themselves through a roof scuttle on East 113th Street. Cassidi had a bit of the outlaw in him: in 1895, when he was a patrolman, he'd been charged with attempting to extort a large sum of cash from a suspect. The accuser was an ex-surveyor who claimed that Cassidi had threatened him with false arrest, then assaulted him when he refused the deal. The detective maintained his innocence, and charges were dropped two years later. As virtuous and clean-living as a priest, Petrosino was still willing to take a risk on flawed men.

Once the squad was up and running, Petrosino proved to be an unusual boss, intensely hardworking and brilliant, yet not quite trusting. His phenomenal memory, along with years of working on his own, had made him self-sufficient. He'd never had fellow cops he could rely on, and the constant insults from the brotherhood of Irish officers had made him paranoid. One squad member, eager to start his first day of work, was told to follow certain suspects through the city streets, but Petrosino refused to tell him what the men were suspected of or even what the case was about. This went on for weeks. Petrosino had suffered bitterly from Italians' calling him out on the street and revealing his presence to the mafiosi. How was he to know these detectives were any different?

Despite their varied backgrounds, there was one force that bonded Petrosino and the others — dubbed "the mysterious six" by the *Evening World* — to one another: the hostility of their fellow cops. The detective bureau, which was heavily Irish, froze out the newcomers, as did its commanding officers. "They had no office," noted one newspaper, "no gold-lettered door, no shiny desks, no direct line telephone, no stenographer, no messenger." They lacked even cabinets to store their files. In the beginning, Petrosino carried around the squad's files in his head, as he was accustomed to doing with his own cases. His apartment became the Italian Squad's temporary headquarters. In the mornings, they would attend the daily lineup at 300 Mulberry; then, when the members of the homicide squad and the detective bureau returned to their offices, the six Italians would retire to a small alcove off a busy hallway and plan out their day, talking in low voices. The Irish cops watched, delighting in the "forlorn" expressions of the Italian misfits.

The squad's orders were "to deal with the peculiar problems constantly arising in the Italian districts." Essentially, McAdoo had just handed over half a million Italians, spread across several square miles of territory, to six men. For comparison's sake, the citizens of Rome, who numbered around 500,000 in 1904, were overseen by thousands of policemen and *carabinieri*, with the full support of courts, prosecutors, and police officials. The squad was expected to do the same work with laughable resources.

And the burden increased daily. Italian immigration into New York continued at a torrid rate throughout the squad's early days. The year of the unit's founding, 1904, saw 193,296 Italian men, women, and children enter the United States. By 1905, the total had jumped to 221,479, and the figures for the following two years were even higher: 273,120 and 285,731. Inevitably, some of those immigrants were criminals. "There are thousands of Black Hand robbers and assassins in New York and Brooklyn," Petrosino admitted to the *Times* in October 1905, "and they are a rapidly growing menace." Later, he put the number of Italian criminals working in Manhattan at between 35,000 and 40,000, with more arriving every day.

Alberto Pecorini, a newspaper editor who studied the Society, agreed. He estimated that 95 percent of the small businessmen, shop owners, organ grinders, bankers, and unskilled laborers in the Italian colonies were paying the Society a weekly extortion fee to keep their businesses and families safe. If this figure was correct, it would mean that there were hundreds of thousands of Black Hand victims in New York alone. But even that number was incomplete, as it excluded those immigrants who'd fled the country in fear for their lives. "The Black Hand," wrote journalist Frank Marshall White, "has ruined and driven out of the United States thousands of honest and industrious Italians who might otherwise have made the best kind of citizens."

It's possible that those numbers were exaggerated. The fact that most Black Hand crimes went unreported made it difficult even for someone like Petrosino or Pecorini to gauge their true number. But there was ample evidence from other sources — victim lists confiscated from Black Hand members, reports from journalists in St. Louis, Chicago, and other cities — that the number of victims was high, certainly in the thousands every year in New York alone. Especially for a small businessman, if you'd amassed any kind of wealth at all in your years in America, you could expect to be threatened.

The demographics were against Petrosino. The Italian Squad was a thin line of men standing on the Atlantic seaboard facing east, braced against a wave that never crested but only kept climbing higher. Many observers believed that the NYPD had made a token gesture by creating the squad while withholding the institutional support the unit needed. "It seemed like a hollow victory to many," wrote one historian, "a PR stunt."

As Petrosino trained his men in the intricacies of the Society, he pushed for funds to open a proper squad office. Finally, McAdoo consented. The detective wouldn't be allowed to house his unit at 300 Mulberry — or perhaps Petrosino requested a place away from the Irish — but he was allowed to rent space at 175 Waverly Place, in what is now Manhattan's West Village. Petrosino rounded up what supplies he could muster, found a few old desks to haul up to the office, and hung a sign in the window that read "REAL ESTATE." Any citizens who knocked on the door asking about property in the neighborhood were quietly turned away. The business was simply a cover for the Italian Squad's real work.

When the squad was firmly established in its new home, the *New York Times* sent a reporter to do an in-depth interview with the chief of this exotic new bureau. He described the man he found waiting for him:

The eyes are the intelligent eyes of a student. There is generally a kindly light in them, a light that makes one feel easy in mind. They invite you to be confidential, and when the straight line of the lips breaks into a smile, you can readily imagine that you are talking to some gentle and thoughtful person who has your interest at heart.

Petrosino began with a tour of the office. Photos of Italian criminals lined the walls, and on a wooden table sat a display of weapons confiscated by the squad: stilettos, revolvers, blackjacks. The detective held up what looked like a pencil sharpener. "Look at this," he said. It was, in fact, a knife taken off an extortionist.

The little inspection over, the two sat down for the interview, and the reporter asked Petrosino how he planned to destroy the Society of the Black Hand. The answer was perhaps a surprise, coming from the notoriously tough detective. "Enlightenment," Petrosino said. He explained:

> We need a missionary more than a detective in the Italian quarters of New York. A missionary who would go among the newcomers and impart to them a reasonable amount of knowledge concerning our government. It is ignorance of the blessings he might enjoy in this country that is holding back the Italian-American citizen. They do not know their constitutional rights. They don't even know the glorious history of the Republic.

Even as he launched this new experiment in law enforcement, Petrosino argued that policing wouldn't be enough. Italians didn't feel part of America; they needed teachers, ambassadors, social workers. The detective strove to emphasize that his countrymen loved freedom, just like Americans, but were confused about how America worked or if, in fact, the system should be trusted at all. Petrosino urged Americans to have patience with his people. The average Italian, he said, "works hard, has simple pleasures, loves the things that are beautiful and sends his children to the public schools. He is worth enlightening."

The journalist filed his story and a copy editor slapped a headline on it. "PETROSINO," it read, "DETECTIVE AND SOCIOLOGIST."

• • •

EVERY MORNING, THE MEN OF THE NEW ITALIAN SQUAD ARRIVED AT 175 Waverly dressed in workmen's outfits, wearing the wide-brimmed felt hats then in fashion with the *contadini*. Their chief sorted through the hundreds of leads he'd gathered from his *nfami* and divided them up among the detectives. The men then left the premises in ones and twos and ambled down Waverly heading for their assignments, disguised as laborers being sent out to repair rental properties.

The Society's violence was ratcheting up with unnerving speed. Bombs were being detonated in Little Italy, Brooklyn, and the East Side. Three policemen were guarding a Williamsburg store when its brick front launched into the street with an earthshaking roar. A dynamite charge had been set without the men realizing it. The shop was torn apart. No one saw the bomber, and police were mystified as to how he got the explosives onto the premises. Letters to other businessmen promised the same. "If you don't pay, great coward," one read, "you will suffer. Resistance is useless. Death now stares you in the face."

Serrino Nizzarri was a baker who ran a shop at 98 Bayard Street in what is now Chinatown. A Black Hander, Anthony Fazia, had already made one attempt on his life, calling him out of a barber's chair and attempting to sink a knife into his chest before Nizzarri managed to dodge the thrust and flee. A letter spelled out whom Nizzarri was dealing with: "Our society is composed, besides Italians, of policemen and lawyers, and if you make known its contents, we shall know at once." When he was ready to pay, the Society letters told him, he was to leave a red handkerchief in his window. But the red handkerchief never appeared. Nizzarri had decided to resist.

One evening, the baker was making bread in the basement of his shop, with his daughter and her baby nearby. Sensing a presence, he looked up and saw a man walking slowly down the stairs into his workplace. It was Fazia. The Black Hander spotted the baker and pulled out a gun, pointing it at Nizzarri's chest. The basement echoed with two shots. The bullets missed the baker, but in the excitement his daughter knocked into a pot of boiling water and spilled it on her child, who let out a horrible cry. The baby was scalded to death.

The Italian Squad hunted down Fazia and brought him to the downtown detention center known as the Tombs. He declined a lawyer, went to trial, and declared defiantly from the stand, "I'll go to jail, but he," meaning Nizzarri, "will pay the penalty. My friends will look after him all right. Read the letter. It tells all." Fazia was defiant, but the squad could take satisfaction in a small victory. Nizzarri had stood up and testified against his persecutor, and the man would spend the best years of his life in Sing Sing. If they could string a number of such cases together, the Society would be crippled.

The battle between the Black Hand and the Italian Squad was the talk of the city. Even jewelry designers took note. Early on in the craze, a newspaper reported that the "Black Hand Is Now the Rage" and went on to explain that "since the recent declaration of Detective Petrosino of the New York police force that there is no such thing as the Black Hand Society" — this was a misquote, Petrosino having said no *national* organization existed — "the whole thing has been taken as a joke." Street vendors began selling small black hands made out of metal for use as watch charms or buttons. The demand, the newspaper reported, far outstripped the supply. Stores in Manhattan even sold special stationery with the Black Hand insignia at the top of the letter, with matching envelopes, so one could send one's girlfriend or great-aunt in Rochester a "Black Hand" letter. The symbols of death and horror had been taken up by the smart set; it had all "become a proper fad."

But violence continued to bubble up everywhere. In nearby Westfield, New Jersey, John Clearwater, a "white" (non-Italian) owner of a restaurant, was walking home at 1 a.m. when a Black Hand gang that had been threatening his life confronted him. They pointed revolvers at him as Clearwater whipped out his own gun and began firing.

Two bullets slammed into the restaurateur's body and he dropped to the ground. The Society members fell on him with their daggers, stabbing him in the neck and face. He bled to death in the road.

No business was exempt. When the steamship *Sibiria* sailed into New York Harbor and docked at Pier 1 with a load of fruit from the West Indies, there were bundles of mail waiting for its Sicilian crew. One of the sailors opened a letter and found a note from the Society. If the crew didn't pay the Black Hand $50 each, the seamen would be murdered one by one. The captain told his men to show the message to the Italian Squad. "No!" the men replied. "For God's sake no! That's one of the things we mustn't do. They would kill us right away." The Sicilians refused to leave the ship and stayed holed up in their cabins, "huddled together like sheep, hands on revolvers, which most had borrowed, others having clubs." The sailors closely watched every longshoreman who came onboard to unload the fruit as he entered the hold. The men didn't rest until the ship sailed away from New York.

Italians were frankly terrified. In Brooklyn, Tony Marendino, the young son of a contractor, vanished from the streets one afternoon. When the Italian Squad approached the boy's father, he refused to talk to them. Even without the family's help, the squad was able to track down the kidnappers, Salvatore Peconi and Vito Laduca. Peconi was a known Black Hand associate who'd been arrested before for kidnapping a child. The pair was arrested and held in jail to await a grand jury. When word reached the victim's father, he rushed to the courthouse and tried to pay the kidnappers' bail, even going so far as to claim that Peconi was his best friend and should be released immediately. Marendino feared that if Peconi went to jail for stealing his son, his life would become unlivable. He refused to testify against the pair, and the Italian Squad was forced to drop the case.

Intimidation was rife; when one star witness appeared in court during a Black Hand trial, detectives watched the crowd to try to catch anyone giving her "the death sign." Just as she was about to name a Society chief, she saw something in the crowd that caused her to stop dead. She nearly fainted, but continued on. Only when another signal was passed did she stand up, screaming, "I swear by the God in heaven! I swear on the grave of my sacred mother! I swear I know nothing! I can tell nothing! I will say no more!" One judge in Baltimore ordered the jury box and the witness stand picked up and turned around so that the men in the audience couldn't see the faces of those giving testimony.

Reports poured into the office at 175 Waverly. Men appeared at the door holding letters, or telling stories of children who'd disappeared, mysterious fires, explosions in the night. Petrosino was just coming to understand the extent of what he was facing. He estimated that for every Italian who came to him, there were 250 who kept silent. The Black Hand scourge was already reaching epidemic proportions.

5

A GENERAL REBELLION

I N THE SUMMER AND FALL OF 1905, A QUITE LETHAL CLOAK-AND-dagger game unfolded across the length and breadth of Manhattan. On grand avenues, in tenement hallways, in malodorous, gaslit alleyways, in the "chianti cellars" where it was rumored that Society men gathered to plot their crimes, the Black Hand and the police clashed again and again. It was a test of the Society's strength in America. A test, really, of whether it could be stopped at all.

Some of the Italian Squad's cases were simple. When a butcher at 211 Bleecker was targeted by extortionists, the squad showed up early one morning before the street came alive with shoppers. They hid in the butcher's freezer and stayed there for hours, drinking hot cocoa and dancing to keep warm. They sat on slabs of ice and told stories about their childhoods or the slick thugs they'd encountered in the Tenderloin. Finally, late in the afternoon, a man identified in the *Washington Post* as Gioacchino Napoli walked into the shop and accepted $50 in marked money. The detectives staggered out of the freezer one by one, half-frozen, and threw handcuffs onto Napoli. In a later case, the detectives worked behind the counter of a drugstore at Second Avenue and 12th Street, dressed as clerks and even serving customers their laudanum and nerve pills, while they glanced through the windows at the cousin of a Black Hand victim who was nervously pacing, waiting for a bagman to appear. The squad men watched as the cousin spoke to a young Italian, who was accompanied by two other men. The cousin handed the stranger something, then took out a handkerchief and wiped it quickly across his lips. It was the signal. The detectives rushed from the drugstore, but the three Black Handers were already running toward a departing streetcar, which was flying down Second Avenue at nearly twenty miles per hour. The trio managed to hop aboard the streetcar. A squad member reached the doorway and pulled himself on, but one of the Society men, Paolo Castellano, saw the detective enter and dove through the streetcar's open window, plunging headfirst to the cobblestones before picking himself up and running.

The detective and a patrolman who happened to be onboard pulled out their guns and began blasting away at Castellano. "The car was in an uproar," reported the *Times*, "men, women, and children screaming and ducking out of range of the revolvers." A bullet struck the black-mailer in the hip, spun him around, and sent him crashing to the pavement. The detectives jumped off the streetcar and dragged Castellano to the nearest precinct along with his two accomplices.

Petrosino taught his men how to read Black Hand letters, to notice certain turns of phrase and bits of dialect that could reveal their author's identity. There were too many threats to take them all with equal seriousness, so the detectives had to learn to distinguish a genuine letter from a bogus one. Some threats lacked the proper touch, such as the one received by a Mr. Nussbaum of Manhattan in the fall of 1905. "See here," it began. "We ain't going to fool with you no longer. If we don't get $50 on September 30 before 11 a.m., we're going to kill you and your girl. I am president of the Klick and can write plainer letters than the rest." It was signed the Black Hand, but the culprit turned out to be

Mr. Nussbaum's fifteen-year-old daughter, Nellie. She'd written the note "just for fun."

A different letter, sent to a Manhattan barber whose shop had been destroyed by a bomb, indicated a far higher level of danger. "You know what to expect now," it read. "This is just a beginning . . . You are doomed because you will not obey . . . We are the men who visited Palibino in 116th Street and Ciro, the grocer, in Elizabeth Street." That kind of message demanded immediate attention. Later in the history of the Society, a Chicago man received a letter from his son's kidnappers, written by the boy. "Please, papa," it read, "pay the money or you will never see me again." The Black Handers added a postscript: "Would you know your boy's head if you saw it?"

Petrosino estimated that tens of thousands of New Yorkers were being extorted by the Black Hand. These were the men digging the subway tunnels, carving out the city's water reservoirs, building out the skyline. How many did the Black Hand have under its thumb? And how, Petrosino wanted to know, was the Society getting the name of every man working on these gargantuan projects?

It took months of legwork, but Petrosino and his men finally unraveled the scheme. When a new building project was announced — a railroad line, an aqueduct — a Black Hand member was assigned to get a job on it. He would show up at the work site, disguised as a common laborer, just as Petrosino did on his investigations, and apply for one of the spots. When he got it, he would head to the camp and mingle with his fellow laborers. Once established there, he would pretend to receive a Black Hand letter, which he'd have brought with him for this very purpose. "He tells one or two and pretends he is almost scared to death over hearing the news," Petrosino explained. "It quickly spreads until every man in that camp fears every other man, not knowing who or how many in the camp are members of the *Mano Nera*." The workers became afraid to talk to one another, fearing their neighbor might belong to the Society. Once the men had been demoralized and isolated, another Black Hand member was ordered to show up at the camp on payday and begin collecting their tribute.

Other aspects of the Society's operations dwarfed that particular scheme. Petrosino soon discovered that members of Black Hand gangs were getting jobs as tellers at savings banks all over the colonies and keeping records of the deposits of small merchants. Essentially, they were acting as moles, reporting on the financial holdings of potential targets. Those assets were substantial. By the end of the decade, Italians in New York would own $120 million in property, $100 million invested in various businesses, and $20 million in bank deposits. The Society was keeping track of who was prospering in order to terrorize them. Black Hand members congregated in barbershops, restaurants, bars, places where immigrants socialized, and trawled for gossip on who had recently gotten married (wedding gifts were not exempt from the Society's greed), whose uncle or father had recently died (nor were inheritances), or who had sold the family farm back in Calabria or Sicily.

Then there were the stores. By talking to the victims of the Society, Petrosino discerned a pattern: many of the victims had done business with shops owned by particular merchants. Soon one name kept coming up. Giuseppe Morello, Petrosino's adversary from the Barrel Murder. Morello and his partner Ignazio "the Wolf" Lupo had established a mammoth grocery store on Elizabeth Street, and branches soon opened across the city. A large part of the operation was to extort the businessmen who came into one of their shops. If a merchant ordered a large number of items, he would soon receive a Black Hand letter at his place of business. If he didn't pay, his own store was bombed and his children threatened.

The two gangsters could hardly have been more different: the troll-like Morello and the stylish, urbane Lupo, who traveled down Mott Street in a buggy pulled by a gleaming white horse, wearing bespoke suits and a hat "tilted rakishly to one side." Lupo had grown up in a wealthy family in Palermo before murdering a rival over a business dispute and fleeing the country. He was moon-faced, with wide, staring eyes, and he spoke in a high, fluting voice that lent his words a kind of singsong eeriness. In the often brutal, testosterone-rich Italian underworld, Lupo was an oddity. "I give you my word," said William Flynn, head of the New York office of the Secret Service, "Lupo had only to touch you to give you the feeling that you had been poisoned."

The two partners preyed on the honest businessmen around Mulberry Street. One such merchant, Salvatore Manzella, imported wine and Italian foods for his store on Elizabeth Street. Lupo arrived at his office and threatened his life, eventually forcing him to pay $10,000 for the right to continue breathing. Manzella was slowly bled of all his money, his once thriving firm driven into bankruptcy. Like so many of the Society's victims, he came into public view only as his life reached its ruinous end.

The sophistication of the racket — and the scads of money devoted to it — outmatched anything Petrosino and his men could put together. "Theirs is a secret information bureau more complete and accurate than any . . . ever devised," Petrosino told one journalist about the Society. "The exact status of every member of the various Italian colonies . . . is known to the powers that prey." The Black Hand was compiling dossiers on every prominent merchant in the city: their net worth, their home addresses, the members of their extended families. The Society that was taking shape before the detective's eyes resembled less a criminal organization than a shadow government: it taxed its subjects, it surveilled them, and it killed its enemies.

• • •

AS THE MONTHS PASSED, PETROSINO COULD TELL THAT THE Society was evolving. It seemed to sense the squad's presence on the street, to anticipate his thinking.

When Petrosino began arresting its bagmen, the Society hired unwitting dupes to pick up the money, many of them straight off the boat from Sicily. When the squad donned disguises, the Society responded with its own. On one occasion, members of the mysterious six were assigned to a stakeout, to keep their eyes on a dummy package that was placed at a designated spot on a Manhattan street. The men tried to behave casually as they watched the streams of pedestrians walking past the bundle. Hours passed. Businessmen, peddlers, housewives, textile workers — no one so much as glanced at the package. As the light softened into dusk, a hunchback turned onto the street. He had a broken nose that was visible even from a distance, and he walked with a peculiar lurching gait. The detectives studied him as he approached the package and were startled when he suddenly dashed over, stooped down, and snatched it up. The hunchback darted ahead with amazing agility and rounded a corner at speed. The detectives broke cover and turned the same corner seconds later. But there was no hunchback in sight: all the men walking along the street were straight-backed, normal. Inspecting the ground, the men found a small piece of putty: the "hunchback's" crooked nose. The bagman, whoever he was, was walking away, his back straight, the money tucked inside his coat. He was never found.

When Petrosino started marking currency, some gangs insisted that victims pay in gold and silver coins. When he identified certain phrases or bits of handwriting as belonging to one Society band, form letters were introduced, the same note sent to hundreds, perhaps thousands of victims, so that the squad couldn't identify any particular gang by the expressions it used. When Petrosino tracked one too many bagmen to their tenements, one gang rented a mailbox.

The men of the Italian Squad became amateur handwriting experts and could identify gangs by the letters they sent out. When the squad found a few scrawled words on a scrap of paper wadding that had been part of an exploded bomb, they rounded up every suspected Black Hander in the city — by now, the list had grown to the thousands — and brought them into local precincts and made them sign the register. The writing of one of the suspects matched the note in the wadding, and he was arrested.

The Society switched to typewriters. Or other methods. A note arrived addressed to Captain Cullen at the Liberty Avenue police station in Brooklyn threatening the lives of the leaders of the police department. It was composed of letters cut out of newspapers.

Sometimes the message took a different form altogether. One victim who'd received a number of letters took them to the Italian Squad. Petrosino assured him that his detectives would investigate the case as soon as they had time; his men were already sleeping at their desks, so not every case could be followed up immediately. A few hours later, a bomb went off in front of the man's shop. He was ruined for having dared approach Petrosino.

The city was on edge. In late September 1905, a hundred-pound boulder smashed through the door of a tobacco store at 230 West 30th Street, nearly flattening a customer before taking out the fanlight and wrecking the interior woodwork. "Screams of 'Black Hand!' rent the air," reported the *Times,* and rumors quickly circulated in the neighborhood that the Society had acquired a gargantuan catapult that was capable of launching boulders over entire city blocks. The truth was more prosaic: the stone had been blasted out of the ground three blocks north, where crews were excavating for the new Pennsylvania Station, and had rolled all the way down Seventh Avenue before colliding with the tobacco shop. The city counted its blessings. At least the Society hadn't yet acquired super-weapons.

The tension was occasionally broken with macabre humor. The sheer volume of Society crimes led to the occasional mistake. Adolph Horowitz, the president of the U.S. Framing & Picture Company of Manhattan, had been threatened with death by the Society if he didn't pay up. One morning he arrived at his shop to find that, overnight, the premises next door had been demolished by a bomb. That day a letter was dropped into his mailbox. "One of our men was sent to carry out our threat, but he made a mistake," the writer explained, "and blew up the store next door." The letter was meant to assure Horowitz that the error in no way affected his obligation to pay the Black Hand its money.

Newspaper wags pounced. The *Washington Post* sent a writer to the verdant suburbs north of New York City, where Society attacks were increasing. "Up in Westchester County is the place to see the people getting shot," the reporter wrote after returning from his excursion. "If you . . . are looking for a new sensation, just take the train from New York, drop off at Katonah or any other pastoral spot in the tombstone belt and straightaway the Black Hand of excitement will be extended to you in welcome." The reporter found that a "general rebellion" was under way in the woods which had changed things for the upper class and their servants. A butler at a fancy home "was now expected to be a rough rider, boer, and a wrestler, and clever enough with the family shotgun to shoot the Black Hander out of a family tangle on the lawn without permitting any birdshot to enter the aristocratic persons or the family youngsters." Children, he reported, were being staked to poles pounded into the front lawns of mansions for their own protection, and "kidnapping alarms" were flying off the shelves of the local stores. (No such devices existed, of course.) He did manage to slip in some real news: fifty deputies from towns all over the region had formed an alliance against the Society and were patrolling Westchester's shaded lanes, armed to the teeth. With a ghastly flourish, the writer ended: "Westchester looks fondly toward the time when their troubles will right themselves by the Italians killing all the negroes and the negroes killing all the Italians."

The satire played on the city's taut nerves. But unlike citizens of other afflicted cities, Manhattanites could comfort themselves with the thought that they had Petrosino and his five loyal men on their side. And indeed the Italian Squad, though overworked and underfunded, was on a tear, arresting hundreds of the most notorious Black Handers in just its first year. Crimes committed by the Society plummeted by 50 percent. The *Times* reported "a calmness that is certainly curious and not to be explained." But the explanation was, in fact, rather clear: Petrosino had fixed a price on Black Hand terror, and fewer criminals were prepared to pay it.

The Italian Squad had evolved from "a homeless, drifting little band of outsiders" to a well-oiled unit that had earned Manhattan's admiration. The "mysterious six" were a new phenomenon in an American city: sworn officers of the law risking their lives to turn back the tide of a looming terror — and they were Italian. To New Yorkers, Petrosino and his men were some of the first immigrants to appear recognizably American. "That little band of zealots," the *Washington Post* would later call them, in admiration.

• • •

THE SQUAD HAD PROVEN ITSELF. COMMISSIONER McADOO, WHO'D resisted its creation, even gave permission for Petrosino to take on more detectives. He went looking for recruits. Petrosino had a wide circle of friends in Little Italy: musicians, storekeepers, fathers and mothers whose families he'd helped out when the Society struck. Among them were the Cavones, a family who'd brought their son Rocco with them from Italy when they'd emigrated some years before. Rocco was a bright kid. "He had shown capacity and management and understanding of the human animal," wrote one reporter, "especially those born with Italian temperament and traditions." He was also, like the young Petrosino, ambitious. By the age of ten, he'd become an errand boy for a wholesale fruit firm. (Like so many Italian children, Cavone quit school to help his family.) By sixteen, he'd become managing clerk of a store, and soon after that he moved on to become a production manager in a Manhattan factory, a heady perch for an immigrant teenager.

One day, Petrosino paid Rocco a visit at work.

"We need you in the police," he said. "I need you."

It wasn't a request to be considered casually. Cavone was on his way to high places in the business world, a rarity for someone so young, especially when one's name ended in a vowel. Yes, the Italian Squad was alluring — they were the idols of much of the colony. But joining would earn Cavone the hatred of many of his countrymen; his life would be in constant danger.

Yet simply to receive a visit from Joseph Petrosino was a high honor. And the pay of a policeman, though low, was still better than what the factory owner was paying Cavone; Italians, even production managers, often earned less than their peers. He accepted the offer.

Cavone quit his job and became a regular patrolman in the department.

Ten days later, he suddenly and quite mysteriously disappeared from the ranks. No one knew what had happened — had he quit? lost heart? — but a day or two later a youth dressed in ragged clothes began hanging around the taverns of Little Italy. He resembled Cavone, but the name the young man gave was different. This newly arrived Italian soon joined in all of the vices that were on full display in the colony. "He was a hanger-on in low basement dives," according to the *Evening World,* "a gambler, a frightened, doubtful pupil of blackmailers and kidnappers." Rocco Cavone was under what would later be called deep cover.

He stopped sleeping in the family home and laid his head on filthy, flea-infested pillows in one of the Mulberry Bend flophouses. These establishments resembled seedy army barracks, where laborers exhausted after a day blasting subway tunnels lay down next to criminals hoping to make their fortune in the Society. Cavone made friends with bartenders, with enforcers and killers. He traded in his business lingo for the special argot of the underworld. He was heard to say things like "Take a slide off Broadway and stay off."

After a few months of this life, Cavone began feeding Petrosino clues about emerging Black Hand gangs: who was leading them, whom they were targeting. Petrosino didn't make any cases with the information. He wanted to know the full range of the outfits' activities before making a move. For months, Rocco Cavone immersed himself in the low life of the Italian colony.

Then, his files filled with Cavone's notes, Petrosino struck. Scores of the criminals the undercover cop had befriended were arrested. Others hurriedly left town. "The few that remained," the *Evening World* reported, "declared war on 'Petrosino's boys.'"

With men like Cavone, directed by Petrosino, the Italian Squad appeared able to take on the Society and win. In the first flush of battle, it seemed that the forces of order might actually prevail.

• • •

THERE WAS ONE PLACE WHERE THE DETECTIVE WASN'T LIONIZED, despite his growing fame and his success with the squad: the NYPD.

His fellow cops constantly sabotaged Petrosino's unit. "Every possible handicap was thrown in his way," according to the *Washington Post,* "and at no time could he count on the cooperation of his superiors or inferiors in rank. All bore themselves in the same contemptuous manner toward the Italian Squad, and when the chance came they would stop at nothing to retard [its] work." Soon after the squad was formed, Petrosino became convinced that members of his own department were spying on him. "There were certain politicians in the city," reported the *Post,* "who were bitterly opposed to the formation of the Italian Squad, and those men had sufficient influence over the members of the uniformed force to compel them to report direct to them." Petrosino was so concerned about informers that, at the beginning of an investigation, he used telegrams to let his detectives know where to meet him. He didn't want his men followed from 300 Mulberry Street to the squad's offices, and he didn't trust telephones.

One of the essential tools of a homicide detective in a city like New York, where tens of thousands of new immigrants were crowding the streets every year, was the mug shot. Suspects were brought to 300 Mulberry Street and "mugged," or photographed, and their pictures entered into the department's vast collection. But when Petrosino brought his suspects to headquarters, the officers in charge refused to shoot the pictures. The detective was forced to have one of the squad members strike up a conversation with a suspect on the street while Petrosino pointed a camera at the criminal, hoping to get a decent likeness. The pictures were often useless; Petrosino was a terrible photographer. The trick also exposed his men to the suspects they were supposed to be following secretly.

At their headquarters on Waverly Place, the behavior of the Italian men in broad-brimmed hats began to attract attention. Who were these dark-haired strangers, tramping in and out of the rooms at all times of the night? A "young and ambitious" roundsman patrolling the block studied the swarthy strangers, who seemed to act "in what he regarded as a suspicious manner." After observing the Italians for a while, the cop ran back to headquarters and reported that a gang of potential Black Handers had moved into 175 Waverly Place.

Captain John "Ginger Jack" O'Brien was given the assignment; ironically, Petrosino had worked under O'Brien earlier in his career. The captain collected a squad of men and they hurried over to Waverly, where they found the door of the "real estate" office locked. O'Brien ordered one of his men to break into the apartment. The man threw his weight against the door and it shuddered open. The cops slowly walked through the rooms, taking note of the assorted weapons spread out on one table and the photos of menacing-looking Italian men tacked to the walls. O'Brien's men proceeded to tear the rooms apart looking for fake currency or other evidence. (As well as kidnapping and murder, the Society was believed to have its hand in the counterfeiting racket.) They pulled out the desk drawers and dumped the contents on the floor and tore up the carpet to study the floorboards.

At that moment, an unsuspecting Petrosino, still in disguise as an Italian laborer, returned to the building after chasing down a lead on a developing case. His panicked landlady met him at the front door, "begging him to fly at once, as the police were after him." As the detective tried to calm her, a cop spotted him and informed Ginger Jack that the leader of the gang had arrived. O'Brien rushed down to the foyer and, failing to recognize Petrosino, tried to wrestle him to the ground. But the detective was much too strong for that. He gave the captain "a hip-lock back heel" that sent O'Brien spinning into a wall and then collapsing to the floor. O'Brien staggered to his feet, pulled out his service weapon, and slowly walked forward, bringing the gun to within inches of Petrosino's face. "Would you like to go to the station," he asked, "with or without the trouble of sending for a hearse?"

Petrosino froze. He knew too many Italians who'd been killed by cops for resisting. He reached slowly for the lapel of his jacket, and pulled it back inch by inch. There, pinned to his shirt, was his detective's shield.

O'Brien let the gun drop away.

The story made the papers the next day, and Captain O'Brien quickly disappeared from his precinct. It was later reported he was "rusticating in Greenpoint"—that is, he'd been demoted to a beat patrol in the far reaches of Brooklyn. But Petrosino bore no grudges toward the other officers. He even recommended the roundsman who'd spotted his "gang" for a promotion to detective sergeant. Petrosino loved an intelligent cop.

Still, it was a moment to savor. An Italian-born detective had prevailed over a red-haired captain named O'Brien in the New York Police Department in 1905. "'The Dago' had become a superstar," wrote one historian of the era. "His bosses, desperately in need of his case-closing skills, did not dare silence him."

Petrosino had truly arrived.

6

EXPLOSION

ON THE AFTERNOON OF OCTOBER 16, 1905, JOSEPH PETROSINO was standing in a doorway, watching the entrance of a small Italian grocery at 13 Stanton Street. The shop was owned by the Gimavalvo brothers. One of the brothers had come alone from Sicily and then worked until he had enough passage money to bring his sibling over. The process had been repeated until the entire family was reunited in Manhattan, all achieved through the proceeds from their little shop.

Then the Black Hand letters started arriving. The Gimavalvos had immediately called Petrosino. Their perch in America was fragile. Could he save their American destinies by sweeping these animals from their doorstep?

A letter from another Black Hand victim to the *New York Times* echoed the Gimavalvos' terror. It came from a man who could speak for every casualty of the Black Hand. "My name is Salvatore Spinella," it began. "My parents were of honest station in Italy. I came here eighteen years ago, and went to work as a painter, like my Father. I married. I raised a family. I am an American citizen fifteen years."

Spinella had prospered as a house painter and bought two buildings, at 314 and 316 East 11th Street. "My family all are happy," he wrote. Then a Black Hand letter arrived, demanding $7,000.

> I tell them to go to hell. They try to blow up my house. I go to the police and fight them as well as I can. They set off another bomb; two, three, four, five bombs. My business is ruined. My tenants leave, all but six of thirty-six families . . . I am a ruined man. My family live in terror day and night. There is a policeman in front of my house, but what does he do? Only my brother Francisco and myself can watch my wife and children, who dare not go out. How long must this endure?

Spinella and his brother bought shotguns and guarded their houses around the clock. Spinella's hair turned gray in a few days and he became known around Little Italy as *l'Uomo Che Non Dorme,* "the Man Who Does Not Sleep." One of the letters he received, which were addressed to "Piece of Carrion" and "Spy and Traitor," told him that "the entire Police Department of New York is unable to save you." The writer was correct. Spinella, after months of torment, lost both houses and was forced to seek work as a manual laborer. There were so many men like him in New York that Petrosino lost count.

Petrosino studied the pedestrians who came down Stanton Street, hoping to recognize a face from the thousands he'd memorized. As he waited, he wondered what his next stop should be: a meeting with the fruit peddler on the Brooklyn Bridge whose life was in mortal danger, or a rendezvous with the Society men "who say they are not afraid of hell because they have chosen to be bad men on earth," each of whom held an Italian family in terror? Or should he go to the West 3rd Street shop of Carmello de Giacono, who'd recently been visited by a stranger who told him that he and his fellow Black Handers had voted on de Giacono's fate, and it "was unanimous for murder"? One member had told de Giacono: "They have been wrangling about how you shall go to your death. Some want to stab you, others would shoot you, but most are in favor of blowing you and your shop up with dynamite."

Petrosino had few resources to dedicate to these desperate people. Little Italy had been chronically underpoliced for years. The editors of the *New York Journal,* owned by the multimillionaire William Randolph Hearst, confirmed this in an editorial. "The Italians pay their taxes," the paper argued, "and pay their rent, and do a great deal of hard work. They are entitled to police protection AND THEY HAVE NOT HAD IT." Not only did the police ignore calls for more patrols and prosecutions, but also they actually prohibited many law-abiding Italians from getting guns. "If the police had been paid *not* to detect," wrote the journalist Sidney Reid, "they could not have done it more successfully."

This presented Petrosino with a dilemma: How does one choose whom to save and whom to let die?

As he watched the front of the Gimavalvos' store that afternoon, with customers entering empty-handed and leaving with paper bags stuffed with eggplants and lemons, Petrosino made his decision: the fruit peddler's case was the most pressing. Everyone else would have to wait. When his appointment drew near, he spotted one Sergeant Funston, whose precinct included 13 Stanton Street, and called him over. He told the officer that the store needed to be guarded continuously until he could return. Funston wrote a note to one Captain Murtha, an Irish officer, with Petrosino's instructions that he put at least one guard on the store, then assured the detective that the store would be watched around the clock.

Satisfied, Petrosino began walking toward the Brooklyn Bridge. There he met the fruit peddler and pretended to be the man's assistant as they set up the humble cart in the middle of the span. Once the fruit was displayed in its boxes, the two rested, watching the crowd and waiting for the extortionists to appear.

Almost immediately there was a snag. A policeman stopped by the cart and told Petrosino and the peddler to move on. Petrosino explained who he was — as a detective he actually outranked the cop — but the cop made such a public commotion that the chances of a rendezvous were ruined. Petrosino was furious. Clearly, the officer saw only two wops making a nuisance of themselves. Petrosino gave up, spoke with the fruit seller, and made his way home to bed.

That night, at 3 a.m., a "terrific explosion" ripped through the Gimavalvos' apartment building, smashing through brick walls and tearing the oak front door off its hinges. The family members were knocked out of their beds and covered in flying glass and splinters of wood. Windows were shattered up and down the block. When the cops arrived, Italians throughout the tenement were on their knees, praying for protection. "A thirteen inch shell could not have done more damage," reported the *Times*. A passing pedestrian had his face badly cut by flying glass. Miraculously, no one was killed.

Petrosino heard about the bombing and couldn't understand what had happened. Where was Murtha's man? Where was the NYPD? He stormed off to Murtha's precinct and there learned the truth. When the bomb throwers had arrived on Stanton Street in the middle of the night, there wasn't a cop to be seen. Captain Murtha had lied about protecting the Gimavalvos.

At this, Petrosino's famous *pazienza* finally gave way. The accumulated rage that had been building for months, if not years, the memory of insults, slights, and aspersions against his race and family, finally broke through. Petrosino erupted. He found a *Times* reporter and told him to take down what he said. "When I . . . learned of the explosion in Stanton Street," he told the man, "I hit myself on either side of the head with my two hands. And then I said to myself things about Captain Murtha for which I am sorry." Clearly, though, he wasn't sorry. The Italian Squad had resolutely protected the family, but the moment the assignment was handed to an Irish cop, the Gimavalvos had been attacked. Petrosino could not contain his fury or his feelings of helplessness. "We have worked so hard and faithfully to suppress this brigandage. We have gone without sleep and food, and subjected ourselves to indignities." Petrosino rarely, if ever, spoke publicly with such naked emotion. But he was no longer willing to stand up for the NYPD while it allowed Italians to be bombed.

What the detective was trying to get across to the *Times* and its readers was that each and every battle in the war on the Society mattered. The attack, Petrosino knew, would become a recruitment tool for the Black Hand. At that very moment, reports of the successful bombing were most likely being repeated all over Little Italy "to the eager ears of Sicilian boys." Brave Italians would be silenced and cowed. The murderers would "gloat over our defeat." And they would seek new victims.

The NYPD was losing the trust of the city's Italian Americans. "There is very little hope, to my mind, of ever breaking up these secret bands," admitted one police captain. Every time an Italian was victimized and no one was punished, it made Petrosino look like an *nfami,* a *spia* — an informer in the pay of the oppressors.

Never before had the detective publicly expressed his anger with the NYPD and its Irish leaders. But now he'd had enough. And he wanted New Yorkers — all Americans, in fact — to realize that they could be next. "They are getting bolder," he told reporters about the Society's minions. "In time they may find a way to prey on the general public. They are clever enough, I believe, to find that way." Petrosino had been saying this for months, but now he added a new twist: "Their society is governed by an Executive Committee, with headquarters in various cities of the United States. The committeemen are called chiefs, and are obeyed absolutely."

This was nonsense, and Petrosino knew it. His investigations had uncovered no national network of Society members, no "executive committee" or headquarters or any such thing. But now he claimed that he had. Perhaps he believed that only by playing to the nation's fears, by confirming its worst nightmares about a vast conspiracy of Black Handers embedded in the heartland, could he reach Americans and shake them out of their apathy.

Even in the midst of his outburst, Petrosino had an objective. The

Italian Squad was outmanned. They needed powerful allies to defeat the Society, and Petrosino had one in mind. "We may be able to run them down in time," he said, "but there is only one way to get rid of the terror, and that is through the Federal Government."

What was Petrosino asking for, specifically? Three things: For the federal government to demand that Italy fine any official who granted a passport to a known criminal. For Congress to pass laws that would allow for the deportation of anyone with a criminal record back to Italy. (Almost every Black Hander arrested in New York was found to have committed crimes back home.) And, finally, for the Secret Service to join the war against the Black Hand.

No one had ever suggested that the U.S. government enter the war against the Society. But Petrosino clearly felt that without it, the effort was doomed. The request also came with a personal significance for Petrosino. He had a painful, even tragic history with the Secret Service that reflected on the present crisis. To illuminate that shared history, we must look back five years.

• • •

IN THE SUMMER OF 1900, A THIN, MUSTACHIOED SILK WEAVER named Gaetano Bresci left his factory job in Paterson, New Jersey, and the anarchist newspaper he'd founded and sailed for the port of Le Havre, France. Once he landed, he made his way to Paris and spent hours walking through the grounds of the Paris Exposition; he bought a silk handkerchief for his wife, with his name embroidered in crimson in the corner. He appeared to be just another tourist taking in the sights of the magnificent fair. Bresci then boarded a train and traveled to the town of Castel San Pietro, Italy, not far from Bologna, where he roomed with a relative. Bresci purchased a five-shot .32 revolver and practiced shooting at targets in the yard. He was training for the mission he'd come to believe was his life's work: to assassinate King Umberto I, in revenge for a cold-blooded massacre of ninety Italian radicals during riots in Milan two years earlier. On July 29, as the young and dashing king was leaving Monza after awarding medals to a group of athletes,

Bresci ran toward the royal carriage and fired four shots into the monarch, killing him.

The Italian government believed that Bresci hadn't acted alone, and that the keys to the true motives for Umberto's death lay in Paterson, which was acknowledged by just about everyone to be a nest of anarchists. "This country," remarked a writer for *New Outlook* magazine, "is without doubt the center and headquarters of the Italian latter-day Anarchy, which is far more dangerous than any of the forms which have preceded." The Italian government asked President McKinley to order an investigation of Bresci and his associates, but the Secret Service conducted only the most casual inquiry before giving up on the case. The reason was somewhat embarrassing. "Panic reigned in Washington for a time," reported the *Post*, "when it was discovered there wasn't a man among the operatives well enough qualified to go and live among the anarchists in this country and wring from them the inner secrets of their clan." In fact, the Secret Service had not one Italian-speaking agent on its staff. Rome continued to press McKinley for answers. Finally the president mentioned the matter to his vice president, Teddy Roosevelt, whose mind immediately flashed back to his rambunctious days as police commissioner of New York City. "I have just the man for this job," Roosevelt told McKinley. "His name is Joe Petrosino, and he's one of the best detectives in New York." A call was placed to 300 Mulberry, and Petrosino immediately agreed to go to Paterson, infiltrate the anarchist clique that Bresci had been a part of, and learn as much as he could about the group and its intentions. He would carry out the mission in total secrecy and report his findings directly to the president.

It was a moment Petrosino could only have dreamt of. Here was a chance to prove his patriotism, his skills as a detective, and his friendship with Roosevelt in one fell swoop.

Petrosino walked back to his apartment and went straight to his famous closet. For the Paterson mission, he chose an outdated suit typical of the *grignoni*, men who always arrived in America wearing unstylish clothes that marked them irrefutably as greenhorns. He placed some laborers' shirts and trousers, along with underwear, in a suitcase. Taking on the guise of Pietro Moretti, an unlettered middle-aged laborer who'd recently arrived from Italy, a type that would blend in easily with the textile workers and blue-collar idealists who populated Bresci's circle, Petrosino left his apartment and boarded a train for Paterson.

On his arrival, the detective checked into Bertoldi's Hotel, which was known to host meetings of the local anarchist societies. Bresci, the assassin, had stayed at the hotel and had even met his wife there. True to his usual style, Petrosino set about looking for work and eventually landed a job on a construction site. He spent his days laboring in the sun and his nights pretending to be a budding revolutionary.

The detective remained in Paterson for weeks, talking, eating, and arguing with the anarchists who worked in the textile factories. He listened to their wild monologues about world capitalism, read along with them articles from *La Questione Sociale,* an anarchist journal published right there in New Jersey, which decried the greed of the ruling class and its puppets in the palaces and parliament buildings across Europe and the Americas. When he returned to his room, Petrosino made careful notes about what he'd heard, then collapsed onto the threadbare blanket and slept. After three months, he felt he'd learned all he could, and one night Pietro Moretti suddenly disappeared from Paterson, never to be seen again. Hours later, Joseph Petrosino, dressed in his derby hat and black suit, reappeared in New York and quickly made an appointment to see Roosevelt and McKinley at the White House.

When he sat down with the president and vice president, Petrosino eagerly poured out his findings. What he'd learned in New Jersey was shocking: the group that Bresci had emerged from was made up of dedicated revolutionaries who had drawn names from a drum to determine who would kill Umberto. But there was still more worrying news: the group's work, Petrosino said, wasn't finished. More assassinations of world leaders were planned. And at the top of the anarchists' target list was President McKinley himself.

Petrosino probably expected that his news would produce alarm, at the very least, in the two formidable men who sat before him. But McKinley only smiled gently and said nothing. The president, possessed of a genial and trusting nature, believed he didn't have an enemy in the world. To him, talk of an assassination was nothing but rash gossip. Roosevelt, too, seemed unimpressed. He made an offhand comment about not wanting an anarchist to make him president, and then the two men thanked Petrosino for his hard work and sent him on his way.

The detective took the train back to New York filled with bitter disappointment. He'd spent three months on a highly dangerous mission in which he'd uncovered a plot to kill the American president, among others. But McKinley and Petrosino's friend T.R. had treated him like an excitable amateur, a man completely out of his depth. It was clear that McKinley and the Secret Service agents whose job it was to protect him weren't going to take his report seriously. Perhaps they simply wanted to be able to tell their counterparts in Rome that a thorough investigation had been conducted and nothing urgent had been found.

Months later, on September 6, 1901, President McKinley was shaking hands inside the Temple of Music on the sprawling grounds of the Pan-American Exposition in Buffalo, New York, when a man with mad-looking eyes and a heavily bandaged right arm approached and fired two shots into the president's abdomen at point-blank range. Eight days later, McKinley was dead of gangrene. His assassin, Leon Czolgosz, was an anarchist.

Moments after those shots rang out, the phones on Park Row in lower Manhattan — Newspaper Row — began to ring. The editors learned of the assassination and immediately called their reporters at 301 Mulberry, opposite police headquarters. The reporters rushed across the street to get the NYPD's reaction. When a few of the journalists came across Petrosino, they told him the news. The detective listened to their reports in stunned silence. Then, to the reporters' astonishment, he began to sob. He wept "as copiously and hysterically as a woman," one reporter wrote; his public display of grief "came as a revelation to his comrades" and to the gathered journalists as well. The newspapermen found it hard to believe that the legendary hunter of men could show such deep emotion. Perhaps a few were even shocked to find that a member of a despised minority would feel so strongly about the killing of an American president.

But Petrosino loved America with the unreasoning love of the immigrant. "No native-born American was ever a more ardent patriot," wrote Frank Marshall White. "He considered himself under an eternal and illimitable debt of gratitude to his adopted country for the opportunities it had given him and so many others of his race." Petrosino had taken the request to help protect the country's leader with deep seriousness, and now McKinley was dead.

After a few moments, Petrosino gained control of himself. "I warned him!" he said to the assembled journalists. "I told him the anarchist criminals wanted to kill him. But the President was too good-hearted and believed too much in other people's goodness." The reporters ran back to their offices and filed long stories headlined "PETROSINO WARNED HIM!" and "ITALIAN DETECTIVE TRIED TO SAVE MCKINLEY."

In the years since the McKinley tragedy, Petrosino had worked closely with the Secret Service on a number of cases, including the Barrel Murder. Italian criminals were often involved in counterfeiting, and sometimes Black Hand gangs dabbled in the game themselves. Over the course of several years, Petrosino had come to believe that the agency's leaders in New York knew the names of "nearly every man" engaged in Black Hand work. On the face of it, this sounds like a preposterous statement. Why would the Secret Service have the names of Society members but refuse to act? But Petrosino had an unimpeachable source for his belief: the agency itself.

On a hot August day in 1904, a special delivery letter appeared at the office of Joel M. Marx, the assistant district attorney for New York City. Marx was a hard-charging prosecutor who'd gone after Italians who were selling false citizenship papers; scores of them were now languishing in jail. The letter read: "Mr. Marx, I wait for you at door yesterday evening. I see you but I say I give one more chance: if you don't stop this business, we will kill you . . . and the Italian detectives. Let the poor people go . . . If you don't stop we kill you and your children. Revenge."

The letter was signed with a heart pierced by an arrow, flanked by two crosses, well-known symbols of the Black Hand.

Several Secret Service agents were attached to Marx's office, and he put them on the case immediately. "This is the first time the Black Hand properly has come within the jurisdiction of the Secret Service," Marx told the *Tribune* in a front-page story. "My men are hot on the trail of the gang, and expect to break it up before we are through."

But he was fudging on the jurisdiction issue. The Secret Service had no power under its charter to pursue criminals who threatened government employees. Marx had simply deputized his men to investigate a threat against an important constituency: himself.

Petrosino must have been startled by this news. He and his men had received hundreds of death threats from the Black Hand, and not once had the agency volunteered to hunt down the culprits. But even more intriguing information was to follow: Marx went on to say that the Secret Service kept thorough files on the Society. "We have a description," he told reporters, "of practically every member of the Black Hand."

This was almost certainly bluster. There were thousands of Black Handers in New York, with new recruits joining daily, and it would have been impossible for the Secret Service to keep track of them all. The only near-complete file of Black Hand criminals resided in Petrosino's head, and that was constantly evolving. But clearly the agency had kept tabs on Black Hand activity, and it was possible they were aware of the major players. That information would have been invaluable to the Italian Squad.

• • •

NOW, IN OCTOBER 1905, AFTER THE ATTEMPTED MURDERS OF THE Gimavalvos, Petrosino publicly appealed to the Secret Service, which had once called on him in their time of need, to join the fight. He'd risked his life to assist the Secret Service and protect the president, but the issue went much deeper: Italians were being imported to build America's infrastructure. They were contributing millions of dollars to the economy every year. They were, by and large, decent, devout, hardworking citizens. And they were being preyed on by criminals of extraordinary cruelty, but their government offered little or no help. Did Italian Americans deserve the same protection under the law that any other citizen received? Petrosino believed they did. The day after his interview with the *New York Times*, he raised the stakes in another newspaper interview. "You may think I am foolish," he said, "but unless the federal authorities come to our aid soon, New York will wake up some day to the biggest catastrophe it has ever seen."

After his appeal was published, Petrosino sat back and awaited an answer. It arrived in the October 21 edition of the *Times*. An unnamed official from the Treasury Department, which oversaw the Secret Service, formally replied to Petrosino's request. "If Detective Prosini," the official said, mispronouncing the detective's name, "wishes to obtain the assistance of the Secret Service bureau in his fight against the Black Hand or Mafia, he can do so by paying our men the same as if they were members of a private detective agency." The Society had "confined their operations to individuals," and until they moved against the government itself, the agency was "not at liberty to intervene."

There were practical reasons for the response. The Secret Service office in New York had only twenty agents, engaged full-time in chasing counterfeiters. It was important work, and it consumed significant amounts of both time and money. To take on the Black Hand would have placed an enormous additional burden on the office. And the Secret Service wasn't technically allowed to investigate crimes such as Black Hand cases, although Roosevelt and his administration had rendered that restriction meaningless by 1905. They'd expanded the agency's role to many types of crimes — corruption, land fraud — that its agents weren't legally authorized to investigate. And the Secret Service had taken action against the Society before, in the case of Assistant District Attorney Marx. The reality is, if the agency had wanted to go to the aid of Petrosino and his people, it could have.

But it didn't. And the statement from the faceless bureaucrat wasn't just a rejection. It was an insult. If Italian Americans wanted protection from murder and extortion, the agency was telling Petrosino, they would have to pay for it.

Why would a spokesman for a government agency choose to humiliate publicly, in the *New York Times,* a cop who was trying to prevent American citizens from being murdered? We have no evidence, other than the cutting nature of the words, of what lurked behind the agency's reply; its archives are silent on the subject. It might have been simple prejudice against Italians; it might have been pique that a dago was making demands of the agency in such a public way. But whatever motivated the statement, its substance was clear: Italian immigrants would receive no help in their life-or-death struggle with the Black Hand. American citizens or not, they were being thrown to the wolves.

7

WAVE

AS PETROSINO MADE HIS WAY THROUGH LITTLE ITALY ON A TYP-ical summer morning, the streets swarmed with life. Peddlers hawked prosciutto, fresh bananas, and brightly colored hand-drawn portraits of the king and queen of Italy. Delivery wagons trundled down the narrow streets, scattering pedestrians and trailing small children waiting for scraps to fall from the back, which they scooped up and carried home to their mothers. He passed theaters featuring traditional Italian puppet shows, tenements where open windows emitted the squawks and hoots of monkeys as from a zoo's big house, as entire floors were given over to the raising of the animals for the organ grinders who roamed the city. He passed the offices of marriage brokers promising honest virgins from the old country, and undertakers whose signs advertised the cost of shipping a body back to be buried in Italian soil. In the alleys as he strode past, crap games were in progress and religious processions were forming up, carrying the statues of saints pinned with dollar bills, meant as offerings for deathly ill relatives or friends. As the black derby moved through the crowd, above it the fire escapes were crisscrossed with lines of laundry, while on the rooftops, bedsheets were laid out, covered with yard upon yard of crushed tomatoes drying in the sun before being turned into tomato sauce for the family's evening pasta. Men's straw hats fluttered in the breeze, stolen from the heads of their owners by small boys and clothespinned to lines strung from one side of the street to the other.

Newcomers who'd arrived only days or even hours before on a steamship from Genoa passed the detective on the streets. Italian immigrants landed in New York and were often sped on their way into the heartland, to jobs in Kentucky or Michigan or Pennsylvania, to lend their backs to the industrial revolution that was transforming the country. Petrosino could have told you their histories after one glance. They were from Maida or Padua or Naples, and they'd seen a billboard in their town square that promised *"Buoni Lavori!"* (Good Jobs!), high wages, and cheap steamship tickets. There was even one poster that showed a textile mill with a bank across the street, and laborers striding from one to the other carrying bags of money. The men would have left their homes and boarded the ship, some carrying a ball of yarn in their luggage, leaving a cousin or girlfriend on the pier holding the other end. When the horn sounded and the boat moved away from the dock, the yarn would slowly unspool, the line of thin wool floating in the air until the last turn of the roll, at which point the string hung in the air, kept aloft by the shore breeze.

Once they landed in New York and were processed through Ellis Island, the men flowed across the country in search of work. In Chicago, Italians toiled in the foundries and factories. In the rail yards spreading out into the Midwest, Italians laid track. In West Virginia, they mined coal. Among the ones who stayed in New York, the men dynamited and dug the subway tunnels while the women sewed in the garment factories. In Brooklyn, they welded ships. In upstate New York, they dug out reservoirs and sealed the banks of the aquifers with concrete. In Michigan, they mined iron ore. In New England, they quarried stone and granite. In Kansas City, they slaughtered cattle in the stockyards. In St. Louis, they forged bricks in that city of a hundred brick plants. In Delaware, they picked peaches. In Florida, it was cotton. In Louisiana, rice and sugar. Everywhere they sweated beneath the sun, building roads and canals. Italians, who were often hired for the most dangerous work, suffered 25 percent of all industrial accidents in the country, with one in five men who came to America maimed or killed on the job. "Your railroads, your public buildings, your coal are wet with Italian sweat and blood," said the writer Enrico Sartorio.

And they were sometimes beaten and enslaved. One Calabrian at a labor camp remembered trying to help a fellow Italian on the run.

My attention was drawn to the other side of the creek, where an Italian was shouting for help — appealing to us as fellow-countrymen to aid him. He had been felled by a blow of a heavy stick dealt him by one of the guards. Cervi, my friend, and I tried to cross over to help him, but were prevented by our boss, who drove us back at the point of a pistol; all I dared do was to shout to him not to resist or he would be killed and to go back; the man who had struck him lifted him bodily by his coat and pushed him on, striking him every time he stumbled or fell from exhaustion.

"I am nailed to the cross," wrote one immigrant from some unidentified point in the American interior. "Of the 100 *paesani* who came here, only 40 have survived. Who is here to protect us? We have neither priests nor *carabinieri* to look after our safety." Even in death, the Sicilians and Calabrians were worth less than their fellow men. When, in 1910, an explosion ripped through the Lawson mine in Black Diamond, California, blasting fire out the mine mouth and shooting eight-foot timbers half a mile from the shaft, twelve miners were killed, all of them foreign-born. Families of the Irish and other nationalities were given $1,200 for each of their loved ones; the Italians received $150.

But they came anyway, pulled by the promise of America. And secreted in the carts and railcars were one or two men who carried with them the germ of the Black Hand. By 1906, the Society seemed to be everywhere.

Bombs tore apart homes in St. Louis; the bodies of Italians turned up on the slopes of hills in Appalachian coal country with dozens of stab wounds; children went missing in Detroit and were never heard from again; families in Los Angeles abandoned their businesses and fled on steamships back to Italy. In October 1906, a Black Hander walked into a Connecticut home where Giuseppe Vazanini was eating his supper, placed a gun to his chest, and shot him dead. In Pennsylvania, violent gun battles between Society sympathizers and Italian residents broke out in the mining town of Walston that left three dead and a dozen seriously wounded; in another village, a Black Hander tossed a stick of dynamite into a shack occupied by miners the Society believed had informed on them, blowing three men to shreds.

Governor Samuel W. Pennypacker of Pennsylvania became so alarmed by the mayhem that he ordered in the state constabulary, the third time he'd been forced to call in troops in a single week. "The murderous spirit of the Black Hand," one newspaper observed, "is beginning to manifest itself all over the state." Society members who were arrested in one town "sneered at the officers" and "declared that the society was so strong that it would be impossible to break it up, and that eventually it would rule the country." In Westchester County, New York, laborers were being shot, knifed, or beaten to death. In response, local sheriffs swore in and armed posses of men, who went roaming through the countryside with orders to kill any "desperado" molesting the workers. "WHOLESALE MURDERS IN WATERSHED REGION," the *Times* reported that August. "TRAINS CROWDED WITH ITALIANS FLEEING FROM THE BLACK HAND."

Americans were spooked. A Chicago woman stabbed an Italian detective who'd staked out a Black Hand rendezvous, thinking he was the bagman. A Pennsylvania man shot and wounded a man who charged past him at a moment when he was expecting a Society member to show up. It turned out the victim was an innocent pedestrian running for a streetcar.

It became abundantly clear by the spring of 1906 that Petrosino's warning that non-Italians would soon fall victim to the Society was quickly becoming a reality. Letters had begun to arrive in far-flung cities and towns where the Society had been merely a report in the local newspaper, some of them written in languages other than Italian or English. There were notes in German, in Greek (signed *"Maupa Xepi,"* which transliterates as "Black Hand"), notes in Yiddish and Hebrew and, later in the Black Hand era, even one verified missive composed in Latin. And it wasn't just day laborers and other workers who were receiving these threats. Inevitably, as the Black Hand expanded geographically, its appetites increased, and the rich and powerful came within its sights. In fact, in the first months of 1906, it looked as if the stain had spread all the way to the House of Representatives.

The affair began with postcards sent to various members of the legislature. On one side was a drawing of a black hand. Beneath were the words "Only four days to come." The appearance of the cards caused a commotion in Congress. "Members began to ransack their brains," reported the *Cleveland Plain Dealer,* "in an effort to think of what act they had committed to gain the enmity of the Black Hand."

Two days later, another batch of notes arrived. Again there was a sketch of a black palm print, along with the words "You only have two days more." The countdown caused "nervous prostration" among the legislators, and security inside and outside the chambers was increased. The following day brought additional letters, which read, "You have only one day more."

The next morning, as the Capitol waited, hypnotized with dread, the final batch of notes arrived in congressional mailboxes. The mystery was revealed. "No more Black Hands," the letters read. "Use Blank's soap." It had all been a marketing campaign.

The congressional scare was diverting, but a far more revealing case was unfolding farther north, in the quiet burg of Springfield, Massachusetts. That same winter, a Black Hand letter arrived at the home of Daniel B. Wesson, the "Revolver King," of the firm Smith & Wesson. Wesson's guns had helped turn the tide in the Civil War and win the West; and at the ripe old age of eighty-one, he was enjoying his money in high style. The gun mogul was worth north of $30 million, and he'd spent a fair slice of that fortune on his gargantuan house, a "magnificent pile of masonry" that many mistook for a large hotel.

The threats terrified the elderly mogul. Police and private detectives converged on the mansion and questioned anyone approaching its front entrance. "Half a dozen of the most experienced men in the police department were secreted in the underbrush," reported the *Washington Post*. Patrolman Simon J. Connery played a particularly dramatic role in the case. One evening he entered the mansion, donned a false beard, along with one of Wesson's business suits, and spent a few minutes practicing speaking in the millionaire's "peremptory tone." When Wesson's barouche was called to the front door, pulled by two fine horses, Connery emerged from the house and sang out, "To the corner of Library and Carew streets!" with an actorly flourish. No extortionists or assassins appeared, however.

But the industrialist, gripped by fear, refused to leave the house. As the weeks went by, "his nervous system gradually broke under the strain." On August 4, Wesson died. The coroner reported that heart failure "superinduced by neurosis" was the cause of his passing, but many of his neighbors believed that the strain of the Black Hand threat had contributed to his death. Wesson was buried in Springfield, in a steel vault, to prevent the Society from tampering with his remains.

But the most interesting feature of the Wesson case was the identity of the agency that had been called in to protect him: the U.S. Secret Service.

As it turned out, despite their declaration that Black Hand crimes didn't fall under their jurisdiction, Secret Service agents had arrived in Springfield soon after the letter was dropped into the Wessons' mailbox. Why, when they'd rejected Petrosino's urgent request for the exact same services? "The writer of the Black Hand letters," reported the *Boston Daily Globe,* "comes under U.S. jurisdiction by virtue of having sent the letters to Mr. Wesson through the mails." *But,* Petrosino could

have cried, *so did every Black Hander who threatened a poor Italian!*
The Wesson case revealed what Petrosino knew well by 1906: the Secret
Service *was* willing to go into the field to protect Americans against the
Black Hand, but only if they were rich.

When four-year-old Horace Marvin, the blond, blue-eyed child of
a prominent doctor in Delaware, went missing one day, apparently
snatched off the top of a haystack on the family's sprawling 537-acre
farm near Delaware Bay, President Roosevelt himself wrote the boy's
father in sympathy:

> My dear Dr. Marvin:
> I am in receipt of your telegram of the twenty-second. Anything that
> the government can do to help you will, of course, be done, for save
> only the crime of assault upon women, there is none so dreadful as
> that which has brought heartbreaking sorrow to your household. I
> have at once communicated with the Post Office Department, asking
> that all aid we have in our power be given along the lines you men-
> tion, or along any other that may prove practicable.
>
> > Sincerely yours,
> > Theo. Roosevelt.

A group of Secret Service agents, led by a general superintendent, were
dispatched to Delaware soon after and began interviewing witnesses.

The response to the lost boy with the blue eyes couldn't have
been more different from the one afforded to the dozens of dark-eyed
boys and girls snatched away from their families by the Black Hand.
Roosevelt never once sent agents to find an Italian child, never wrote a
note of condolence to his or her parents, never spoke out, never acted.
The two sets of children existed in separate categories of American life.

How empty the president's common-man rhetoric must have
sounded to Petrosino in those moments.

· · ·

THE ONSLAUGHT SPARED NO ONE. GOVERNORS, MAYORS, JUDGES, even the heir to the Coca-Cola fortune, Asa G. Candler, earned the Society's wrath. (Candler's persecutor turned out to be a fellow member of his Methodist church, who was promptly arrested by the Secret Service.) A justice of the peace in Paterson, New Jersey, who had helped police track the Society received "an infernal machine" in the mail. When he opened the package, it exploded, blowing the man to pieces. The scourge even crossed the Atlantic. Count István Tisza, the former prime minister of Austria-Hungary, received Black Hand letters from America threatening his relatives with death unless he paid $2,000. Papers around the world gaped at the audacity. The Secret Service traced the letters to Lebanon, Pennsylvania, where suspicion soon fell on Ignace Wenzler, an iron molder who worked in one of the local steel mills. A Secret Service agent befriended Wenzler and asked him to write a letter in German to a friend of his. Wenzler agreed. The agent took the letter, thanked the iron molder, then rushed back to the agency's temporary headquarters and placed the new note alongside two Black Hand missives. The handwriting was a match. Wenzler was arrested.

Despite the squads of Pinkerton men, police chiefs, postmasters, and Secret Service agents dedicated to protecting the rich, no millionaire was ever shot, bombed, stilettoed, or otherwise physically assaulted by the Black Hand, though quite a few were scared out of their wits. The tormentors who pursued these wealthy men often turned out to be Black Hand impostors — that is, nonviolent (and non-Italian) opportunists who saw their chance to make a quick dollar. As Italian Americans died or watched their homes go up in flames while their persecutors remained free, the rich, far more often, saw their victimizers caught, convicted, and jailed.

By the end of 1906, the Black Hand held sway in cities from coast to coast, and many citizens feared that darker days were on the way. "A reign of murder and terror has existed which steadily grows worse," proclaimed the *New York Tribune*. No easy remedies presented themselves.

There was no national law enforcement agency willing to go after the Society or capable of doing so; the FBI wouldn't come into existence for another two years.

Like an epidemic or a natural disaster, the Society even created a new class of internal refugee in America: the Black Hand victim on the run. "From the moment he stepped on American shores," noted the *Cincinnati Enquirer* about one such refugee, "he has been haunted from city to city, from house to house by desperate men bent upon inflicting vengeance. He moved from town to town, but everywhere were new, mysterious, dangerous figures lurking for him in dark corners and alleyways." One morning the refugee would be gone from the new city where he'd only just arrived. The sight of a face seen once too often in one too many places would send him fleeing to the next way station.

In the tiny Pennsylvania town of Hillsville, two hundred Italians left for Italy in the space of six months. "Many more" had fled the larger town of Newcastle, leaving neither explanations nor forwarding addresses. It was easy to stumble into the nightmare: one could do so simply by overhearing a conversation. Benjamin de Gilda had immigrated to Philadelphia and built up a shoemaking business through hard work and scrupulous saving. His roommate, a man named Morelli, was secretly a Black Hand member, and soon became convinced that de Gilda had overheard a conversation that implicated Morelli in a murder plot. The Society gave de Gilda a choice: join or die. He refused. "Persuasion and dangerous threats," according to a local newspaper, "did not move the shoemaker."

De Gilda moved to another town and tried not to draw attention to himself. Then one afternoon, as he was repairing a customer's shoe, he looked up from his workbench and saw Morelli staring at him through the shop window. De Gilda's heart sank. But Morelli smiled and motioned to him. The shoemaker put down his tools and edged toward the window. In a pleasant tone, Morelli called for him to come outside for a talk: there was nothing wrong; he would do de Gilda no harm. De Gilda finally opened the door of his shop and the two men went for a stroll. When they came to a secluded spot, Morelli pulled out a razor and swept it quickly at de Gilda's throat. The victim flinched at the last moment and the blade missed its target, instead slicing a deep cut diagonally across de Gilda's face. Bleeding profusely, de Gilda ran for his life. When Morelli was caught by a policeman, he confessed that he was a member of a Black Hand gang, and the leader, a man named de Felix, had paid him $75 to silence the shoemaker forever.

The police told de Gilda they planned to arrest and prosecute the gang leader, but the young shoemaker, his location exposed, his face scarred and instantly recognizable, knew that his life was effectively over. He bought a gun. One day he closed his shop and boarded a streetcar to Philadelphia. When he arrived, he began to prowl the streets, looking for de Felix at his favorite haunts. When he spotted the Black Hand chief walking with his father, de Gilda drew out his pistol, aimed, and fired. De Felix fell to the ground, blood spilling from his wounds. A red mist now descended on de Gilda: he shot at de Felix's father, but the bullet flew wide. Taking out a knife, de Gilda plunged it into the elderly man's chest, killing him. Then he picked up the gun, put it to his own temple, and fired. He stumbled several hundred yards to a field, where he dropped dead.

Several victims committed suicide rather than run. On June 23, 1906, a Pennsylvanian put a gun to his head and pulled the trigger after receiving a series of Black Hand threats. He left a wife and six children to deal with the aftermath. In West Mount Vernon, New York, Max Bonaventure, a saloonkeeper, shut his store seven days before Christmas and hung a sign on the door: "This store is closed on account of a death in the family." He walked to the back of the saloon, threw a rope over a beam, and hanged himself. Men from the Society had demanded $500 or, they vowed, he would die before Christmas morning. Bonaventure didn't have the money. His son, who came across the body swinging from the rafters, also found a note: "My dear Lena, goodbye. Charlie, Lena, Anna and Frank, I loved you all of my life. Goodbye."

Many others were simply terrorized into silence. A few months later, back in New York, one of Petrosino's Black Hand cases would be thrown into chaos when a Mrs. Fiandini, whose husband had been killed by the Society, stood up in a Manhattan courtroom and declared that her husband hadn't been the victim of a murder. In fact, she refused to grant even that Mr. Fiandini — who was at that moment lying on a slab in the city morgue — was dead. The court was stunned. No prosecutor in memory had ever had to deal with a chief witness in a murder case denying that a loved one had, in actuality, ceased to exist. The reports of the case don't mention whether the prosecutor considered bringing the corpse into the courtroom for the jury to examine, but eventually the case was dismissed. Mrs. Fiandini clearly knew the cost of offending the Society, and she declined to pay it.

• • •

IN AMERICA, UNLIKE IN ITALY, THE SHEER SIZE OF THE COUNTRY could make it easier for Black Hand victims to disappear — or so one would think. John Benteregna was a barber in New York who'd fallen in with a Black Hand gang but tried to leave, either because of a dispute or in disgust at its methods. When one of his associates attempted to kill him on the street, he fled to Chicago, "where the Society made life miserable for him." He ran to St. Louis, then Omaha, then Denver, then — giving up on cities altogether — an isolated ranch farther west, where he hoped to hide out while working as a farmhand. But in each place he was discovered and his life threatened. Finally, he reached the end of the continent: Los Angeles, which must have seemed, with its sun and openness and lack of Italian ghettoes, a kind of oasis.

But soon after his arrival in California, letters postmarked Manhattan were slipped under his door. "Leave here," read one note, adorned with a skull and crossbones. "This is your last chance." Benteregna tore up the letter. Another arrived and he gave it to the police, who did nothing. While he was walking along the street one day, someone fired at him. Benteregna ducked five bullets, then went into hiding. Nearly broke, he took some of his remaining money and rented a chair at a barbershop, where he began working.

The *Los Angeles Times* reported what happened next. One day, a man appeared outside the barbershop where Benteregna worked.

"His assassin tapped on the front window to attract his attention. As Benteregna turned around, a shot was fired through the window, the bullet entering his left side and piercing his intestines." Through his final conscious minutes, Benteregna refused to say who'd killed him, though he admitted it was one of the Black Handers who had pursued him so doggedly from city to city.

There were instances in which men were told the hour and minute they would die, and the sentences were carried out to the last tick of the clock. And another in which a man testified in court against the Society, with whom he'd been involved in several crimes, and requested that the judge sentence him to twenty years in the penitentiary, "because that means twenty years of life." After being threatened with having his throat cut, a Newark baker sold his business for a pittance and fled, like so many others before him, back to the hometown in Italy he'd left, nearly penniless, years before. Three days after his arrival, his body was found in the road outside his house. He'd been shot and, as a matter of punctilious duty, his throat had been neatly opened from ear to ear.

Americans in the 1900s, at least city dwellers, weren't innocents. They lived with corrupt governments, filthy streets, news of horrifying industrial accidents, global epidemics, scandals large and small. They'd weathered crime waves before, including the political violence of the Molly Maguires and the mass brainings of demented Irish gang members by other, even more demented Irish gang members. But the Black Hand was different. There was something almost occult about it, a whiff of some darker, more corrupt conception of life than the one envisioned by the Founding Fathers. It was an old sickness in a young country.

The tales of long pursuit ending in murder fascinated and appalled Americans. "The far-reaching power and relentless vengeance of the *Mano Nera* have no equals in the history of crime," declared an article in the *Washington Post*. "Across deserts, rivers, seas," wrote another journalist, "the long arm of the Black Hand reaches. In every State of the Union, its crushing grip may be felt, and even in Europe it may strike and to its enemies bring death."

How could a young nation make sense of such bewildering acts? One way it tried was through its growing popular culture. By 1905, the Society was increasingly featured in movies, novels, pulp magazines, poetry, and stage plays. When the melodrama *Kidnapped in New York* opened at the Bijou in Manhattan, audiences watched as Jack Dooley, an Irish newspaperman and amateur detective, tracked down a kidnapped girl who has been abducted (apparently) by her lily-white governess, Mary. After several wild turns, Jack uncovers a Black Hand conspiracy, rescues the girl, and marries the governess. The plot of *A Midnight Escape,* a play that made it at least as far as Hartford, Connecticut, ran along the same lines, with the hero and his betrothed "bound in the dark chamber of the Black Hand Society" and realizing they are facing an execution squad of eight men with rifles. "There were two good-sized audiences present yesterday," the *Hartford Courant* reported, "and at both performances nervous women screamed." The plots were creaky, but in each of them the Society went down in defeat.

Bat Masterson, the celebrated real-life western lawman and friend to Wyatt Earp, was a celebrity in 1900s America. His fame soared to such heights that he became a fictional character in the "Bat Masterson Library," a serial that ran in major newspapers beginning in March 1905. The inaugural issue, "Bat Masterson in New York, or On the Trail of the Black Hand," opens with a U.S. marshal crying out, "You cur. You have stabbed me!" The marshal had been alone in his office when he was accosted by Vito la Duca, "dread bulwark of the Black Hand," who informs the lawman, "You shall not escape me this time." La Duca buries his dagger in the lawman's chest three times and is about to finish him off when a stranger, his spurs jangling — never mind that he is in midtown Manhattan — appears. "Back," he cries, "or Mary Jane, the trusted revolver that never misses her target, will hark in your vitals." The stranger and the Society thug fight, and the stranger executes some jujitsu moves before tossing the villain over his shoulders. "Who are you?" the marshal asks the man. " 'Bat Masterson, the blood stained avenger of Butte,' cried the latter — for it was he — tearing off the whiskers from his handsome countenance." In the absence of an actual solution to the problem of the Society, the serial's writers had turned to a fading legend to defeat it.

• • •

AS THE TERROR WAVE ROLLED ONWARD, AMERICANS BEGAN TO worry that the Society would no longer stop at individuals but would seek to infiltrate and control governments. What if the Society's ultimate target wasn't money but power? Perhaps, theorized a writer at *Collier's* magazine, the individual groups were not only in touch with one another and coordinating their attacks but also now awaiting "the electrifying touch of executive power from the *alta* [high] mafia and then will come — hell." This was a persistent fear. Even the police commissioner believed it was a possibility. If a "master hand" molded the gangs together, he said, "what a monster we would have to contend with! To successfully fight it would be impossible."

In fact, the Society had already taken over governments within the United States. If one had visited Hillsville, Pennsylvania, in 1906, one would have found a town that was operated by and for the benefit of the Black Hand. Immigrants arrived in Hillsville to work in the enormous quarries owned by the Carbone Limestone Company, which were said to be the largest in the world at that time. The little town featured all the normal institutions: a mayor, a police force (on loan from nearby Clinton County), laws, and statutes, as in any other village or city in America. But Hillsville — nicknamed "Helltown" by its inhabitants — was actually ruled over by one Joe Bagnato, the leader of the local Black Hand. Every payday, Bagnato would wait a few feet from the window where the miners came to receive envelopes filled with their wages. Each laborer would open his packet and give Bagnato his tribute. "The money collected," reported the *New York Times,* "was understood to be the price of life and liberty until next pay day." Workers who managed to accumulate some savings in the local banks regularly disappeared; days after they vanished, bank drafts would arrive for the total amount in their savings accounts, down to the last penny.

When the children of Helltown went out raspberry picking on the hillsides near the mines, they knew to avoid the mounds that dotted the slopes. These marked the graves of those who failed to pay the Society. "There are people buried up here, yet nobody knows where," one miner said. "The Black Hand ran everything." The police were overwhelmed and outnumbered. If they found the victim of a "dago killing," they would lay the body out by the roadside for his family or friends to pick up. Many times, no investigations were conducted. Hundreds of emigrants were driven out of the town by the terror and fled back to Italy. "I lived in fear," said one resident. "We were all scared to death."

Some of the Helltown thugs were said to be graduates of a school for the Black Hand discovered one night during a raid in rural Pennsylvania by fifty detectives from "all over the country." Inside a secluded house, the astonished lawmen found a group of seventeen Italians sitting in front of a teacher and a rubber mannequin; the men were "intensely interested in a lesson explaining the exact spot on the human body in which a stiletto should be plunged to ensure instant death." The business operated under the pretense of being a "fencing" school and was run by a man named John Jotti, a longtime criminal from the town of Santo Stefano d'Aspromonte in Petrosino's home region of Campania. In addition to the rubber mannequin, marked at the spots where a blade would do its most effective work, was a trunk containing Black Hand form letters, along with daggers and revolvers. One of the letters contained threats against Baltimore detectives. "Use not clubs against these policemen," it read, "but kill." The place was, in effect, a vocational college for Society members.

Pennsylvania officials knew that Helltown was only the most notorious of several similar villages ruled by the Society. In May 1907 they interviewed Italians from all over the state who had "mustered up courage enough" to talk about their lives. They found that there were agents of the Society in nearly every mining village and town in the coalfields. Helltown was the capital of the Pennsylvania Black Hand, but it was hardly unique.

If the Society could take over a place like Hillsville, American officials and law enforcement officers feared, they could eventually run a Scranton or a Cincinnati or a New York. The police already saw links between the Society and Italian anarchists who were quite explicit in their desire to overthrow the government. At times, the two terms, "Black Hander" and "anarchist," were used interchangeably. While chasing the suspected Black Hand murder of a prominent local Italian, Pennsylvania authorities stumbled on a group of anarchists who regularly met in a shack near the town of Baird. In the shack were letters from fellow radicals urging the thirty-one members to assassinate Governors Pennypacker of Pennsylvania and John M. Pattison of Ohio. When arrested, the members were found to be wearing badges with the picture of Gaetano Bresci, the man who had killed King Umberto I.

More and more, newspaper editors, police chiefs, and politicians came to believe that the terror practiced by the Society was a prelude to something deeper and more permanent. The hysteria around the figure of the Italian immigrant mounted. The crime spree elevated the Society in the minds of some Americans from a diabolical gang of cutthroats to nothing less than a threat to the future of the republic.

8

THE GENERAL

BACK IN NEW YORK, PETROSINO MARKED THE SECOND YEAR OF
the Italian Squad's campaign by bolstering its ranks. In 1906 the unit
grew to forty men and added a Brooklyn branch, headed by Sergeant
Anthony Vachris, who would become one of the detective's closest
friends. As the Black Hand atrocities earned headlines, spreading the
Society's message and intimidating the public, the newly expanded
Italian Squad struck back with major public victories. Even the case of
Willie Labarbera, the boy kidnapped off a street while playing with his
friends, had a happy ending.

One Monday, weeks after the boy had vanished, Petrosino was
working late at night. He was reading police bulletins from across the
city, searching for any clue to Willie's whereabouts, when he came
across a report among hundreds, this one from Brooklyn: a crying boy
had been found wandering the streets, mumbling something about
"Barbara." The child had been brought to a nearby precinct station,

then to a local branch of the Society for the Prevention of Cruelty to Children.

Petrosino reread the description of the boy, then rushed to Brooklyn. He asked the matrons for the child, who had not been able to give his name, and they brought forth a sleepy boy. It was Willie. It was now three o'clock in the morning. Petrosino brought the boy some food and took him to police headquarters at 300 Mulberry Street in Little Italy. On the streetcar, the boy fell asleep on his shoulder. Once the detective had deposited the boy at headquarters, he made his way to the Labarberas' house.

When the door to the home opened, an object emerged. A revolver.

"Metti via la pistola," Petrosino said. "Put the gun away." The Black Hand had frightened the public to such a degree that Italians could now be arrested just for owning a pistol. "It's Petrosino," he continued in Italian.

William Labarbera opened the door, peering at the figure lit by pale moonlight.

"Have you got my boy?" he asked.

"I've got him."

William lowered the gun and called back into the house in rapid-fire Italian. After a few seconds, the figure of Caterina Labarbera appeared in the doorway. She fell to her knees on the threshold and bent down to kiss Petrosino's feet, then gestured upward, as if to the particular saints she'd called on to find her boy.

Petrosino calmed the pair, told them to dress, and then brought the couple to 300 Mulberry Street. When she walked in, Caterina grabbed her son and embraced him. "I thought she would eat little Willie," Petrosino said later, amused. Willie disappointed his mother by saying he only wanted to see his sister Rosie.

Most of the children kidnapped by the Black Hand never forgot the ordeal. Some returned home unable to speak about it, having been told by the Black Handers that if they gave any details, their families would be slain. Some were murdered. Others carried the scars from straps or ropes that had been tied around their wrists; at least one bore marks of burning on his body. A Chicago boy was described this way: "His eyes have the haunted look of a scared child, and his little body is emaciated."

But on the night of October 9, the Labarbera boy was safe in his bed, and Petrosino, a devout Catholic, was thankful. That time, at least, he and his men had won.

Even Enrico Caruso, the great Italian tenor, called on the squad's services. When Caruso, then at the height of his fame, came to New York to perform, the Black Hand threatened to kill him if he didn't pay them $2,000 in protection money. He paid. Almost immediately, new letters arrived, until the opera star had collected a stack "a foot high." Caruso went to the NYPD for relief. A crowd of cops and reporters gathered around the desk where an officer was writing up a report and listened to him tell his story: the threats; the three Italian bodyguards he'd hired to go everywhere with him; the sharpened sword that lay within the black cane he walked with, ready to be drawn out; the pistol he kept tucked inside his coat. Even in a grim police office in the middle of Manhattan, the flamboyant Caruso couldn't resist putting on a performance. "I will give nothing to these blackmailers except cold steel or bullets!" he told the crowd. "Let them come on. I am prepared. They are a set of cowards." The American officers, even the Irish ones, beamed at the diminutive singer. Here was an Italian who would not only talk back to the Black Hand but also meet them bullet for bullet. "His face wore the gladsome smile of a child," wrote one journalist, "who feels that he has done something worthy of applause, and all the Americans in the office were smiling at him." But among the onlookers, one man — an Italian, as it turned out, an educated official who assisted the police in suppressing crime — scowled at the famous tenor. "The fool!" he exclaimed to the reporter. "He gives Italians a bad name. He ought to keep his —— mouth shut!"

But the threats from the Society continued, and Caruso's courage faded. The singer grew increasingly nervous about venturing out in public. Around this time, he was introduced to Petrosino, and the two became friends. Caruso eventually confided to the detective that a new demand for $5,000 had arrived, and he'd decided to hand over the money. Caruso was not merely a fabulous earner—he made over $2 million from his contract with the Victor record company alone—but a shrewd investor. By the time World War I broke out, his annual tax bill alone totaled $154,000. The amount demanded was a trifle to him.

But Petrosino was horrified: Caruso, his hero, the flower of Italian opera, the man with a tone so pure he performed in large stadiums without a microphone, was going to bow down to these animals? In Petrosino's own city? The detective knew the demands would only grow, until they consumed Caruso's entire fortune. "It's an empty pit," he told the singer. He begged Caruso to reconsider and came up with an alternate plan. The tenor, after careful consideration, agreed to it.

Caruso sent a message to the extortionists. He agreed to pay the $5,000. But he would only hand over the money at a rendezvous in Manhattan. Petrosino would impersonate the tenor at the handoff. The Society agreed to his terms. On the appointed day, Petrosino dressed in a cape and suit resembling the singer's own, and hurried to the meeting. He met with the thugs, overpowered and arrested them, then brought back the cash to a relieved Caruso. The story of Petrosino's gambit circulated on the streets of Little Italy for years.

It was a heartening triumph for the detective, but the wave of terror continued to roil the streets of lower Manhattan, and the outcry in New York newspapers became a drumbeat. Tammany Hall, with its quivering antennae for anything that might disturb the smooth progress of its reign, realized that the crime issue needed attention. Mayor George McClellan Jr., the son of the Civil War general George B. McClellan, began looking for a new commissioner to replace William McAdoo. He found his man in a profane, colorful, and altogether American military man named Theodore A. Bingham, nicknamed "the General."

Bingham was an imposing Yankee, an army man through and through. He was tall and rangy, with a body that reminded one reporter of "a starved panther," constantly in motion. "He is a soldier in every particular," observed the *Los Angeles Times,* "an animate picture of vigor, rough grace, and daring." The General's bloodline was divided between divines and warriors; it included a handful of Revolutionary War soldiers and Connecticut clergymen. He made valedictorian at Yale before following his ancestors to West Point, after which he received a commission as a second lieutenant. But Bingham was destined never to see warfare. His field was engineering, and he came to Washington, D.C., in 1897 with the rank of colonel to oversee the capital's public buildings. After a successful tenure, he moved on to the White House, where, in the words of one newspaper, he served President McKinley as a "major domo, drum major, social secretary or something to that effect." It's difficult to imagine this brusque and irascible man as the White House social arbiter, but he had a mind for organization, and the McKinleys were well satisfied with his work.

When Teddy Roosevelt became president, however, things did not go so smoothly. There was "friction and fire" between the men. "The White House was not big enough for two Theodores," wrote one journalist, and a mysterious altercation at a White House dinner — the details of which were never revealed — finalized the breach. Bingham was promoted to the rank of brigadier general and sent off to an engineering project in upstate New York, where, in the course of his duties, a seven-hundred-pound derrick collapsed on his leg. Doctors amputated the limb, and from then on the General was required to use a stout cane, which he often flourished like a war club. His military career was over. The appointment as commissioner of the NYPD came at a low moment in his life.

With his bristling handlebar mustache and bright blue eyes, Bingham was a dynamo who fed on illimitable reserves of energy. As for his personality, he seemed to await the arrival of an Evelyn Waugh to do him full justice. He was blunt, outrageous, politically naïve, and possessed of one of the most original vocabularies on the American scene. Everything he said was expressed with force. "It is said," wrote one reporter, "that when he gets ready to express an emphatic opinion or utter a firm resolve, his jaws click loud enough to awaken the office cat." For emphasis, Bingham would slam his cane on a lectern or any handy surface. He was known for swearing like a marine, for saying "you all" (a habit he'd picked up while on an assignment in the Plains), and for a blazing intolerance of fools.

Bingham was surprised to get the job of NYPD commissioner but accepted with alacrity. His introduction to his men and the city's press corps was a memorable one. Journalists publicly lamented the fact that they couldn't reproduce his opening speech for their readers because it contained so many words "which render it unfit for reproduction in any great religious journal," but one newsman jotted down an expletive-free bit of it:

> Men, I'm glad to meet you. You look like a manly lot of officers. I love a man. I try to be a man myself. I've been sent here to do a certain piece of work, and I'm going to do it if I can and if I've the strength . . . We are strangers now and I come here with nothing against you, no suspicions . . . But, by the nine gods of war, you've got to deal with me on the level . . . That's a straight tip. See to it that you do your work, and don't go back on the hand I've stretched out to you.

The cops loved it. The press loved it more. The speech, according to one journalist, "went off, biff, bang, bing — Bingham." When asked what his politics were, the new commissioner shot back, "You know an Army man is just an American citizen, damn it!" which struck the right note in a city that was so bitterly divided between Republican and Democrat. The newspapers invented a new verb, "to Bingham," which meant "to talk as if you meant it."

Bingham reminded many of Teddy Roosevelt, but without the political cunning. He certainly worked as hard as T.R. (including, to the bluecoats' disgust, on Saturdays) and had strong ideas: he demanded his men greet him with a crisp military salute, introduced a modern card-file system to the department, and bolstered the police's recruiting methods. He kept a record of every individual policeman in a separate envelope and vowed to crack down on any malfeasance. "It's going to be the business," he said, somewhat inscrutably, "or the torture." Any cop who neglected his duties or took bribes would be fined for the first two offenses, "and then I'll reach for the ax."

He freely admitted to trusting no one, not even himself. The job of commissioner was a feeding trough for the corrupt, he acknowledged, and all he could promise was to try to resist the lures of the city. "I'll watch myself," he told the *Los Angeles Times.* "Up to date, I have been satisfactory. Can't say anything, however, about tomorrow. No decent man can. My only danger is money. May be seized, you understand, with the universal frenzy. 'Get a million,' says the devil. After that, it can be easy disgrace, with horses, automobiles, Jersey cows, and a house in the country—the insane asylum or the penitentiary." In fact, it would be ruthless ambition—not corruption—that would haunt Bingham's administration and his relationship with Petrosino. But at least in the beginning, he seemed determined to master himself and his flaws.

Bingham was a hit with the public from day one. New Yorkers wanted someone who would be tough on crime, and Bingham fit the bill. The General's gruff talk and martial metaphors indicated he was ready to go to war with the Society. "The people of New York," wrote one observer, "expect the Black Hand to be pretty stiffly Binghamed before the police administration goes out."

Petrosino was delighted with his new commissioner. McAdoo had been an adroit politician and had approved the Italian Squad, but his heart never seemed to be in the struggle. Bingham was itching for a fight. He ordered that suspected leaders of the biggest Black Hand gangs be placed under continual surveillance and offered any policeman who could find evidence to convict the men a promotion to detective first class. "At last," Petrosino announced, "we've found a commissioner who understands us." The "us" might have referred to cops or the squad or Italians or all three.

To serve in his new administration, Bingham hired Arthur Woods as deputy police commissioner. Woods was another Yankee, tall, personable, and scholarly. He'd grown up in Boston in a prominent and wealthy family, attended the Latin School, and went on to Harvard. The young graduate began teaching at Groton, where one of his students was Franklin Delano Roosevelt, but the prep school's idyllic campus proved too tame for Woods. Inspired by the burgeoning Progressive movement, he left for New York and became a reporter for the *Evening Sun*, earning a paltry $15 a week. He took rooms at the Harvard Club and joined the Racquet Club to keep in shape.

Before Woods accepted the deputy commissioner job, he asked for time to go to Europe and study the methods of the police there, at his own expense. He analyzed the procedures of the men at Scotland Yard, then returned to New York. Woods proved an innovative thinker who was far better at showing the human touch than his boss. When one reporter sat down for an interview, he found that Woods "gave a strong impression of eagerness, kindness, quick senses of humor, joy in his work, love of a square deal, and a powerful liking for people." One of Woods's assignments in his new job was to oversee the Italian Squad.

If one cloud darkened the General's early days, it arrived from the direction of Tammany Hall. The political machine, led by Big Tim Sullivan and his quiet, diminutive cousin Little Tim Sullivan, were cool to the appointment of this military man and outspoken reformer. Big Tim Sullivan was the undisputed ruler of Manhattan below 14th Street. He was handsome, tall, gregarious, and sharp as a new knife, "the greatest overlord the politics of New York ever saw." That he was corrupt goes without saying, but he was a highly effective politician who looked after his constituents. When an Irish gang began tormenting a number of Orthodox Jews in a Tammany district, word soon reached Big Tim, who immediately ordered the NYPD to swoop down on the outfit's clubhouse and turf the hooligans out of their nest. When the gang was gone, and the premises cleared, Sullivan personally signed a lease for the space, procured a Torah, converted the club into a synagogue, invited the Orthodox Jews back in, and met them at the door with a handshake. Such gestures made Sullivan a legend, and his high living only added to its luster: in his suite at the fabulous Occidental Hotel, he ran a poker game that went on for five straight years without a break. His interests in vaudeville, gambling, and outright graft had made him a millionaire, but for the Irish he was a demigod, the living symbol of what was possible for their kind in America.

His cousin Little Tim was the shadow to Big Tim's great light. He was small, tightly wound, and bristling with anger. He'd come up the hard way as well, shining shoes on Broome Street just as Petrosino had, before becoming a runner for journalists on Park Row and getting his law degree by a special act of the state legislature. His sharp elbows and conspiratorial turn of mind had made him into a formidable opponent. But he believed sincerely in the Irish way of doing things. "The Tammany man," Little Tim once told the *New York Times*, "must feed the starving, clothe the naked, bury the paupers, and be good friends with everybody."

This odd couple seemed never to have a serious political disagreement. "Their fondness for each other was more than fraternal," observed the *Albany Evening Journal*. "It was almost feminine in its tenderness." They didn't tolerate traitors, however; it was said that Big Tim perfumed the ballots on election day so that he could make sure his constituents had actually voted by sniffing out the scent on their hands. Over the years, the pair had fought off several waves of bright-eyed reformers, gnawing at their ankles whenever they stepped onto the Sullivans' downtown turf and sending them howling back to their mansions on Fifth Avenue, crying about "moon-faced Irishmen" and the death of democracy. For the Sullivans, Commissioner Bingham fit a familiar type: a Protestant blueblood eager to take back what the Irish had earned through hard work and honest graft. They weren't about to let that happen.

The cousins wielded financial power in the city through the Board of Aldermen, which funded a wide range of city agencies, including the NYPD. As soon as Bingham set foot inside 300 Mulberry, the Sullivans and their allies on the board began to attack him in the press as a bumbling outsider, hopelessly out of his depth. "He does not know enough about the city to describe any three of its streets," said Big Tim. "In my opinion, the Board should not pay any attention to a man so incompetent and arrogant as General Bingham."

The first showdown between the two came with Bingham's proposed budget for the NYPD. It was an eye-opener. The General requested two thousand new officers to patrol the streets, one hundred new detectives, and improvements to the precinct stations that would cost, together with the new manpower requests, $1.6 million. With the extra policemen, the department could take on the Black Hand, one of Bingham's top priorities, with far greater effectiveness. But the Sullivans' gambling and other illegal interests south of 14th Street would have been negatively impacted, to say the least, by a more robust NYPD. The cousins responded by vetoing the additional cops and, for good measure, actually cutting the General's budget. If Bingham was to be believed, they also installed men inside 300 Mulberry for the sole purpose of committing espionage. "My headquarters," the General told reporters, "was . . . full of spies."

Despite the commissioner's trials, a new, forceful leader was in place at the NYPD, giving Petrosino reason to be hopeful. He was working practically without rest. He recruited new men to the Italian Squad, as some moved into other bureaus or simply quit, exhausted by the pace he set. Perhaps with this fire-breathing general backing him, and with the fresh alarm about the spread of the Black Hand, the city would finally meet the Society with the kind of force it deserved.

• • •

MANY EVENINGS, AFTER HIS DAY WAS DONE, PETROSINO — WHO apparently never learned to cook — would find his way to Little Italy and a small restaurant called Saulino's. It was an unpretentious place where the waiters spoke in dialect and the owner, an Italian war veteran named Vincenzo Saulino, sat with the customers and chatted as the wineglasses clinked and Italian folk music played. Saulino had emigrated from a small town called Agnone, a hundred miles east of Rome, the site of a famous bell foundry. Agnone was surrounded by hills dotted with monasteries and hermitages; hundreds of years before, during the Kingdom of the Two Sicilies, it had been a "royal town" and an important trade and craft-making site. But by the time Saulino was a young boy, the place was stagnating, taxes were high, and starving peasants were being thrown in jail for stealing the wheat of the gentry, the *galantuomini* (literally, the "gallant men") who ruled the town. With few options, Saulino joined the Italian Legion and fought during the Crimean War at the siege of Sebastopol, in which the two thousand members of the Legion battled the Russians. Saulino had already seen a great deal of blood and sorrow in his short life.

After the Crimean War ended, the soldier returned to Italy and fought in the War of Italian Unification. When hostilities ceased in 1871, Saulino apparently found that even a unified Italy had little to offer him. He left for America with his French-born wife and found his way to a restaurant in Little Italy, where she cooked and he ran the front of the house.

At Saulino's restaurant, Petrosino found decent food and genial companionship. Saulino's specialized in the Mediterranean dishes of southern Italy, the food that the detective loved. He often called ahead to order before he arrived, knowing that the more time he spent in such a public place, the more dangerous his life became (plus, he didn't have time to wait for meals to be cooked). He always chose a table against the wall, so no assassin could take him by surprise from behind. On those occasions when he wasn't pressed for time, Petrosino would play cards with Saulino, working himself up into such a rage when he lost that he would take the cards in his thick, strong hands and tear them to pieces. This amused Saulino so much that he would ask the detective if he could tear the cards himself. It was an honor, to a certain type of Italian, to have Petrosino eat in his restaurant, to sit at his table.

But there was another reason, known only to Petrosino at first, why he chose Saulino's for his evening meal. The owner had a daughter, Adelina, who often served Petrosino. She was eleven years younger than the famous detective, handsome rather than pretty, with a strong nose and chin, and eyes that sloped downward at the corners. In pictures, she wears her chestnut hair piled in curls. Her English was rudimentary, so she and Petrosino spoke in Italian as she arranged the cutlery in front of him and set down a bowl of minestrone or a plate of seafood farfalle. "She was an outgoing person," says her granddaughter. "She liked to read the society column and loved to sing. She loved adventure —she would take the boat back and forth from Boston alone, which in the nineteen hundreds was very unusual for a woman."

Unknown to anyone but himself, Petrosino had fallen hopelessly in love with Adelina. "He was just smitten," says the granddaughter. Adelina had been married to a man in Massachusetts but had returned home to the restaurant after her husband died. At first, according to her granddaughter, "she lived alone in Boston, but her father said, 'It doesn't look right, a woman living alone. Come to New York.' And she did." Over many evenings, over the sound of conversation and folk music, the waitress and the detective grew close.

Eventually, Petrosino made his feelings known to Adelina, and then to her father. It was a good match: the detective had a steady job, was known to be honest and hardworking, and was a hero to many in the colony. An Italian widow in her thirties didn't have a wide range of romantic choices in early-1900s America. But Petrosino was in for a shock: Saulino refused the offer of marriage. The reason? The detective "was in constant danger of assassination," and, having watched his daughter suffer through the loss of one husband, Saulino apparently wished to spare her the pain of losing another. Perhaps he also worried that the bombs that the Black Hand planted would someday find their way to the detective's home and kill everyone inside, including Adelina.

Petrosino refused to give up. He was in love and would wait for Adelina as long as it took. Perhaps he thought that Saulino would yield, after a few more dinners and conversations. So Petrosino would enter the restaurant around dusk, hanging his derby on a hook, and sit down at a table with a red-and-white-checked tablecloth. Adelina would come to serve him. The two apparently never saw each other outside the restaurant. The courtship rituals of Mott Street could be as strict and unyielding as in the most conservative Calabrian town.

Year after year, Petrosino returned. But Saulino steadfastly refused his entreaties to consider the marriage.

And so Petrosino would nod to Adelina, sit down to eat his pasta and drink his Chianti. "Waiting made him extremely nervous," said one biographer of Petrosino's time in the restaurant. His friends assumed this was because of the danger of being exposed in a public place, but perhaps the detective also found it painful to be near the brown-eyed waitress whom he yearned to call his own. If the anger that filled him when he lost to Vincenzo at cards was tinged with another sort of rage, Petrosino kept it to himself. Hadn't he himself said years before that there was too much death in his business, and that "a man hasn't the right to bring a woman into it"? Now he was being held to that rule.

If Joe and Adelina ever talked about doing something rash, running away together like the Americans did, getting married and setting up house, it was a private conversation that never entered the public domain or even survived as a whisper in Petrosino family legend. The detective apparently never thought of leaving New York; it was where his life's work resided, and that work was unfinished. And he was in many ways a traditional Italian man with values to match. To run off with Adelina would have been an act of unthinkable disrespect to her father. So he kept silent.

Throughout New York, families were suffering the theft of their children, the slow diminishment of their dreams, bankruptcy, violent death, and loss of faith in America. But Petrosino may have been the only enemy of the Society whose punishment was to be barred from marrying the woman he loved.

9

"THE TERROR OF HURTFUL PEOPLE"

Ayear after the blossoming of his deepest ambition, the thing that would make him a "Supreme Venerable" of the Italian community in America and would raise his people from the palpable disdain that was their lot in America, Dr. Vincenzo Sellaro was afraid. An enormous bomb had gone off in the handsome red brick building at 203 Grand Street in the heart of Little Italy where Sellaro had his apartment and his offices. He'd been asleep upstairs when the explosion shook the building, waking him. His neighbors were already in the hallways, running down the stairs in their nightclothes to the streets, brick dust everywhere. "Men, women, and children appeared on the fire escapes," read one report of the bombing, "screaming that there was fire and begging for help." Windows for a hundred yards in every direction were shattered.

Sellaro knew that the bomb was a warning. To him.

Letters signed "THE CHAMPIONS OF THE BLACK HAND" had been arriving at his apartment for months, demanding $5,000. The Society warned him to send them the money, in a sealed envelope, or his house on Grand Street would be blown to smithereens. There was one further instruction: he was to send the money "in perfect silence . . . without any knowledge of Petrosino . . . he will do you a great deal of danger." Such warnings were not uncommon. Black Handers often instructed their victims not to contact the detective and even designed their schemes to evade him. "It became," according to the *Baltimore Sun,* "one of the features of plot-making to find a way to throw Petrosino off the scent."

Sellaro had refused to pay the ransom. How could he, of all people, bow to these murderers who were dragging the Italian name through the muck and the grime? For a year before, Sellaro had taken a step that he hoped would redeem his people from the taint of degradation epitomized by the Black Hand and would alter the course of Italian American history forever.

On a brilliantly sunny June day in the summer of 1905, the doctor had waited in his beautifully appointed apartment for his visitors to arrive. The occasion was the culmination of many years of dreaming and planning for Sellaro, and he was dressed, as was customary for him, in a good-quality dark suit, which played up the luster of his brown eyes. He wasn't a conventionally handsome man; the line of his dark hair crested over a large forehead, and his eyes were hooded and brooding. There was something of the basset hound in the good doctor's appearance, but the mildness of his expression belied a granite will.

Sellaro was a Sicilian, born in Palermo, who'd received his medical degree from the University of Naples. In 1897, he took the boat for America and enrolled at Cornell Medical School. By 1904, he'd saved enough money to open his own practice out of his offices at 203 Grand Street, on the corner of Mott. His practice thrived. Many of his patients came to him after nearly losing their lives in New York hospitals where the doctors and nurses didn't speak Italian and an interpreter often couldn't be found. How could a woman suffering from tuberculosis or a pulmonary embolism explain her symptoms in sign language? Later, Sellaro would be among the founders of the Columbus Italian Hospital, where doctors were required to speak both Italian and English.

By 1905, Sellaro had grown prosperous and well respected, but his ambitions ran further: he wished "to emancipate Italians from every prejudice." (He would later join the Masons, not because he particularly wanted to, but simply to prove that a Sicilian could.) So on this summer's day he'd called some of the prominent individuals in the New York colony to his gracious apartment on Grand to found an order that would begin the ascent of the Italian American into the highest reaches of American life.

The men arrived one by one: The pharmacist Ludovico Ferrari was from Piedmont. The attorney Antonio Marzullo was from Campania, home to the much-maligned city of Naples. The prominent sculptor Giuseppe Carlino came from the central region of Lazio. And the two unnamed barbers — often men of high standing in the colonies — hailed, like Sellaro, from Sicily. Though the theme of the evening was pride and unity, the men gathered that night were mostly from the south, the sun-stricken and often despised regions that had supplied 90 percent of the mass immigration to America. The men here knew, painfully, the reputation of their *compatrioti*. And they were here to redeem it.

Sellaro greeted the men, and we can imagine that he pressed glasses of wine into their hands. It was a hot day, and this was a celebration as well as a meeting. Sellaro stood and addressed his friends. "The Almighty has brought us all together for a purpose," he announced. The aim of the gathering, he said, was to found a new society, Figli d'Italia, the Sons of Italy. Sellaro acknowledged to his compatriots that evening that the Italians were the poorest and the least educated of the Europeans; in their old lives, they'd been common laborers, tenant farmers, field workers, shepherds, gardeners, and fishermen. Four hundred years after Columbus had sailed from the Spanish port of Palos, the Italians had finally followed him, "the last to come to America." But they had come of their own free will, to work and prosper, to free themselves of the corruption of Rome. "It is because of this that today I have a dream," Sellaro said to the five men, "and hope that someday, even if it takes a hundred more years before we are fully accepted, our children and our children's children . . . will be able and proud to continue our traditions, our culture and our language . . . I want to believe that someday we will become a very important part of American history." The men raised their glasses and toasted Sellaro and this new beginning.

After that summer's day, the Order of the Sons of Italy had thrived: it was well on its way to becoming the largest and most powerful of the Italian fraternal societies in America. There were already eight lodges in the city, and many others were planned throughout the country. Sellaro, who'd been named "Supreme Venerable" of the society, was planning to open schools to teach English to immigrants from Naples and Palermo and Milan, as well as centers where they would learn how to become American citizens. There would be orphanages and homes for the elderly. He dreamt of other things, such as mortuary funds for those unfortunate souls who died carving out the subway tunnels. (Just a few years before, nine workers, mostly Italian, had been caught under 195th Street in a dynamite explosion and perished, their names and families unknown, forcing the city to load them onto the "dead boat" and bury them in unmarked graves on Hart Island.) Credit unions, welfare societies, scholarship funds, all were being planned.

But now the Black Hand was threatening to murder Sellaro. How could he uplift his people when these killers mocked everything he dreamt of building?

Sellaro and his friend Joseph Petrosino were in the vanguard of a group endeavoring to repair the Italians' reputation. There were other idealists in New York as well, fellow travelers in the struggle. A young lawyer named Gino Speranza had founded the Society for the Protection of Italian Immigrants in 1901 to help the newcomers but also to counter the backlash against their arrival, a backlash he saw everywhere. "We hear a great deal nowadays of the 'problem of integration,'" Speranza wrote. "Orators and statesmen, newspapers and magazines, never lose the opportunity of talking of the 'foreign peril,' of the danger from an influx of immigrants who do not readily assimilate with the elements and institutions of the Republic."

Speranza and his volunteers met newcomers at Ellis Island and herded them away from the "runners" who were there to steer them toward overpriced housing and abusive jobs; he ventured down to the labor camps of West Virginia where Italian workers whispered their stories of beatings and whippings. (He always wore a fine suit on these trips, both to gain the respect of the laborers and to ward off the abuse of their overseers.) "I have been in certain labor camps in the South where my countrymen were forced to work under the surveillance of armed guards," he wrote. "I have spoken to some who had been bound to a mule and whipped back to work like slaves. I have met others who bore the marks of brutal abuses committed by cruel bosses with the consent of their superiors." And yet these men were the ones accused of being ungrateful for the freedom they found in the new land. "What conception of American liberty," Speranza wrote, "can these foreigners have?"

Finally, in Brooklyn, a brash young prosecutor named Francis Corrao was working his way into the borough's Democratic machine. The youngest Italian lawyer ever to practice in the borough, the flamboyant and pugnacious Corrao was a pioneer who craved acceptance and power for his people and himself. But first, he knew, the Black Hand must be defeated. Corrao's brother "Charly" was a member of the Italian Squad, known for the brilliance of his disguises.

The lawyer lobbied publicly for the Brooklyn district attorney to hire an Italian prosecutor. Who better than a man who spoke the language and knew the culture to prosecute Black Handers? Finally, on April 2, 1907, Corrao himself was awarded the position, with a handsome salary of $5,000 a year. It was another "first" for the Italians, and Francis envisioned himself and his brother, along with the rest of the squad, sending the scum of Sicily away for long terms and freeing his people from this curse. Petrosino and his men would arrest the lawbreakers; Corrao would prosecute them.

Petrosino was the most visible and arguably the most influential of these men, all of whom lived in New York and traveled in the same circles. But the detective knew that even his power was severely constrained. He was arresting hordes of Black Handers, but he couldn't get the authorities in Manhattan or Washington to engage fully in his war, and he couldn't get Italians to testify in sufficient numbers. How could the Italian American rise when even a man like Vincenzo Sellaro was held hostage by their oppressors? The detective asked himself this question over and over again.

How does one spark a resistance?

. . .

IN MARCH 1907, THE STEAMSHIP *CALIFORNIA* WAS CHURNING ITS WAY across the Atlantic, headed west. The ship had left the port of Le Havre, France, weeks before and was bound for New York. Aboard were hundreds of immigrants, their cheap suitcases tied with grass rope, stacked in steerage.

A steamship depended on coal for power. Day and night, in the depths of the ship, stokers shoveled anthracite into the four furnaces. Covered in soot, with only their eyes and teeth flashing white in the glow of the fires, the men worked four-hour shifts in extreme temperatures that sometimes reached 160 degrees. In between shovelfuls of coal, a stoker would dash to a metal pipe that rose all the way to the ship's surface and gulp down the cold Atlantic air that flowed through the tube. It was the work of the stokers that enabled millions of Italians and other immigrants to find their way to Ellis Island on boiling gusts of steam.

If the passengers of the *California* had been paying close attention to their crew, they would have noticed something peculiar. There was one stoker who never seemed to dirty himself with coal dust and in fact seemed to do no work at all. He was a slight man with olive-tinted skin, "piercing" eyes, and a prominent scar that dipped from his left ear to the corner of his mouth. He was quiet and purposeful, and he exhibited that quality that the Italians called *pazienza*. This stoker was "a man who meditated much and spoke little until aroused, when his phrases poured forth in a torrent, proving that his ideas had been carefully arranged—a man little given to impulse." If asked, he gave his name as Giuseppe Balstieri.

If any of the passengers were from Naples, and had crossed the man's path before, they most likely avoided him for the duration of the trip. For he wasn't a stoker or a run-of-the-mill stowaway, and his name wasn't Giuseppe Balstieri. His real name was Enrico (also known as Erricone) Alfano, and he was the king of the Neapolitan Camorra.

Alfano was a figure of terrifying reputation in Italy, with a string of murder accusations in his past, a requirement for any mafioso. "The populace considered Alfano the light of a demi-god," said the *New York Tribune* of the people he'd left behind. "He was thought to be invulnerable to bullets and able at all times to escape his pursuers." Alfano was allegedly powerful enough to get men elected to Italy's parliament; he even charged the Naples power company a monthly fee for not stealing their electrical wires.

It would be a mistake to believe that figures like Alfano and the other great mafiosi generated nothing but fear in their countrymen. It was a deeper, richer, far more complicated gaze that the average Sicilian would have cast on a figure like him. He was a *uomo di rispetto,* a man of respect, who had defied the fate laid out for him as a boy, the life of *miseria,* of endless physical labor and suffering, by becoming a bandit. And yet more than a bandit. "The Northern Italian of any class . . . is perpetually busy accumulating wealth," wrote the historian Henner Hess. "The Southern Italian . . . above all wants to be obeyed, admired, respected, feared, and envied."

Over the door of one Sicilian village church is etched a tribute to one of the most famous *uomini di rispetto* of the region, a man who surmounted his humble origins to become a powerful mafioso. "With the ability of a genius," the inscription reads,

> he raised the fortunes of the noble family. Clear-eyed, dynamic, untiring, he gave farm laborers and sulphur workers prosperity, constantly

worked for the good, and made his name highly respected, in Italy and beyond. Great in his enterprises, much greater still in misfortune, he always kept smiling, and today in the peace of Christ, reunited with death's majesty, he receives from all his friends and even from his enemies, the finest testimonial: he was a *galuntuomo*.

That is, a gentleman. Alfano, too, saw himself as a *galantuomo*, a man who had overcome his beginning. A complete man in the Sicilian mold.

Alfano had taken passage on the *California* because he'd found it necessary, like so many men in his position before him, to flee to America. He'd been accused of masterminding a pair of sensational murders that had originated in the Piazza San Ferdinando, in the aristocratic quarter of Naples. It was a neighborhood full of palaces, "still occupied by families who were prominent under the viceroys of Spain" in the sixteenth and seventeenth centuries. But not every resident of San Ferdinando had such illustrious forebears. A few, in fact, had much darker pasts. But they could pay the rent.

At seven o'clock on the morning of June 6, 1906, a servant girl rang the bell of the fifth-floor apartment at number 95 Via Nardones, where one such couple lived. When she received no answer, the girl alerted the owner of the building, who — knowing a bit about the two people occupying the flat — ran across the street to the police station for the San Ferdinando district. There he explained his dilemma to one Agent Simonetti, who agreed to return with him and investigate the strange occurrence. Simonetti asked for and received a master key to the apartment, then the two men walked across the street and ascended the stairs to the fifth floor. Once the door was unlocked and opened, Simonetti found himself inside an apartment decorated with expensive furniture and luxurious drapes, still and calm in the morning light, and apparently unoccupied. Entering the dining room, he saw that the meal from the night before, including some half-eaten tarts from a nearby pastry shop, hadn't yet been cleared. From the dining room, Simonetti entered the first bedroom, an elegant space with new walnut furniture upholstered in red, but now strewn with clothes and the contents of jewelry boxes. The shutters were closed against the strong Italian sun, and the night lamp still glowed. In its light, Simonetti could make out a figure on the bed. It was a woman, her dark hair splayed above her white silk nightgown. Lifting the gown, Simonetti saw that the woman's torso had been punctured with thirteen dagger wounds that reached up to her neck. "Blood," he remembered later, "was everywhere."

The woman's name was Maria Cutinelli. In life, she'd been a notorious beauty "who had led a most adventurous life among the most intelligent and aristocratic elements of the *mala vita*" — that is, the Neapolitan underworld. At thirty-nine, she'd married Gennaro Cuocola, the son of a respectable leather merchant who had fallen into "evil companionships" in the Vicolo di Santa Lucia quarter of Naples, known for its crime and high living. Cuocola was a member of the Camorra, specifically a *basista*, a crime strategist. His wife had been an *adescatrice*, a stool pigeon for the police. Both were dangerous occupations, but Maria's, in corrupt and gossip-ridden Naples, was slightly more so.

Simonetti reported what he'd found to his superiors, and one of them wrote out a report identifying Maria's death as a classic "uxoricide," the murder of a wife by her husband. This official was on the verge of signing the report and ordering the arrest of Gennaro Cuocola when an officer rushed into his office with news: a carter walking the Cupa Calastro, on the shore of the Bay of Naples, a beautiful stretch of land known as a place where lovers met and strolled on summer evenings, had come across another corpse. The body had been violated even more thoroughly than Maria's; it displayed forty-seven knife wounds, whose triangular shape matched the gashes on the body of the victim at 95 Via Nardones. The man was identified as Gennaro Cuocola. The police official quietly put his report away.

The murders of the beautiful Maria and her raffish husband became a sensation in the Italian newspapers. Victor Emmanuel III, the king of Italy, who'd been looking for an opportunity to clean up the cesspool that was Naples, ordered the minister of war to investigate the crime, using the *carabinieri reali*, the military police known for their discipline and efficiency, to take on the case, fearing that the local police were

too corrupt to complete the job. The *carabinieri* combed the haunts of
the Camorra and pressed their informants for tips; there they learned
that Enrico Alfano, the *super-capo* of the Camorra, had suspected that
the couple was giving information to the police about his group's activities. He was promptly arrested.

Alfano's many friends and benefactors went to work to free him.
(How much work was needed is debatable, however; Alfano's star sat
high in the Italian firmament.) His godfather, an influential priest, was
eventually able to get the suspect released from prison, but the charges
still stood. Alfano saw the storm building and left Naples, moving "from
village to village under various disguises in his efforts to escape capture." Police in the town of San Leucio learned that the suspect was
staying in a local house and quickly surrounded it, but Alfano managed
to escape and took a train to Rome. There he decided America was his
only hope. He had a false passport made by one of his associates and
booked passage aboard the *California*. New York, the lifeline for so
many criminals of the south, beckoned. The very thing that Petrosino
had decried for years, the easy transit of killers from Italy to America,
now had its most famous example. The powerful and universally feared
Enrico Alfano, head of "the most monstrous criminal organization the
world has ever seen," was headed for Manhattan as perhaps the world's
number one fugitive.

• • •

PETROSINO KNEW ABOUT ALFANO'S ARRIVAL ALMOST FROM THE
moment he stepped off the boat. The detective's informers told him
that Alfano had passed through immigration on March 21, that he was
traveling under the name Giuseppe Balstieri, and that he was said to
be carrying seventy thousand francs in French currency. It was also
rumored that the members of the Neapolitan Camorra who had settled
in Manhattan, some of whom were involved in the Society, intended
to hide their *capo dei capi* in order to prevent his extradition. But
Petrosino's informers could tell him no more. Once Alfano stepped off
the pier, he'd disappeared.

Petrosino put out the word to his sources and his *nfami:* Find Alfano. Quickly.

For nearly a month, nothing. Alfano was hiding somewhere in the Italian colonies, most likely in the area around Mulberry Street, but no one had seen him. Then, on April 17, two members of the Italian Squad, Detectives Carhipolo and Bonanno, found themselves sitting in an Italian restaurant in the subbasement of a house at 108 Mott Street, near the corner of Hester. How they had come to be at this particular spot at this particular hour remains a mystery. Did they receive a tip that something unusual was happening? Did they follow a suspect down the steps into the dark tavern? Or did they happen to be having lunch when the situation presented itself? Whatever the case, they were witnesses to a gathering that did not seem possible: a dozen feet from where the two detectives sat, six men were holding a lively banquet for a man who resembled — this was all they could say — Enrico Alfano.

But *was* it him? The two detectives couldn't be sure; there were no photographs to go by. And why would the head of the Camorra flaunt his presence in Little Italy in such a public place? The pair took one last look at the man, then exited the restaurant and went in search of their leader. A reporter from the *Evening World* revealed what happened next.

According to the reporter, he met Petrosino on Mulberry Street that afternoon. They were walking along the crowded street when Petrosino stopped in front of a restaurant: 108 Mott. "I'm going to lunch here, come," the detective said, and the two descended the stairs into one of the basement eateries that dotted the neighborhood. Petrosino sat at a table near the door and studied the menu nonchalantly while stealing glances at six "villainous-looking men" who were gathered around a table halfway down the bar that ran along one wall of the restaurant. Some were standing, others sitting, and all were engrossed in an "almost worshipful attention to a spare, bold-eyed Italian" who had a deep scar running from his left ear to the corner of his mouth. The men were speaking Italian, flattering their guest of honor, and he was basking in their praise.

The reporter was oblivious to what was taking place. He was hungry and studied the menu while making small talk with Petrosino. After scanning the offerings, Petrosino laid an arm softly on his, as one would to a friend engrossed in the playbill when the theater curtain rose. The reporter looked up. The detective was standing now, looking toward the table of talking men. All of a sudden he called out "Alfano!" in a booming voice, "as one might call a cringing dog." The room went silent.

The *capo dei capi*, who wasn't used to being addressed in such a disrespectful tone, stood up from the table and whirled around to face Petrosino. The other Camorrists, who must have recognized Petrosino immediately, stayed where they were.

As the reporter gaped, Petrosino strode across the room straight toward Alfano and "fetched him a mighty slap" across his cheek. Alfano staggered back and toppled against the wall, where he sat propped like a marionette, his back to the bricks. Moving quickly, Petrosino brushed past the Camorra men and approached Alfano, leaning over and slapping him briskly across the face, then again. Then he reached behind the killer, grabbed his collar, and, as the reporter watched in stunned silence, dragged the *capo* across the restaurant floor "with his toes face down." When one of the Camorrists took a step toward him, Petrosino said, "Get out of my way, lest I take you to jail with this cowardly dog" — this although, the reporter later learned, all of the men were armed (Alfano had a knife secreted in his waistband), and "every one of them was a murderer, either in fact or in prospect."

News of the arrest ran in papers from Salt Lake City to Los Angeles to the small town of Paducah, Kentucky ("STRANGE ROMANCE OF BANDIT CHIEF WHO CAME TO AMERICA AS A STOKER"). Days later, Petrosino put his captive on a ship back to Le Havre, where he was arrested and brought to Naples. The proceedings that eventually resulted, though it took five years for them just to begin, expanded to embrace the entire Camorra leadership: forty-seven defendants, including twenty-seven Camorra bosses, went before a judge on charges of murder, corruption, assault, and other grave offenses. Italy was transfixed. "Not since the case of Dreyfus," reported one journalist, "has a criminal trial so stirred a nation." After seventeen months of testimony that was collected in sixty-three volumes of transcripts, the defendants were convicted and sentenced to 354 years of imprisonment. The arrest of Alfano broke the Camorra in Naples. The trial was a major landmark in Mafia prosecutions, the predecessor of the "maxi-trials" that emerged in Italy during the 1980s. And it had all begun with Petrosino's slap.

Still, the detective's performance — for it was a performance, as precisely thought out and choreographed as anything in his beloved *Traviata* — remains curious. Why risk being shot to catch Alfano himself when he could have brought a dozen armed cops to take him down? Petrosino hadn't even bothered to draw his gun. Why become, as the *Times* called him, "the terror of hurtful people" on a public stage?

Why? For the same reason that the Black Hand sometimes chose to mutilate its victims, and once arranged for a rendezvous to take place in a cemetery in front of a freshly dug grave: it was excellent advertising. Petrosino wished to show Italian Americans that they should fear no one, not even the head of the dread Camorra. He wanted to stiffen their backbone, while deflating the myth of the all-powerful Italian criminal. The detective also knew that publicity was a force multiplier. He and his men were outnumbered a thousand to one; the arrest of a *capo* like Alfano made the Italian Squad appear more powerful than it really was.

• • •

THE ALFANO AFFAIR WASN'T AN ISOLATED INCIDENT. IN THE absence of willing witnesses and good prosecutions — of, really, a functioning justice system — this kind of treatment became an unofficial policy of the Italian Squad. Petrosino went after Black Hand men any way he could. "If the courts send these criminals back into the streets," he told a reporter, "we'll make life so tough for them that they'll have to clear out whatever way they can."

Petrosino had declared his own private, semi-legal war on the Society. And it was to be a dirty war.

Members of the Italian Squad began "bracing" the best-known

suspects: accosting them on the street, throwing them up against a wall, threatening them with arrest or worse if they didn't leave town. They surveilled their apartments. They introduced them to what was known as "the nightstick cure." They noted their associates and braced them as well. Petrosino even disguised himself as a common criminal and had his fellow cops bring him in handcuffs to the Tombs, where he was locked in a cell with Society suspects. There he would sit, appearing dejected and listless, but in fact listening closely to his fellow prisoners discuss their crimes and organizations. Once Petrosino was "released," the Italian Squad would begin targeting the Black Handers.

The officers of the Italian Squad were rough on their quarry. They knocked men around; they broke noses, jaws, clavicles. "The gangsters who had dealings with him bore the marks of the 'interrogation' for months," noted one writer. Knowing that most criminals, even the guilty ones, would be given light sentences or released without charges, Petrosino sometimes beat them during his interrogations, or challenged them to mano a mano battles on the streets. If they could outlast him, they would walk free. He often ended the sessions with the words "This way you'll remember who Petrosino was."

The practice extended to Italian criminals who weren't necessarily Black Handers. In one particularly loathsome scheme, criminals would trawl small Italian towns looking for women desperate to leave or to get married; with so many young men gone to America, it was difficult for young women to find husbands. The men would tell these girls about a lonely bachelor in America who was searching for a wife of good morals, who could keep house, to love and marry. If a woman agreed, the men would buy her a steamship ticket and send her off to New York. Waiting in New York was, of course, not a fiancé but a brothel owner and his associates, who forced the woman into a life of degradation and unimaginable horror.

When Petrosino broke up one such prostitution ring, he convicted the entire gang, including its leader, and sent them away to prison, except for one: a twenty-seven-year-old named Paolo Palazzotto, from Palermo. Palazzotto escaped prosecution for unknown reasons; but he was found to have been a convicted criminal in Italy and was scheduled for deportation. Before the suspect left, Petrosino decided to exact some revenge for the women whose lives he had ruined, and to give the white slaver a reminder never to return to Manhattan. He entered the room where Palazzotto was being held, a bunch of keys clutched tightly in his right fist. By the time Petrosino left the room, Palazzotto had lost a significant number of teeth.

The squad's reputation spread. Police brutality, if one can rightly call it that—the concept hadn't even entered the public consciousness in 1907—was so prevalent in the NYPD that it was rarely remarked upon, and it enjoyed a healthy dose of public support. "Guns flashed, clubs whacked, and men fell" is one description of a typical encounter between criminals and Manhattan cops. Clubber Williams, Petrosino's old mentor, once famously said that "there's more law in the end of a policeman's stick than in a decision of the Supreme Court," and many New Yorkers would have agreed with that sentiment. Even Teddy Roosevelt liked a rugged cop. During his reign as police commissioner, one legendary officer came across a gang of wiretappers and instantly "leaped on them, knocked them down and kicked them bodily out of the police station, across the sidewalk and into the street." Roosevelt's response was a hearty "Atta boy!"

Petrosino was relentless. The detective, one Brooklyn alderman complained, "knocked out more teeth than a professional dentist." These were not one-way battles, however, or not always. One journalist recounted that, after years of street battles with Society members, Petrosino "had scars all over his body." But there was one difference between what he did and the actions of the ordinary cop: Petrosino targeted only those suspects he was convinced were guilty and likely to escape punishment. This was wholly unconstitutional, of course, and it's possible that Petrosino, even with his excellent sources, assaulted more than one innocent man. But the detective was desperate to blunt the rise of the Society and to save as many Italians as he could.

The strategy did result in some lighter moments. A suspect named Giamio, whom the squad suspected in a kidnapping, was taken to headquarters to be questioned. The detectives brought Giamio to the photographer's room for his mug shot and placed him in a wooden chair. A bright light buzzed above the Italian's head, catching the nervous man's attention. Maybe it was the buzzing or maybe it was Petrosino's grim expression, but the idea came to Giamio, who no doubt had heard stories of the vast powers of the Italian Squad, that Petrosino had dispensed with a trial and had placed him in the infamous "electric chair." In Giamio's mind, the bantering he heard around him was the prelude to his own execution. Unable to contain himself, the suspect jumped up, shouting that he did not wish to die and calling on the saints to help him; then he "flopped to the floor" like an ungainly fish.

Petrosino and the others watched it all happen, laughing themselves sick at this *grignono,* this greenhorn, making an ass of himself. Then they picked Giamio up off the floor and explained that, in this case at least, the chair was just a chair.

Nevertheless, many disappearances of gangsters and would-be assassins could be traced to a visit from the detective. Ignazio "the Wolf" Lupo, the stylish, high-voiced criminal mastermind who'd teamed with Giuseppe Morello to defraud and terrorize dozens of honest merchants in Little Italy, was by October 1908 a wealthy crime boss, a role he kept hidden behind his position as a Little Italy merchant. Lupo's magnificent flagship store at 210–14 Mott Street was a seven-story building filled to bursting with Parma hams, long tubes of mozzarella, and exotic spices. It was "easily the most pretentious mercantile establishment in that section of the city," according to the *New York Times,* "with a stock of goods over which the neighborhood marveled."

The smooth-faced criminal, however, had lately found Petrosino impinging on his business. The detective not only pursued him relentlessly for acting as the intelligence network for the Black Hand in New York, but also lost no opportunity to warn Italians not to deal with the Sicilian and his friend Morello, "attacking their credit wherever he could." This had so enraged Lupo and his associates that he'd sent a lawyer to the detective's office, who told Petrosino that if he didn't stop blackening the name of his clients, he was going to file a criminal libel suit against him.

Petrosino, confident in his sources, didn't let up. He wanted to drive Lupo and his gang out of New York. Finally, the boulevardier struck back. He told friends and associates that if Petrosino didn't stop his campaign, he, Lupo, would hurt him. The threat was soon out on the street.

One afternoon, the Wolf was in his shop overseeing his business, working, as usual, in one of his tailored suits, when the door opened and Joseph Petrosino walked into the store's gleaming ground floor. He inspected the stacks of Parma hams and Asiago cheese, then called Lupo over. The Wolf approached him; Petrosino leaned over and said a few words in a low voice. Before Lupo could respond, Petrosino's right fist shot out and knocked the Wolf to the ground. As Lupo's employees and customers watched, Petrosino proceeded to administer a severe beating on the floor of the Wolf's fine establishment.

Within a month, Lupo's buggy was no longer seen on Mott Street with its owner snapping the whip at his immaculate white horse. Petrosino had driven the Wolf from the city. A year later, the merchant filed for bankruptcy.

Few men who encountered the chief of the Italian Squad ever forgot the experience. One prominent politician from Palermo, Raffaele Palizzolo, announced he was coming to New York to help his compatriots fight the Black Hand. Twenty thousand Sicilians, many of them wearing buttons with Palizzolo's face on them, met his ship at the pier and cheered him lustily as he descended the gangway. But Petrosino discovered that Palizzolo had an unsavory reputation back in Sicily, where he was known as "the King of the Mafia" and had once been sentenced to prison for murder. His opposition to the Black Hand was a charade. The detective followed Palizzolo from event to event, breaking up his lectures by force and announcing the man's true history to stunned crowds of immigrants; he even knocked on the politician's hotel room door one night and "threw some fear" into him.

After weeks of these confrontations, the politician cut his visit short and boarded a ship for Europe. At the pier, he made his way to the side of the vessel and looked down mournfully at the relatives and well-wishers waving up at the departing passengers. As his eyes scanned the skyline and then the crowd, Palizzolo was stunned to make out a familiar figure amid the jostling crowds below: Joseph Petrosino, standing among the throngs as if the politician were his favorite nephew leaving on a trip back to the old country. Palizzolo stared at the detective with mounting rage. Before the ship slipped into the ocean currents, he raised his fist and shook it at Petrosino, crying out to the receding figure below, "If you ever come to Palermo, God help you!"

10

ONCE TO BE BORN, ONCE TO DIE

IN INTERVIEWS, STREET BATTLES, AND CONFRONTATIONS WITH the Society, Petrosino set a tone for dealing with the Black Hand, and it was one of defiance. He insisted that his countrymen stand up to the killers, no matter the cost. Those who paid up he regarded with an almost violent disdain. There were times, said an Italian journalist, when the detective was "more furious against the victims than the criminals." It's not that Petrosino lacked sympathy; he understood very well the terror that entered a person's life the moment he or she opened a Black Hand letter. He'd experienced it himself. But regarding his own death as almost certain, as in fact long overdue, he didn't understand people who sought to save themselves while behaving, as he saw it, atrociously. Perhaps it was because he had no children. But it honestly perplexed him.

Not everyone surrendered. Whether inspired by the detective or simply acting on their own sense of moral outrage, a number of Italians in Manhattan and across the country followed Petrosino's example and said no to the Society. One such man was John Bozzuffi. His story is one among hundreds.

Bozzuffi was a self-made man, a prominent banker in the small Italian colony on the Upper East Side. One day, three men came to see him. The first, Mr. Christina, was a cobbler with a thriving shop who'd earned enough in America to hire three assistants. He'd received a letter in red ink saying the Black Hand would drink his blood if he didn't come up with a certain sum of cash. The second, Mr. Campisi, who owned a grocery shop near Mr. Christina, had been warned that he would be cut into small pieces and packed into a barrel if he didn't leave the city. Not too far from his store was the First Avenue barbershop of Mr. Fascietta, which had been partially demolished with a bomb not long before. All of them were friends of Bozzuffi's, and they had come to his bank on Seventh Avenue to ask for help. The three were thinking of paying or fleeing the city. No other choice seemed possible. "Virgin Mother," swore Mr. Campisi, "I will get out before they kill me or kidnap one of my children!"

Bozzuffi understood their fear. He, too, had a business that catered to Italian customers. He also had seven children — the eldest, Antonio, named after his grandfather, who had brought the family to America, "and who slaved as a laborer in the trenches of the streets of New York in 1872 to give his own eldest son a chance at a public school education." John Bozzuffi had started as a ticket taker on the elevated subway and worked his way up while earning extra money as a notary public on the side. He bought a little grocery store, then moved on to insurance and banking. It had been difficult all the way up, but Bozzuffi was respected, and he was honest. He was proud of the family's rise, an Italian patriot as well as an all-American booster. "I'm not ashamed of my people, family or nation," he said. "But I'm an American by the sweat of my father's brow."

Bozzuffi had received his own letters from the Society. But to give in to them was, for him, unthinkable. If he capitulated, the Bozzuffis would surely be pushed back down the economic ladder into the stinking tenements, which were so ridden with disease that one journalist of the time wrote that they "might well earn for New York the title The City of Living Death." His children would have to reenact the fate of their grandfather. But it was more than that: it would be an insult to his race. "For the sake of decent, honest, hard-working Italian citizens," the banker said, "I will sacrifice everything I have." And so, when the three men came to see him, Bozzuffi had a simple message for them: Resist. "Stick it out!" he said. "Not for your own sake, but for the sake of the decent Italians who are making their way in the world, and will be easy victims of the *banditi* if you or I give tribute to such cattle."

He managed to calm the men and sent them back to their businesses. But more letters arrived at the trio's shops, and they returned to see Bozzuffi once again weeks later. "Don't pay blackmail," he insisted. "Die first." One chink in the armor of the three friends would mean the Black Hand would never let them go.

Every weekday, Mr. Fascietta opened the shutters of his shop. Customers filed in, and he cut their hair and shaved them. He knew his tormentors were possibly among the crowd, but he persevered. Meanwhile, the cobbler, Mr. Christina, had a method for steeling his nerves. Every time the Black Hand was mentioned, every time he received a letter, he would whisper a word to himself. *"Petrosino!"* The detective's name was for him a kind of talisman.

This went on for months. Then one day, Mr. Bozzuffi's eldest son, Antonio, was leaving Dilmer's drugstore near his home. Antonio was fourteen and a good student; the banker "hoped to see [him] distinguish himself in Harvard or Yale some day." On this afternoon, a man Antonio didn't know walked up to the teenager. "Hello, Tony," he said. "Will you do me a favor? We have some letters from the old country at my house and we want you to translate them."

Antonio agreed. The pair walked down Second Avenue to 59th Street. The man gestured toward a door leading to a second-floor apartment, and Antonio, unsuspecting, opened it and walked up the stairs.

When he stepped into the apartment, he found himself facing three men in black masks. The man who'd brought Antonio to the apartment closed the door behind him. Antonio heard the lock slide into place.

One of the men pulled out a revolver and pointed it at the teenager's face. "Tony," he said, "if you don't holler and do what we tell you, we will do you no harm. But if you yell and don't do what we tell you, we'll kill you." Another man pulled out an axe; it hung in his hand, bright, newly store-bought.

They seated Antonio at a table and told him to write a letter. One of the men recited the words: Bozzuffi the banker would pay $20,000 or Antonio would be returned to him as a corpse. When Antonio heard this — the amount was an absolute fortune — he broke down. He was shaking so hard he was unable to write.

The men began to shout at him and curse his family. Antonio couldn't regain his composure. He felt something cold against his temple: the barrel of the revolver.

Slowly, the teenager pulled himself together. His hand stopped shaking and he finished the letter. If the police or Petrosino himself was contacted, the men instructed him to write, his death would follow.

The kidnappers bound Antonio's arms and legs with ropes and stuffed a handkerchief into his mouth. He was terrified. He tried to think, to gather clues. From the noises that came through the thin panes of glass, Antonio suspected he was above a saloon. Meanwhile, on 62nd Street, Bozzuffi received his first ransom letter. From the start, he held out little hope. "He considered his son dead," reported the *New York Times*. "He had been kidnapped by the same class of Sicilians that had promised to drink the blood of the cobbler, to pickle the grocer, and had ruined the beautiful barber's pole of Fascietta."

Bozzuffi ignored the letter's instructions and contacted Petrosino. The detective arrived at the Bozzuffi home and began to chase down leads, with the father "on his heels." First, Petrosino called all the hospitals in the area to make sure Antonio hadn't been wounded and brought in for treatment. Nothing. Then he started making inquiries in the neighborhood.

The contents of the letter quickly became known in the tight-knit Italian colony. Bozzuffi was a favorite banker among the small businessmen on the East Side, and rumors quite naturally began to spread: *Bozzuffi is going to take his depositors' money and pay the Black Hand. Wouldn't you do the same?* Depositors crowded into his bank, holding their books with the modest balances written in ink. Many withdrew everything. Bozzuffi watched from his office as a run on his bank began.

By Tuesday, $7,000 had been withdrawn from his vault, and the panic wasn't over yet. Another letter arrived: the Black Hand now set out the details of his surrender. If he was ready to settle on March 7, he should hang a sign in his bank window reading "SEVEN MEN WANTED." If he chose March 8, "EIGHT MEN WANTED." On the specified day, the captors or their associates would arrive to collect their money.

Bozzuffi contemplated the situation, then looked around his office until he found a piece of pasteboard. He dipped his fountain pen in the inkwell and wrote out a message, in Italian. He poked two holes at the top corners of the pasteboard, strung a piece of twine between them, and took the sign to the window that faced out onto First Avenue, where Italian pedestrians moved up and down the sidewalk at all hours of the day. He pushed a tack into the wooden frame of the window and hung the sign on it, facing outward. The sign read: "THE MONEY IN THIS BANK BELONGS TO THE DEPOSITORS AND IT WILL BE PAID TO THEM IF I NEVER SEE MY SON AGAIN."

Bozzuffi's family and friends begged him to reconsider, but the banker — having encouraged the cobbler and the grocer to stand fast — couldn't do it. "I have six other children," he told them. "They can take them one by one, but not a cent will they get from me in tribute." To pay would be to become party to a crime that was blackening the name of his unborn descendants.

On the third day of the standoff, Antonio escaped. When one of his captors was left alone to guard him, the boy slipped his bonds and ran out the door, dashing up First Avenue. Some in the city believed it was an honest mistake; others theorized that the kidnappers, realizing Bozzuffi wouldn't budge, chose the least humiliating way out of the situation. In any case, Bozzuffi embraced his son and joyfully called Petrosino to give him the news.

The story of the Italian who'd defied the Black Hand made headlines from Los Angeles to St. Louis, from Wilmington to Minneapolis to Walla Walla, Washington. Bozzuffi had broken a cardinal rule of Italian culture: he'd risked his child's life — his firstborn son's life, in fact, which was an important distinction — for a principle. Americans were filled with admiration. "I believe that I have as much of the instinct of a parent as any human," Bozzuffi told reporters who gathered at his bank, "but I have something beyond that. I have never ceased to love my fatherland and the people of it . . . I will give all I have — money and children, home and wealth, life itself — before I will be a means to hindering the honest development of my people as Americans." They could have been Petrosino's words.

Still, the threat wasn't over. Bozzuffi took his children to the studio of a local photographer and had pictures taken of each of them in case they were kidnapped and flyers with their images had to be passed around the colony. But his story had a happy ending. Not only was Antonio returned to him, but also the run on his bank stopped, and his firmness even won him new customers. "Today," reported the *Times,* "the banker stands higher in the regard of the people in the colony than ever before."

It was for Italians like these that Petrosino risked his life.

• • •

NOT EVERY STORY HAD SUCH A SWEET ENDING. IN BROOKLYN, A twenty-four-year-old named Francesco Abate arrived in the neighborhood of East New York, where there was a thriving Italian community. No one in East New York had experienced Black Hand threats before; it was virgin territory, and Abate was determined to claim it. He rented an apartment at 136 Sackman Street, holed up in his room, and began a period of intensive research. He bought books and pamphlets on how to make a bomb, some written in Italian and some in French. He found (where was never discovered, but locally) a volume detailing how extortion gangs had worked their arts in the Argentine Republic. He collected samples of Black Hand letters and "hundreds of clippings" on the workings of Society outfits in New York and Chicago. He found a treatise on dynamite and read lists of its ingredients and procedures for concocting it. "The police of this city," a journalist wrote after Abate's nest had been raided, "have never found so complete a library of what might be specified as Black Hand literature."

Having surveyed the academic field, as it were, Abate put his knowledge to work. Letters began showing up at local businesses demanding tribute. The merchants, who'd heard horrible stories from the colonies in lower Manhattan and Harlem, had no idea who the extortionist was. Fearful for their families, and impressed by the ferocity of Abate's notes, they paid.

It was American self-invention at its purest. By declaring himself a member of the Black Hand, Abate had become a member of the Black Hand.

Soon the young man's lifestyle showed a marked improvement. He "blossomed forth in fine raiment," showed up on Brooklyn's Pennsylvania Avenue in beautiful suits; in no time, he'd made a name for himself as a lady-killer. The local beauties didn't mind the fact that Abate seemed not to have a job, because he always had plenty of cash and wasn't shy about spending it. Abate had a knack for his work. "He surrounded himself," said one journalist, "with an air of mystery that made him doubly interesting." He did this by not only extorting money from the merchants of East New York, but also then paying social calls on those same merchants in the evening. "The young upstart," reported the *Evening World,* "had the unutterable cheek to come into their homes and flirt with their wives and daughters, showering presents upon them." The money for the presents, of course, had come from the fathers of the girls he was courting.

Abate soon found that romancing the women of East New York on the scale that he envisioned was expensive, and so he raised his demands. The businessmen convened a meeting and sent a message to Abate: they agreed to the new prices. The men arranged to meet Abate at the gates of the Acacia Cemetery in Ozone Park to hand over their first installment under the new regime. That night, at the entrance, Abate arrived beneath a bright moon. As best the Italian Squad was later to figure out, the merchants greeted him, then pulled out a collection of knives, axes, and even a pickaxe like the ones used to dig the Manhattan subway tunnels, and fell on the beautifully dressed extortionist. The men cut Abate to pieces and left his remains at the cemetery gate. The Society experiment in East New York was over.

If one knew the local Black Handers, fighting back was easier. One immigrant, "known throughout the Italian community as a robust, strong, and fearless man," bought a gun as soon as he received the first letter. Then he visited some acquaintances whom he knew to have Black Hand connections and told them that if any harm came to himself or his family, he would kill them. He never got a second letter. Another man, who was legendary in the neighborhood for his feats of strength — he would pick people up off the street and carry them for blocks with his arms fully extended, simply to amuse himself — found out that his brother's business had become a target of the Society. The man gathered all the weapons he owned, hid them in his clothing, and walked to his brother's establishment to stand guard. For three days, he never left the storefront, scanning the faces of pedestrians. In seventy-two hours, he saw nothing out of the ordinary. Then on the third day, he recognized a member of the Society walking by. He seized the man by the collar, raised him into the air, and began shaking him violently. As the Black Hander looked down in terror, the man asked him why the gang hadn't come to bomb his brother's store, because he'd been waiting and it had cost him three nights' sleep. He set the Black Hander back on the pavement and told him that if anything happened to his brother or his place of business, he would hunt down each member of the gang personally and eliminate them. Again, no more letters arrived.

Giovanni Barberri, a wealthy baker in Mount Vernon, in suburban

Westchester County, was being pestered by extortion letters; they demanded $500 on pain of death. When he refused to answer them, a man named Antonio Fotti took a train from the city and got off at the Mount Vernon station. He walked into Barberri's shop, pulled out two revolvers from beneath his coat, and pointed them at the baker. Barberri ran into the street, followed by the gunman. Two passing neighbors, both women, saw Fotti emerge and grabbed his arms. He cried out and fired two shots wildly. The baker, seeing his chance, ran back into his shop and emerged with a shotgun loaded with birdshot. Calmly, he told the women to let Fotti go. When they did, he leveled both barrels at the Black Hander and fired. Police followed the blood trail to a hospital in Yonkers and arrested Fotti.

Two days later, on the outskirts of Mamaroneck, another Westchester suburb, hotelkeeper Pietro Caputo was living under the threat of the Society when three men walked into his hotel bar, led by a criminal known as Big Pietro. The strangers ordered drinks, and when Caputo went to pour them, Big Pietro reached over the bar, his knife flashing in the gaslight, and stabbed down onto the saloonkeeper's head, then brought the blade forward and cut viciously across his throat. Caputo fell back and collapsed to the floor. Fatally wounded, his hands grappling for the shotgun he kept behind the bar, Caputo stood up. A curtain of blood gushing from the wounds on his head obscured his vision, but he could make out the shape of Big Pietro; he pointed the shotgun and yanked back on both triggers. The buckshot sliced Big Pietro's scalp from his skull and blew the top half of his head away, spraying his two accomplices with brain matter. Caputo fired twice more before he fainted and bled out. The local Italians formed a posse and went hunting Big Pietro's partners in the woods that surrounded the town.

The Black Hand was so feared that there were few it declined to attack, even mobsters. At one point in the history of the Society, a Chicago group decided to target Big Jim Colosimo, a top gangster who controlled gambling and prostitution on the Near South Side. Colosimo's gang, known as the Chicago Outfit, dominated crime in the

Windy City, and Big Jim, in his spotless white suits and diamond jewelry, enjoyed the profits in high style. Colosimo's connections with corrupt Chicago pols, beginning with Michael "Hinky Dink" Kenna, were peerless, and he was considered as untouchable as anyone in Illinois. He was making $600,000 a year from his chain of brothels (he'd married a famous madam, Victoria Moresco, to get this part of his business started) and eventually expanded the business to two hundred houses.

But Colosimo began receiving letters adorned with daggers and ebony hands, and he took them seriously enough to pay out a total of $5,000 to the Society before realizing, like many merchants and innocent victims before him, that he would soon go bankrupt. Colosimo apparently believed that no one in his own gang was up to the challenge of stopping the Black Hand, so he looked farther afield, to Brooklyn. There he found John "the Immune" Terrio.

Terrio had immigrated to New York as a young boy and worked as a bouncer before graduating to various gangster pursuits. Bright and tough, he was spotted by the New York mobster Paul Kelly, who remade Terrio's appearance (choosing conservative suits), reformed his manners, and offered him business advice. Soon Terrio was running a profitable numbers business. When he was targeted by the Black Hand, he had a simple solution: he killed everyone and anyone connected with the extortion demands on sight.

When he received the call from Big Jim, Terrio knew he faced the same challenge on a grander scale: Colosimo was a far more public figure, and far wealthier, than Terrio was. Terrio took the train to Chicago and set up meetings with the various gangs that were sucking money from Colosimo. Each time the bagmen showed up at the rendezvous, Terrio and his men opened up on them with their tommy guns and left the bodies in the streets as a message to other Black Hand gangs. The number of threats declined precipitously. Terrio was so successful that Colosimo took him on as his right-hand man. Terrio eventually imported another rising gangster into the outfit to act as his bodyguard, an ugly, intelligent, and thoroughly vicious former bouncer named Al Capone. The underground fight against the Black Hand ended up transporting the notorious Chicago mobster to the site of his future empire.

. . .

THESE ACTS OF RESISTANCE SHOWED THAT THE NATIVE COURAGE of the Italian American was still intact. But they were isolated incidents, scattered across the country and over a period of many months. They didn't present an existential challenge to the Black Hand; there just weren't that many Society victims who were comfortable killing other people, even to save their own lives.

Petrosino had another idea: organized resistance. He'd been calling for the creation of protection groups, in which Italians could band together and fight the Society, for at least two years. "If they would form a Vigilance League," he'd told the *Times* on September 22, 1905, "that would drive into the hands of the police Italian malefactors, they would be as safe as any one else and not have as the penalty of their industry and prosperity the payment of large sums to the idle and worthless." Now he went to leaders in the Italian community and begged them to join together. But fear of the Society was everywhere, and the men turned Petrosino away.

By early 1907, it was clear that the Italian Squad, even at forty men, couldn't take down the Black Hand on its own. The Secret Service had declined his appeal. The only hope, as Petrosino saw it, was for Italian Americans to rise up against their oppressors.

But he was running out of time for this to happen. Alarm over the Society had already begun to seep into American politics and popular culture. Soon that alarm would grow into full-blown panic.

11

"WAR WITHOUT QUARTER"

THE WORK OF THE SQUAD WAS GROWING INCREASINGLY DANGER-
ous. On December 28, 1907, Rocco Cavone was climbing slowly up
the stairs of an apartment building in Kingsland, New Jersey, toward
the room where he had reason to believe a young man named Nicolò
Bananno was hiding. Bananno was the leading suspect in the murder
of a young Italian barber in Manhattan on Christmas Day: the victim
had opened his front door, expecting a holiday guest, but had instead
been blasted once in the chest with a pistol round. Cavone had been
staking out the Kingsland building for two days. Now he was closing in
on capturing the fugitive.

Cavone had already been promoted to lieutenant after only a short
time with the squad. He'd recently married a young woman and
installed her and their baby in an apartment at 77 Thompson Street
in lower Manhattan. Catching Bananno would be the latest feat of a
detective on the rise.

Above Cavone a skylight let down a few rays of dirty sunlight into the stairwell. The light threw shadows across his path as he trained his eyes upward. The hallway smelled of cooking: onions, prosciutto, peppers, fresh garlic.

Cavone paused, listening. He placed his foot on the next step and was pushing upward when suddenly two shots rang out. Unbeknownst to Cavone, Bananno had been crouching with his revolver at the top of the stairwell for the detective to get close enough to kill. Cavone whipped his head back and cried out. He'd been shot in the face.

Hearing the shot, other members of the squad raced up the stairs from their positions below. The sounds of their pounding feet mingled with footfalls that echoed from above: Bananno was running up the stairs, toward the skylight. When he reached it, the gunman pushed the glass panes open, hoisted himself up, ran across the roof to the fire escape, and bounded down the shaking structure to the street below.

The cops reached Cavone and found him bleeding from the face and left hand. One of Bananno's bullets had slammed into his forehead at an oblique angle, creasing a furrow down his face before ricocheting through his palm. "Never mind me," Cavone said to his fellow squad members, "but get the fellow who plugged me."

The detectives gave chase. Cavone worked his way slowly down the tenement stairs and out of the building. He made it to the train station and was whisked back to New York. Petrosino was waiting for him at the terminus and rushed him to nearby St. Vincent's Hospital. What Petrosino's feelings were at the time — the dread of having to tell Cavone's parents and young wife that the man he'd recruited had been killed — can only be imagined. But Cavone was lucky. Some of the nerves in his left hand were damaged, and doctors told him he might not regain the full use of his fingers. The head wound, however, was only superficial.

Bananno, alone in a wooded area with the police closing in, put the gun to his cheek and pulled the trigger. He failed to kill himself, however, and the Italian Squad soon took him into custody.

If arrests of men like Bannano burnished the squad's reputation,

Petrosino knew they weren't enough. The detective and his men had enlarged their aims by 1907. They weren't just arresting Black Hand leaders and breaking up their gangs; they aimed now to decode the Society itself, to reveal the nature of its mission in America.

After three years, Petrosino had found that the Society acted more like a terror franchise, in which different branches followed their own rules on membership and initiation, on how to approach a victim, when to inflict violence, and how to guard the Society's name. Every branch, no matter how tiny or obscure, traded on the reputation of the Black Hand. One journalist perceptively quoted Robert Louis Stevenson on sixteenth-century Parisian gangs—"independent malefactors, socially intimate, and occasionally joining together for some serious operation, just as modern stock-jobbers form a syndicate for an important loan." It was as good a description as any.

The Italian Squad found evidence of cooperation between the franchises. "Specialists" were often imported from other cities to kill a victim, so that the gunman wouldn't be recognized and the gang responsible couldn't be identified. When the Society itself was slandered, a local branch might spring into action to protect its good—that is, its bad—name. Donato Zarillo, who lived in West New Rochelle, New York, "spoke sneeringly" of the Black Hand in a local saloon one evening, calling its members a bunch of cowards and vowing if they ever dared to threaten him, he would end their lives. Word got around the neighborhood, and soon after, Zarillo was shot on a New Rochelle street and left to die, along with his severely wounded brother.

The Black Hand was a classic secret society: its members vowed never to reveal its innermost values to outsiders. In fact, very few did. Their oaths were sworn in a ceremony called a *picciotto*. A member who went through one described the ritual: The men met in a secret location, first depositing all their weapons in one place, which was guarded by a member. They formed a circle, linking their arms together. The new recruit was told that the center of the circle represented an abyss "in which everything spoken was to be forever buried." The leader began talking in a strange tongue, uttering a kind of chant or invocation, after which the men kissed one another on the cheeks. If the newcomer was being inducted as a *cameristo,* or full member, five knives were set in the middle of the circle with the blades pointed outward. A handkerchief was laid over the daggers, with the points still visible. The men drew lots, and the member who drew the short stick rolled up his sleeve and presented his bare arm. As "cabalistic incantations" were chanted, the man's arm was sliced across, and the new member had to drink down the spurting blood.

Petrosino learned to identify individual gangs by how they killed. One left a blue sash on the body of a victim; another would stab the victim thirteen times, a third twenty-one times; others would leave a row of wounds across the torso in a certain pattern that never varied. Kidnapping a victim's relative became a familiar tactic that the Italian Squad knew to take seriously; it was called *sequestrazione,* or "seques-tration," a legal term meaning the seizure of assets until a debt was paid. Another common method was the "watch of death," the vigil placed on those whom the Society had selected for elimination. Each step along the path indicated where in the process the case was, sometimes allow-ing the squad to anticipate the Society's next move.

Then there were marks that read like urban hieroglyphics. The *freggio,* the slashing cut across the face, identified an informer. A body found with no ears was a message that the person had overheard some-thing he shouldn't have. If a victim was found with his tongue cut out, he'd talked to police. A missing nose? Petrosino learned this was a case of something called the *troppa bircca,* or a man who'd inquired into things that were none of his business. (*Troppa* means "too much," but *bircca* is untraceable — perhaps a bit of Sicilian slang.) One Manhattan gang sliced a victim's face from mouth to ear with a bale hook, a sharp curved tool used to gather hay. When an Italian Squad detective caught the slasher and asked his victim to sign a complaint, the man pointed to the crescent scar on his cheek. "This time they cut me here," he told the detective. "If I do what you ask me, they will cut me here." The man drew his finger across his throat. He didn't sign the complaint.

There were modern touches, too. One Society gang in Brooklyn had access to a baker's oven. Knowing that murder convictions required a body, they murdered their victims, then baked them in the oven until only ashes and bones remained. "Many times," said a member of the Italian Squad, "the morning bread of the Brooklyn neighborhood was caked on a funeral pyre." Whenever this particular gang struck, the Brooklyn Italian Squad knew it had to find the bodies before the members disposed of them.

The squad had also deciphered the meaning of the letters, which almost always followed a set pattern. In their first note, the Society would instruct their victims to deliver a ransom to a specific location; members of the gang would watch the man but fail to make the rendezvous. By telling him, in a second letter, exactly where he'd gone and what he'd done, the Society gave the victim the impression that he was being watched at all times, stoking his fear even higher. In the second letter, the Society would tell their prey to seek help from a "friend," who might be able to negotiate in his place. Petrosino found that, in almost every case, the friend was in reality a Black Hand associate, acting as a "cut-out" for the gang, protecting them from prosecution. The detective informed police officials across the country about these methods, and they used the information to adjust their tactics in the ongoing fight.

Petrosino's insights into the Society spread from coast to coast through his wide network of police contacts and newspaper articles. He was in such demand that journalists sometimes made up interviews out of whole cloth and published them; Petrosino once came across a long article for which the writer hadn't even bothered to contact him. The detective simply didn't have time to explain the inner mysteries of the Black Hand to every hack in America.

. . .

DESPITE HIS FAME, THE GLOW OF PETROSINO'S EARLY VICTORIES had begun to fade by early 1907. Even the expanded Italian Squad couldn't cope with the sheer numbers of immigrants pouring into the city and the criminals who came with them. New York was being splashed liberally with blood that season. "There was a killing in First

Avenue tonight," reported the *Washington Post* on January 26, 1907, "that would have done a frontier town proud." A Black Hand victim and his tormentor had shot and sliced at each other with guns and razors. At the corner of 48th Street and Second Avenue, the victim spotted his quarry and fired a shot at two hundred feet; the bullet caught the Black Hand man in the hip and spun him to the pavement. Bystanders gawked as the two profusely bleeding men ran north along First Avenue. At the next corner, the pursued man looked back over his shoulder, which gave the gunman time to drop him in his tracks with a bullet through his head. Such scenes were not uncommon.

In August, detectives in the central office were told to wear masks when they did lineups so that Society suspects couldn't identify them. In October, a Black Hander with a dynamite bomb under his coat powerful enough to destroy a city block was found stabbed to death in Brooklyn. In December, the Black Hand burned down a tenement at 5 Rivington Street; the sixteen families inside barely escaped with their lives. A concerned citizens' group in Chicago sent a telegram to the chief of the police department. "New York is experiencing unparalleled outbreaks of crime," it read, "many of which are assassinations by members of foreign secret societies, blackmailing plots, and criminal assaults on women and little girls, chiefly by foreigners . . . Will you state your ideas of how best to cope with the situation, which admittedly is beyond control of police?"

The Italian Squad itself had to change offices several times when suspicious Italian men were found congregating near the base of operations, clearly watching Petrosino's headquarters. His life was under continuous threat. He received letters almost daily telling him he would die for his work; one journalist at the time estimated that the detective received thousands of death notes over the length of his career and was the target of hundreds of murder plots. "They have no imagination," Petrosino told a friend as he read one letter. "They all send me the same kind of message." He never kept the letters but threw them away after giving their contents a cursory glance.

There were suspicious encounters. Petrosino recalled that, more than once, he was bumped into by a stranger on a Manhattan street; as the pedestrian glanced at him and passed by, the detective was overcome by an uncanny feeling that the man was an assassin who'd lost his nerve at the last moment. When he walked the streets, he kept his Smith & Wesson .38 revolver in his pocket, an index finger on the trigger, ready to be pulled out at any moment.

One reporter stopped by Petrosino's apartment building on Charles Street to get details for a story he was working on. It was late at night, and the journalist was waiting in the darkened hallway on the first floor for the detective to arrive home. After a few minutes, the reporter glanced toward the foyer and recognized Petrosino's massive frame as he came through the front door into the lighted vestibule. The reporter, leaning against the wall, was in shadow. When Petrosino entered the hallway and turned toward the stairs, the man spoke Petrosino's name, "not thinking of the caution which must surround this man, who for years had been storing against himself all the vengeance of which the criminal Italian nature is capable." Petrosino jumped, the reporter recalled, not away but *toward* him, moving so quickly that the reporter had no time to speak. The detective pinned him against the wall with terrific strength, knocking the breath out of him. Only then did the newspaperman catch his breath and manage to cry out his name. The detective instantly let him go.

"Petrosino did not laugh," the reporter recalled. He simply nodded and told the man, "I thought it was my time, at last. Someday they will get me."

• • •

THE PRESSURE ON PETROSINO AND COMMISSIONER BINGHAM GREW throughout that turbulent year. The *Tribune* was calling for the "rapid deportation of Italians," arguing that, every other measure having failed, this was now "the only hope for the future." The Italian Squad was still catching and arresting Black Handers throughout the city, and driving out others through intimidation, but it seemed that for every Black Hand member the squad caught, three new ones joined the Society.

On August 20, after another rash of Society violence, General Bingham took action. He shocked New York by demoting two Italian Squad detectives, Frank Bonanno and Felix de Martini, to a lower rank and cutting their pay from $2,000 a year to $1,400. "I want the police to make good on these Black Hand cases," the General told the press, "and when I find that investigations have been shiftlessly handled, off will go the heads of the police officers." Bonanno and de Martini were farmed out to plainclothes duty in the Bronx. The pair were two of Petrosino's best men.

Bingham took pains to emphasize publicly his support for his ally. "Now don't think I'm running down my men," he told reporters on one occasion. "Lieutenant Petrosino and his Italian Squad have done excellent work." But he acknowledged that the squad's success had created problems. The members had become so well known in the Italian colonies that they were being recognized on the job, undermining their investigations. But the neighborhoods where the Black Hand flourished remained "strange and impenetrable" to non-Italian cops, creating no-go areas for the NYPD.

The scourge even invaded the consecrated realm of American baseball. On August 18, 1907, Frank Chance, the manager and captain of the Chicago Cubs, arrived at the Polo Grounds in upper Manhattan to play the New York Giants. He found a letter waiting for him with a bony hand and "clawlike fingers" drawn at the bottom. "Dear Sir," it read. "Your club must not get again pennant this year 1907 from New York . . . If you do not let the Giants win the first place this year, Gang of Black Hands will see you after . . . We will use bombs on your players on train wreck . . . We are cranky on Giants. Yours truly, Black Hand." Police theorized the bad grammar was a giveaway for a Giants fan trying to disguise himself as a half-literate Italian. The letter, sadly for the team's supporters, failed ignominiously: the Giants finished in fourth place in the National League, twenty-five and a half games behind the Cubs. Months later, George Napoleon "Nap" Rucker, a star pitcher for the Brooklyn Superbas (later the Brooklyn Dodgers), got a letter accusing him of throwing games to National League teams and informing

Rucker that he would soon be assassinated. "The charge is absurd," said his manager. "Still, it will not do the pitcher any good."

It didn't. The first game Rucker pitched after receiving the letter, on August 17 versus the Cincinnati Reds, he was shellacked for five runs on twelve hits. Brooklyn lost, 5–0.

• • •

THE DRUMBEAT OF HORROR DEPRESSED ITALIANS. IMMIGRANTS, one priest in Detroit reported, were "filled with a feeling that the Americans despise them." Divisions between immigrants from the south and north of Italy, which had always been present, sharpened. "The Sicilian is bloodthirsty man," read a petition sent to the Manhattan coroner, signed by two hundred women from northern Italy, "treacherous; thief; overbearing; vindictive; liar; counterfeiter. He belongs to Black Hand. He exercises blackmail. Is a dynamiter, and by blood a coward. Therefore if the Government wants peace, if the Government wants quietness in America, we must suppress the immigration from the Sicily."

If there was one sign of hope, it came from a direction Petrosino had long looked to. For years he'd been encouraging Italian Americans to find their courage and join together to fight the Society. Now it began to happen — in Chicago. Prominent Italian Americans in that city called for a meeting on November 17 at Roti Hall. More than a thousand people showed up and crowded into the building to witness the founding of the Society of the White Hand.

At the appointed hour, a Chicagoan named Stephen Malato climbed to the lectern amidst the murmuring of male voices below. As he peered out over the audience of Milanese, Sicilians, Calabrians, and Campanians, each group talking in its native dialect, Malato gestured for the crowd to be silent. "We will clean out the Black Hand within a month!" he began. "We will give the public enough evidence to convict these blackmailers and then it will stop." Malato read out the mission statement of the White Hand Society, one that spoke to the fears and hopes of the Italian community. The men in the room pledged themselves "to remove from the atmosphere the burden of mystery and terror" created by the Black Hand and "to rid public opinion in America of its preconceived notions and prejudices." The White Hand would be not only a crime-fighting organization but also an advocacy league that would restore the good name of Italians. "War without truce" was the call the members heard that night. "War without quarter."

Italian lawyers, merchants, physicians, and bankers lined up to sign their names to the society's list of members. Grand plans were formed: a $50,000 war chest was promised, of which $10,000 was pledged inside the hall. The White Hand would recruit, train, and pay no fewer than one thousand detectives to hunt down the malefactors in Chicago; within a few days, the league had received five hundred applications for those positions, which went by the title "secret agent." The executive committee drew up a list of eleven known Black Hand leaders to give the detectives a head start once the candidates were selected. Until indictments could be obtained against these men, the White Hand promised to maintain round-the-clock surveillance of their homes.

Twenty men were sworn in as deputies, adding to the rather bewildering list of various agents who would chase down Society members. These were not your typical crime fighters — among them were a peddler, a clerk, and a laborer — but they were willing and eager to begin. The chief of the actual Chicago Police Department gave the effort a ringing endorsement, saying the White Hand would be able to track down the blackmailers better than his own men. The Chicago newspapers published glowing editorials, which were reprinted all across the country. The result, one author wrote, was that the Italian community no longer felt it was being treated as "a pack of criminals, cowards, and thwarters of justice, unworthy of being harbored in a civilized country."

Almost immediately, imitators began to spring up all across the nation, in cities and towns large and small. On January 22, 1908, Italians in New Castle, Pennsylvania, banded together as the Catholic Protective Society. Organizations were proposed or opened in Carbondale and Reading, Pennsylvania; Clarksville, West Virginia; Brockton, Massachusetts; New Orleans; Baltimore; and many other places.

As soon as the White Hand of Pittsburgh was founded, its members took up arms against the enemy. The two sides met in a rail yard among the coiling loops of steel tracks, dodging freight cars and engines puffing black smoke. A gun battle erupted. The Black Handers and the White Handers hid behind railcars, ducking their heads out for a view of their enemies before firing their guns. The battle raged over an area measuring three city blocks, with hundreds of shots fired. One White Hander was hit by a bullet and went down; two others chased after the gunman, slipping and tripping on the rocks that bordered the rail beds. Finally, they caught up to the Black Hand member, identified as one Phillip Rea, and shot him dead.

. . .

OTHER VICTORIES FOLLOWED. IN "HELLTOWN," WHERE THE BLACK Hand had effectively taken over the government of the thriving mining village, the local police admitted they couldn't stop the Society, and so Frank Dimaio of the Pinkerton Detective Agency was called in. The agent met with operatives from the U.S. Steel Corporation — the limestone from Hillsville was a key ingredient in the corporation's ovens — and decided to follow the path set forth by Petrosino's infiltration of the anarchist societies of Paterson, New Jersey. The agent and several other detectives disguised themselves as Italian immigrants and boarded a ship outside New York Harbor, then entered Ellis Island. After passing through the immigration halls, the men headed for Hillsville, where Dimaio soon brushed up against the Black Hand. Fearless and daring, he joined the Society and rose to a position of leadership. After months under deep cover, the trap was set. One afternoon, as the miners trudged to the small building where their pay envelopes were distributed, they found a stranger standing next to the cashier's window. When one of the Black Hand suspects entered, the man would tell him there was a problem with his wages and ask him to step into a back room. There, agents would jump on the suspect and put him in handcuffs.

It worked perfectly until a woman allied with the Society noticed that men were going into the back office and not coming out. She ran to the headquarters of the gang to spread the word. As the woman entered the house, a boxcar ran down a railroad siding nearby; the door opened and policemen began pouring out. The lawmen surrounded the house and pulled nine suspects out one by one.

The audacious strike had wiped out a complete Black Hand outfit in a single morning. It seemed to offer hope that an alliance of private agents, police, prosecutors, and Italian witnesses could defeat even a deeply entrenched Society gang. Hillsville was no Manhattan, of course, but the formula had worked.

That same year, the federal government finally delivered the tools needed to fight the Society. Packaged into the Immigration Act of 1907 was a clause that allowed for the arrest and deportation of any immigrant who'd been convicted of a crime in his home country, up to three years after his arrival in the United States.

And finally, in the new year of 1908, the Italians of New York joined the cause. The announcement came at a "big and fiery" meeting held at Manhattan's Bolletino Hall at 178 Park Row. The gathering, held before an overflow crowd, marked the founding of the Italian Vigilance Protective Association. Speakers took the stage throughout a raucous evening and called the gathered men to arms with "impassioned addresses, with the vociferousness and gesticulations of which only members of the Latin race are capable." The Black Hand was condemned and the glories of the Italian people proclaimed. Bootblacks, cobblers, and merchants stood shoulder to shoulder as the speakers fired their volleys, competing with one another in their cries of *"Viva!"* and *"Bene!"* Three hundred men signed their names to the league's membership list that night.

It appeared that the Italian community was at long last going to "open up its batteries on thugdom," as the *Tribune* put it. By March 11 of that year, membership had swelled to several thousand. For the first time, the decent Italian Americans of the city had marshaled a significant army to take on the Black Hand. The ordinary Italians of New York had finally answered Petrosino's call.

12

BACKLASH

BEFORE 1907 CAME TO AN END, THERE WAS ONE LAST BIT OF news — both sad and, in its way, wonderful — that would change the detective's life. Vincenzo Saulino, his friend and the father of Petrosino's beloved, passed away just before the New Year. Adelina, the restaurateur's daughter, never revealed her feelings about his death, but she was a loyal and loving child and must have been deeply distressed. Saulino's passing, however, carried with it one hopeful prospect. It meant that Adelina was finally free to marry the man she loved.

It's not clear when Petrosino first made his marriage proposal. Some said it was in November 1906, when he became the first Italian lieutenant in an American police department and went to Saulino's to celebrate. Others date it much earlier; one newspaper reported that their courtship had lasted a full decade. But all sources agree on the form the proposal took. "You too must be very lonely," Petrosino told Adelina. "We could get along well together." Remarkably prosaic words, but

Petrosino was forty-seven years old; he was speaking the truth. He and Adelina were both lonely sojourners in the city.

In light of her father's death, Adelina abandoned the elaborate plans she'd been privately concocting for her wedding day. Instead, she and Petrosino arranged for a small, quiet ceremony at the old St. Patrick's Cathedral on Mott Street. The detective's penchant for secrecy still ruled the day; he told almost no one what was happening, but rumors of the match began to leak out. The Italian colony was agog. "MUL-BERRY STREET ALL IN A FLUTTER," reported the *Evening Sun.* "There has been whisperings among the friends of Mr. and Mrs. Petrosino for several weeks past," the paper noted, "but neither she nor Joe would admit the truth of them." Then, on Monday, January 6, 1908, Petrosino slipped away from police headquarters and made the short walk to St. Patrick's. Waiting were the bride, her brother, and her sister-in-law, along with assorted relatives and well-wishers. Monsignor Michael J. Lavelle, who was old enough to remember when the streets around Mott were the province of the Irish, presided over the wedding mass. Commissioner Bingham was there, bald-headed and beaming under his handlebar mustache, as well as all the members of the Italian Squad. The iron-fisted detective had revealed a more tender side to his charac-ter, and no one was more surprised and delighted than his fellow cops.

It seemed for so many years that Petrosino had no romantic life, and yet right under their noses he'd been conducting a long-running courtship against formidable odds. The news circulated rapidly at 300 Mulberry, and on Tuesday morning, detectives and bluecoats waited impatiently for the man of the hour to arrive. When a solemn-faced Petrosino walked in, the men stood up and burst into a raucous ova-tion. "Joe was snowed under with congratulations," reported the *Sun.* Deputy Commissioner Woods, inspectors, even rookies clapped him on the back. "[He] was all confusion and blushed like a young boy."

Petrosino was happy. His friends were happy for him.

The couple took up residence at 233 Lafayette Street, a brisk walk of a little over a mile from his office. Adelina set up housekeeping in the apartment, and her brother and sister-in-law moved in one story above.

It was a cozy arrangement. Adelina gradually learned what it meant to be married to "the most famous but also the most hated policeman" in New York. Petrosino gently advised her to keep the shades drawn at all times, to guard against assassins' spotting her silhouette in the window. When she opened the mail that arrived daily, she found, along with the bills and invitations, death threats marked with daggers and coffins. Petrosino must have pointed out that he'd been receiving them for years and yet nothing had happened. Whatever concerns she may have harbored, Adelina always had Petrosino's dinner waiting for him when he returned home after an exhausting day.

It had been late in arriving, but Petrosino finally had the home life he'd dreamt of.

• • •

IF THE DETECTIVE'S PERSONAL AFFAIRS WERE GOING SWIMMINGLY, his war on the Society was not. The fifth official year of the struggle would turn into an *annus horribilis* in which the Society would surpass even the worst outrages of previous months. And if 1905 had been notorious for kidnappings, 1908 became the year of the bomb.

Manhattan now echoed with the sound of explosions on a weekly, often a daily, basis. There were so many explosions in the Italian quarter bordered by 11th Street on the south and 14th Street on the north between Second Avenue and the East River that the Italian Squad gave it a name: "the Bomb Zone." But in fact, no part of the Italian American quarter was safe. After one explosion at a Brooklyn grocery store, a reporter who ventured into the neighborhood found that "most of the Italians were so frightened they could hardly speak."

Many buildings around NYPD headquarters at 300 Mulberry Street had been wrecked, and policemen working inside the elegant building regularly felt the walls and floors shake from the latest explosion. Bingham kept an "official roof tree" atop 300 Mulberry. On March 2, the concussion wave from a bombing on nearby Elizabeth Street nearly ripped the tree out of the soil.

The toll mounted month by month:

February 5: A powerful explosive planted at 254 Elizabeth drives a chandelier two stories up through heavy flooring.

February 20: A bomb in Fairview, New Jersey, blows an entire house into the air and propels it into the yard next door. A new lodger on the top floor has the top of his head sliced off and dies at the scene.

March 1: An enormous bomb tears open the offices of a cheese importer in Little Italy, ripping apart the storefront "from the threshold to the ceiling."

May 23: An "infernal device" explodes in an ash can on Mott Street, killing a young boy and badly injuring five other children.

December 9: A Black Hander climbs to the roof of a four-story tenement at 320 East 63rd Street, opens the skylight, lights the fuse, and drops a bomb down the airshaft. The device explodes halfway down, collapsing walls and badly wounding nine people. The target was a banker, Giovanni Cozussi, whose son had been kidnapped three years before. Cozussi had endured an ordeal since then: Children in tenements he owned were stolen away, men in his houses murdered. His buildings were set on fire, and "firemen reported that the hallways of the houses were smeared with kerosene."

To counter the wave of explosions, Petrosino created the NYPD Bomb Squad, the first in the nation, which would go on over its long history to battle anarchists, German saboteurs, and Palestinian terrorists. He taught his men how to recognize explosives concealed inside olive oil cans filled with black powder and lit with linen fuses. He traced sticks of dynamite (known as "Italian sausages") to construction sites, where laborers were sneaking them away and selling them to Black Hand gangs for pennies on the dollar. He discovered the new alarm-clock timers, which allowed the bombers to escape long before the explosion blew apart a deli or tenement house. He unearthed a note-book, a veritable bible of chemical mayhem, detailing how different bombs were made and how they could be safely defused. The depart-ment even hired an official "Inspector of Combustibles" and gave him an office on East 67th Street, where the expert analyzed the various devices the squad brought him.

And Petrosino went after the bomb makers. He tracked down the evocatively named Pellegrino Mule, "a big, gaunt Sicilian" who was accused of setting off an explosion that injured twenty children. When Deputy Commissioner Woods sent to Italy to see if his suspect was wanted by the law, he learned that the Mule had received a life sentence for decapitating an informer and nailing his head to a post near the vil-lage of Caltabellotta, with a warning to anyone who would interfere in the case. By the time of the trial, he'd fled for New York.

While searching the Mule's house, Petrosino found a pad of paper. The top sheet was blank, but when he turned it slantwise to the light, he discovered an impression of handwriting. Technicians put the note under a microscope and were able to read the words: "Dear Friend, This will be our last answer, so be careful . . . You pig of Madonna, you know that this time . . ." It was the tracings from a Black Hand extortion note that had been written on the page above it and then torn off. The handwriting matched a series of letters sent to Manhattan business-men. Deputy Commissioner Woods cheered the breakthrough. "This is the most important Black Hand arrest since the recent outrages in the Italian colony began," he announced. The Mule was scheduled for deportation and his gang was broken up.

In July, Petrosino began chasing an even bigger target, the man he believed to be the chief bomb maker of the Manhattan Black Hand, an individual named Pronzola Bonaventura. For days, the detective followed him around Little Italy, trying to catch him in the act of con-structing or planting one of his "infernal machines." Finally, he spotted Bonaventura entering the house of a landlord whose tenements had been targeted by the Black Hand. Petrosino and his detectives rushed into the building and found Bonaventura lighting the fuse of a dynamite bomb. The detectives snuffed out the flame and, after a brutal and bloody fight, dragged the bomb maker to jail.

At times like this, Petrosino could be said to be fighting not just the Black Hand but the unintended consequences of progress itself. It was the industrial revolution that had brought millions of Italians to Manhattan, and it was the construction of modern transportation systems and ever bigger, taller buildings in American cities that supplied the dynamite to the bombers. Newspapers printed on fast modern presses not only helped create the Black Hand but also gave it reams of free advertising. The Society was often seen as a throwback to the violence of the past, a thing out of the Dark Ages, but in reality it was a thoroughly modern invention, owned and operated by criminal entrepreneurs. And it flourished in the modern city, feeding on the solitude of the immigrant who often arrived without friends or family, where he felt like a tiny warm speck amid the cold, rushing millions. All this made the Society a product of its times, and so very difficult to stop.

• • •

ACROSS THE COUNTRY, THE REPORTS OF SOCIETY OUTRAGES GREW darker. Half the town of Export, Pennsylvania, was destroyed by bombs on February 5, including a home, a store, a boardinghouse, and the rectory of St. Mary's Church. In Rockland County, New York, a letter was sent to one Arthur Seaman of Piermont, a picturesque village on the banks of the Hudson River known for its hand-cranked drawbridge. By chance, Seaman's eight-year-old daughter Grace opened the envelope and read the note inside. "Its threats terrified her," the *Tribune* wrote, "so that she could not be quieted." For days, the girl refused to eat and was unable to sleep. Her worried parents moved to the nearby town of Sparkhill, hoping to restore Grace's health, but she continued to decline. Eight days after reading the letter, Grace passed away.

In Greensburg, Pennsylvania, two Black Handers knocked on the door of a resident and demanded cash. When he said he had nothing to offer, they accepted the answer and presented him with a small package, saying: "Well, if you can't give us any money, we will give you a gift. Here's a box of candy for your children." When they left, the man pulled the string on the box. It exploded, tearing off his right arm and destroying his house.

A surgeon who was part of a West Virginia gang cut off both arms of a suspected informer just below the elbows, and the other members threatened to take his legs. He was intended to be "a living example of the vengeance of the Black Hand on a traitor," a kind of walking billboard of fleshly horror. The stumps of the man's arms healed well, but he remained terrified. "The least noise startles him," wrote one reporter who was brought in to the police station to study the immigrant up close. "He is exceptionally nervous."

But what of the White Hand societies that had sprung up, the great resistance? They were already foundering. Dr. Carlo Volini, the president of the Chicago organization, received a dark and very Catholic-sounding letter that February. "The supreme council of the Black Hand has voted that you must die," it began. "Your killing has been assigned and the man waits for you. Prepare yourself for death. We will kill your body but we do not want to kill your soul." Volini bought a gun and stopped making nighttime visits to his patients.

Contributions to the White Hand slowed. The "1,000 detectives" who were supposed to be hired never materialized; instead, the group hired a single investigator by the name of Godfrey Trivisonno, whom the White Hand brought all the way from Rome with great fanfare. Trivisonno was named "war secretary" of the league, but instead of breaking up gangs and arresting Society leaders, he spent most of his time trooping around Chicago giving lectures on subjects like "How to Detect the Passwords of the Black Hand" and "How to Reveal to the White Hand the Mystery You Have Solved Without at the Same Time Exposing Yourself or Family to Unnecessary Danger of Vengeance." Various fraternal societies booked him, but there is no record of Trivisonno making a single arrest. The White Hand was effectively silenced. "Never before in the history of Chicago," asserted the city's *Daily Tribune,* "has the Black Hand . . . been such a menace. Nearly every Italian who has acquired a little property lives in constant agony."

Other groups disbanded. In December, James Tassarelli, vice president of the St. Joseph's Italian Society for the Suppression of the Black Hand in Scranton, Pennsylvania, was cornered and "literally cut to pieces" by unknown attackers; it was assumed to be a Society attack. He suffered twenty-one stab wounds to his body, with a single gaping wound to his chest the cause of death. Little was heard from the Scranton league after that.

Even the New York branch of the White Hand fell apart. In fact, if one had listened closely to the speakers on the night the league was formed, it was clear its leaders weren't exactly itching to bring the killers to justice. No, the group being formed that night swore only to protect Italians *"from the 'general obloquy'"* resulting from the Black Hand's crimes. That is, the league never pledged to do battle with the Society at all but rather intended to combat something far more ephemeral: prejudice. The assembly had been a grand and thoroughgoing sham.

A month after the group was formed, the *New York Tribune* weighed in with an editorial titled "Where Is the White Hand?" Through weeks of bombings and kidnappings, "all anxious citizens have whispered, 'Where oh where is the great Italian Protective League which set out a month ago to battle with Sicilian cutthroats?'" The editors pointed out that not a single extortionist had been exposed since the group was formed; no funds had been collected; no reports filed. "Such a collapse of fair promises," the paper charged, "would prove conclusively one of two things: either that the Italians have not the moral courage to attack an evil menacing their lives and property or else that they have no capacity for organization and leadership."

The New York police had thrown their hands up. The Secret Service was interested only in protecting the wealthy and powerful. Now Italian leaders, some braver than others, were abandoning the fight to . . . whom?

• • •

FEARFUL AND ENRAGED, AMERICANS BEGAN TO LASH OUT. IN mid-January 1908, extortionists attacked six lumbermen in tiny

Ellamore, West Virginia, killing two of them. The other workers immediately put down their tools, armed themselves with rifles and revolvers, and went looking for the murderers. "If the posse succeeds in capturing the fugitive blackmailers," an observer wrote, "lynching is almost certain." When a Black Hand member kidnapped a nine-year-old girl in Philadelphia, he was chased by a "howling mob" of Italians, a unit of mounted policemen, and a squad of marines all the way to the banks of the Delaware River, where he leapt into the water. As the pursuers studied the water's surface from the banks, the girl was found alive, bound and gagged beneath a heap of rubbish. But the Black Hander, knowing what probably awaited him should he surrender, stopped swimming and sank beneath the surface.

Ten days later, in Reeds Station, Kentucky, locals became so furious over crimes committed by the Society that they began attacking local immigrants. "Italians are being terrorized," the *Washington Post* reported. "Several of their houses have been burned and a number of them have been given orders to leave the place on penalty of death." The governor of the state opened an investigation—into the Black Hand, not the targeting of Italians. Another attack against dark-skinned immigrants occurred in Illinois, in the city of Clinton, the place where Abraham Lincoln allegedly uttered the words "You can fool all of the people some of the time . . ." In mid-April, thirty Italians who worked for the Illinois Central Railroad were "driven from the town by a mob who intimidated them with a fusillade of shots from guns and revolvers." The throng rampaged through the city in the middle of the night, firing bullets through the windows of the immigrants' homes while "police stood by and refused to act." The United Press dispatch from the scene went out under the headline "RACE WAR: WHITES ATTACK ITALIAN LABORERS IN EAST."

John D. Rockefeller, cofounder of Standard Oil and one of the richest men in the world, voiced the nation's exasperation when he arrived in Manhattan in April 1908 with fifteen detectives in tow. His granddaughter had been threatened in Chicago, and his daughter Edith, Mrs. Harold McCormick, was said to be "verging on a nervous breakdown" because of it. A change of scenery was required. But Rockefeller was made of sterner stuff than his daughter. "I am not afraid of Black Handers, dynamiters, anarchists, kidnappers, or anyone who lives," he told the gaggle of reporters who strode alongside the millionaire down Fifth Avenue on a walk with his grandchildren, as detectives watched every well-wisher who came up to shake the mogul's hand.

In fact, Rockefeller had good reason to fear. His splendid estate in Pocantico Hills, New York, was a hotbed of Black Hand violence: two of his workers had already been attacked; in addition, nearby a deputy sheriff had been stabbed with knives and beaten with clubs, and a road builder had been murdered with a bullet through the brain. Finally, Rockefeller had dismissed all the Italians working at his estate, and locals — that is, non-Italians — were hired in their place. Rockefeller claimed that he just wanted to give honest men a chance at employment, but prejudice and fear were rife in the country, and it's hard to believe they didn't play a part in the mass firing. The move proved highly popular with the press. "Praise for Mr. Rockefeller is heard on all sides," declared the *Times,* which noted that the magnate was even allowing these men to go into his forests and cut wood to burn in their stoves, during a season when temperatures regularly dipped below zero. At the same time, hundreds of immigrant servants, groundskeepers, and laborers tramped away from Pocantico Hills, uncertain where they would find new jobs to feed their children.

The states tried passing new laws to stop the outrages. Legislators in West Virginia proposed a law to bar Italian immigrants from entering the state. New Jersey made extortion punishable by twenty years in prison. New York had already passed a law raising the sentence for kidnapping to fifty years, a direct result of the Black Hand scare. A prominent Detroit clergyman who worked with Italian immigrants called for the death penalty for simply writing extortion letters. "There should be no mercy shown," he said. "This is an epidemic." In July, the Black Hand achieved a marker of international fame: Lloyds of London announced that it was now insuring businesses and individuals against Society attacks.

The terror even began to shape the country's demographics. Farmers in states like Georgia, Alabama, and Mississippi badly needed labor in the early 1900s to plow their fields and harvest their crops. Federal officials estimated that the region was losing $1 million per day because there was no one to till the farmland, with African Americans streaming north to escape Jim Crow laws and virulent racism. Who would fill the void? Italians were solid candidates — thrifty, used to hot climates, and hardworking.

But all over the region, voices spoke out in opposition. "It is sometimes wiser to bear the evils we have," argued an opinion piece in the *Nashville American* in 1906, "than to fly to others with which we are unacquainted." States below the Mason-Dixon Line petitioned the government's immigration authorities for more northern European immigrants while explicitly discouraging them from sending Italians. During its 1908 session, the Virginia state senate passed a motion that urged representatives to "oppose in every possible manner the influx into Virginia of immigrants from Southern Europe, with their Mafia and Black Hand murder societies."

The Society was even thrust into the center of the 1907 race for the Mississippi governorship. "The campaign . . . now under way," reported the *Pittsburgh Post*, "seems likely to turn upon a race issue, but a race issue in which the negro is little concerned . . . It looks now as though the election will be a referendum on whether the Italian is wanted or not." Candidates stumped from small town to small town decrying the devastation that the hordes of olive-skinned southern Italians would bring to Anglo-Saxon Mississippi. Some went so far as to produce "Black Hand scrapbooks," filled with newspaper clippings that described bombings and kidnappings in the North, and passed them around at their campaign rallies, where voters pored over the books with fascination, reading of such things as the *freggio, omertà,* and the blood oath.

Once the modern Ku Klux Klan arose in 1915, its members would attack Italians, burn crosses on their lawns in Mississippi, and chase their families out of Birmingham at the point of a gun. The faces one sees on the sidewalks of Asheville today, the names of civic leaders in Tuscaloosa or Biloxi, the list of alumni at Ole Miss—all are different from what they might have been. The Society created fear where there had been only strangeness.

. . .

FOR FOUR YEARS, THE COUNTRY HAD TRIED VARIOUS COMBINA-tions of police pressure, new laws, violent public condemnation, and the creation of White Hand societies. But little had changed. The Society was, if anything, stronger. The Black Hand was no longer a trend; it threatened to become a permanent part of the national scene. "Unless the Black Hand be wiped out by the most drastic measures soon," warned the *San Francisco Call*, "the system will become firmly grounded in the American social structure." The paper estimated it would take ten years, and the lives of many law enforcement officials, to eliminate the Society. The Black Hand was putting down deep roots. The Manhattan gangs were making so much money, Petrosino found, that they were investing in legitimate concerns, opening stores and even banks on the East Side. Tens of thousands of workers were contribut-ing two or three dollars out of their weekly paychecks. To that extent the Society had become an institution much like the IRS. Meanwhile, Manhattanites—who dwelt at the center of the national panic—existed in "a state of mind bordering on hysteria."

For the first time, newspapers began to direct their mounting anger at the Italian Squad and its leader. "The trouble all along has been in one respect at least, in the personal character of Lt. Petrosino," com-plained an editorial in the *Detroit Free Press*. The writer had clearly never met the detective: he hilariously described Petrosino as "elderly, grey-haired, spectacled, slight of build." The portrait of a frail, vul-nerable investigator was ridiculously off the mark, but it reflected the writer's view of Petrosino's temperament. "He may be morally certain that he has located a gang of [Black Handers]," wrote a *Free Press* editorialist, "and that they are planning a bomb carnival, but he will not arrest without the kind of evidence that will convict in court."

The writer painted the detective as an aging milquetoast who carried the Constitution around in his pocket for frequent, nearsighted study.

It wasn't just policing that was being overwhelmed. In July of that year, Lieutenant Vachris of the Brooklyn Italian Squad confided to a journalist that he had had to drop some Society cases because city officials refused to pay for the extradition of Italian criminals from other states. Black Hand suspects were going free for lack of carfare. And in Brooklyn, the firebrand lawyer Francis Corrao, who'd vowed to take on the Society from his position as the first Italian D.A. in the country, found obstacles in his path, too. Corrao was assigned menial duties that could have been handled by any law clerk, while Black Hand victims were being killed in the streets. "Murder, assault, and robbery of Italians," he fumed, are "looked upon by the District Attorney's office with the most cynical indifference." Corrao couldn't get even simple assaults prosecuted if they involved an Italian victim. "Every avenue and every door was shut to me," he said, "that I might not, even in the smallest degree, aid in putting down an Italian criminality that has outraged the people of my race." The prosecutor realized that his appointment had been mere political window dressing. The Brooklyn D.A., he believed in his heart, didn't care if Italians lived or died.

Even the detective's longtime supporters in the press were growing fatigued. On May 26, the *Evening Herald,* which had lionized Petrosino for years, now skewered the NYPD. "LIVES OF 10,000 IN PERIL BY BLACK HAND," the headline blared; "BINGHAM HELPLESS." The article laid out its indictment on the Black Hand war: An epidemic of smallpox, cholera, or even a disease less dangerous

than either of these which would imperil the lives of 10,000 citizens of New York in less than a year and a half might easily call for drastic action on the part of the authorities. Yet there is affecting New York at this time an epidemic of lawlessness which has extended over five years, gaining strength with time . . . A few hundred ignorant, dirty, low-browed aliens . . . have the metropolis of the United States and the second largest city in the world by the throat.

Another article in the same edition went after the detective himself. "PETROSINO'S SQUAD A FAILURE," read the headline. "Of Petrosino's honesty and ability, there can be no question," the paper made clear, "but his special Italian staff has failed to make good." The Black Hand would have to blow up an entire tenement building, the paper predicted, killing hundreds, before the NYPD came to their senses.

In fact, the Italian Squad, with four years of often bitter experience under its belt, was more effective than ever. In the past two years, its investigators had made 2,500 arrests, 2,000 of them in Black Hand–related crimes, and gained 850 convictions. In November they raided a tenement on Long Island and uncovered nineteen bombs. Three days later, Petrosino arrested a kidnapper who'd snatched a number of children off the streets of East Harlem, putting an end to his spree. Squad members were working flat out, often arriving back at the offices after fourteen or sixteen hours on the job and collapsing on their desks, rising after a few miserable hours of sleep to return to a blackmailing case or the search for a kidnapped child. For one stretch of six months, Petrosino rarely returned home to his own bed.

Ideas for stopping the bombing craze were few and bordered on the extreme. The bloodthirsty *Brooklyn Eagle* proposed a life sentence for anyone convicted of simply possessing an explosive device. If the bomb exploded? "Send him to the chair." Beating criminals was passé; the crisis had become so acute that members of the Society "should be classified with Sherman's Good Indian." That is, the only good Black Hander was a dead Black Hander, and the miscreants should be shot on sight. The *New York Post* didn't go quite that far, but it did demand that kidnappers be physically marked so that their crime would be known. "Let the letter 'K' be branded low on the forehead of the criminal," wrote the editorialist, "then let him be turned loose to meet the living death that would await him in society." This idea was heartily endorsed by the *Times-Union* of Jacksonville, Florida, which encouraged legislators to make it law.

Three years before, Petrosino had told his fellow citizens, "We need a missionary more than a detective in the Italian quarters of New York." Education and loving grace would win out over time. Now the mood of the city, and the nation, had darkened considerably. Americans weren't calling for missionaries. They didn't want detectives. They desired vigilantes.

Commissioner Theodore Bingham decided to comply.

13

A SECRET SERVICE

In THE WINTER OF THAT TERRIBLE YEAR, PETROSINO'S LIFE changed once again. On November 30, 1908, Adelina gave birth to a twelve-pound baby girl. The overjoyed father brought the infant to St. Patrick's to be baptized Adelina Bianca Giuseppina Petrosino. At a party, one woman remembered the detective going around urging guests to eat some cake, like any exuberant new father. "He was so happy and delighted and smiled every minute," she recalled.

The next few months, fulfilling ones, were unlike any the detective had ever experienced. Petrosino "had begun to acquire a taste for family life and the joys of fatherhood," wrote his Italian biographer. He no longer returned to his office after dinner to take up another Black Hand case or study police flyers from Chicago. Now he hurried home to 233 Lafayette to have dinner and play with the baby. His love of music deepened. Musicians would drop by after their gigs around the city to play some arias in his apartment, trying not to wake young Adelina.

Pedestrians walking by could hear the notes of his favorite operas float-ing down from the three windows above. The music might go on into the early morning. Wine, certainly, was drunk.

The mood at 300 Mulberry was not quite as festive. Commissioner Bingham had been brought in to stop crime, particularly Black Hand crime, and he hadn't been able to do it. In plotting a way forward, the General had begun to think past Petrosino. For months, as the headlines had turned darker and more strident, he'd been nursing a proposal to kill the Society off once and for all: a private army of detectives, invisible to the public and answerable to no one but him. A secret service of his own. It would be the first such force in America.

The General revealed the plan to the press. "You ask me what I want to do?" he fairly barked at a reporter for the *Sun*. "Just this: I want a force of from six to ten real detectives, Secret Service men . . . What little crime of this Black Hand sort we could not prevent absolutely we would make arrests and convictions in mighty short order." In fact, he couldn't understand why he hadn't been granted such power long before. "What the people of New York, Italians, and everyone else are thinking of in allowing this campaign of bomb throwing and assault to go on without giving the Commissioner of Police the entirely reason-able and inexpensive aid he asks for, I don't know."

Bingham's plan was to hire at least half a dozen top-notch men whose identities would be known only to the commissioner and who would never testify in court. Bingham would pay them out of a secret fund, and they would report directly to him. He warned that the kind of detective he had his eye on would cost $10,000 a year, around four times what Petrosino was making. One of these super-sleuths alone, Bingham boasted, "could knock out the Black Hand in a month." The General never explained precisely what these detectives would do that Petrosino and his squad weren't already doing. There was a suggestion that some of the methods would fall outside the law. Bingham neglected to answer a rather fundamental question: if the men weren't going to appear in court, how could the evidence they gathered be introduced at trial?

At any rate, Bingham needed funds for his new secret service. The Board of Aldermen, led by Tammany in the inimitable shape of Big Tim and Little Tim Sullivan, held the purse strings. A clash loomed.

The General was undeterred. He spoke about the service to anyone who would listen: newspapermen, civic clubs, police banquets. He wrote an essay for the May issue of the *North American Review* in which he declared that "the police force itself, even the best men, would not recognize a high-grade, first-class, real 'sleuth' if he came down the street headed by a brass band." (Petrosino must have winced at that.) The General was obsessive by nature, and the secret service became an *idée fixe* for him. There were rumors in certain circles that Bingham was nursing political hopes that went beyond being police commissioner. If he was considering a run for higher office, destroying the Black Hand would be a feather in his cap, a coup that no other political leader could claim. He would be lionized far and wide for such an accomplishment.

The announcement of Bingham's idea caused a sensation. The prominent novelist (*The Great God Success*) and journalist David Graham Phillips had become famous for uncovering a Senate corruption scandal. Now Phillips sensed another abuse of power in the offing and wrote to the *Times* in a fury. "Thanks to the carelessness of New Yorkers about decent government," he declared, "our present police force is to a great extent an instrument of blackmail and oppression. A secret police force would be even worse." The Black Hand was evil, he conceded, but a secret service would be a danger to democracy. "I see no politics, no 'grave menace to free institutions' in the doings of ignorant, crazed creatures, issuing from dingy top rooms to run amuck with dynamite. It seems hysteria to me to take them so seriously, to call homicidal mania political propaganda."

William Randolph Hearst agreed. His *Evening Journal* dissected the proposal with a sharp knife. "If Mr. Bingham uses his police force at his discretion," the paper warned in an editorial, "what is to prevent him tomorrow from taking money from Mr. Rockefeller to investigate another class of citizens — labor union men, or recalcitrant legislators, or any others?" The cure, Hearst believed, was worse than the illness.

The argument raged as far away as Nashville, where a local paper took Bingham's side. "The fact [is]," the editors wrote,

> that every New York detective is more truly a public character than the Mayor is. Let a "plainclothes man" sally forth and patrolmen will nod to him, street car conductors will ask no fare, bellboys will pick him out, janitors will make a sign, bootblacks will look eagerly about for his quarry, politicians will wing patronizingly, barbers will stop in the midst of a shampoo, pawnbrokers will get anxious, second story men will duck into the nearest saloon, and the cronies of all of these will note his passage with silent wonder as to what's up.

In other words, Petrosino and his men had become too famous to do their jobs.

That Bingham's remarkable suggestion — a secret police force in the largest American city, answerable to only one man — was seriously considered by Manhattanites speaks to the depth of their anxiety. The proposal was the direct result of the failed war on the Black Hand. By now the Society often seemed indifferent to the police. When the famous tiger hunter and prohibition activist C. D. Searcy received a series of letters in the winter of 1908, one of them advised him to "go kiss yourself goodbye, for we are several hundred strong." This was followed by a taunt: "Now go ahead to your detectives, who are the only friends you got, and see if they can help you. Yes, they can help you get your lights put out."

Bingham's idea received generally good press. But he knew he was facing a battle with the Sullivans and their aldermen. Soon after his announcement, the board called the commissioner in to testify before a special committee. When the session opened, members immediately attacked Petrosino and his men, accusing them of outlandish acts of brutality. Bingham grabbed his cane and levered himself up to direct a blast at Little Tim. "I am the Police Commissioner," he shouted. "I am responsible for everything my men do . . . Petrosino is one of our best detectives. With a handful of men he has to keep thousands of Italian criminals in line. Of course he has to use his hands now and then, but we ought to let him alone."

The aldermen and the commissioner jousted for a few minutes before the discussion turned to the secret service. "You must admit," said one Commissioner Redmond, "that you could turn your secret service not only against the Black Hand, but also in any other direction you thought proper."

Bingham ignored the question. He stated that no one could prevent him from creating a squad to do whatever he, as commissioner, saw fit.

"We can deny you the necessary funds," Redmond shot back.

"I can do without your funds."

The meeting adjourned. Afterwards, the aldermen called for Bingham's resignation.

Bingham was undeterred. Speaking in front of a gathering of five hundred policemen at the Police Lieutenants Association over plates of filet mignon à la Wallace, he proceeded to Bingham the aldermen:

> There are two places within half a mile of where we are now where any crime, from the lowest to the greatest, can be bought for money. And I know it, and many of you men know it . . . I can't touch [the criminals] under present conditions, and I say that to all New York. That's one reason I want some secret service money . . . [but] I do not believe [the aldermen] will give it to me.

The crowd gasped in astonishment, then roared its approval. As to the aldermen's call for his removal, Bingham laughed. "No Patrick this or Tim that or Tom the other or Charlie so and so is going to get me to quit. I am sorry but I will be with you 'til the end." Applause and shouts of "Hurrah!" prevented the General from speaking for several minutes.

Petrosino, swallowing any resentment over Bingham's criticism of New York detectives, lent his voice to the cause by hinting darkly at the nature of the opposing forces. "It would surprise the public," he said, "if it knew the names of some of the men in both parties who have come to me to intercede for some Italian criminals." The subtext was clear: the Sullivans and the aldermen were in league with the New York underworld.

A few aldermen threw their support behind the commissioner; one even suggested that a bomb would bring down an entire building unless they took the war to the Society, and "men and women will disappear." But Little Tim savaged Bingham and his warnings. "This Black Hand business is all fake," he announced at another hearing. "I don't believe it."

"You come up to my office," the General thundered, "and I'll show you some Black Hand data that will make your hair stand on end."

Bingham had clearly gotten under Little Tim's skin with his talk of politicians and their criminal friends. In one short meeting, Sullivan accused Bingham of perpetrating "bunko" (a swindle) and called him both a "four-flusher" (a poker player who oversells his hand) and a "bulldozing bluffer." Publicly Sullivan supported the motion to give the commissioner $25,000 to fund the secret service; in 1908, it paid for a politician to appear tough on crime. But behind the scenes, Sullivan worked furiously to doom the funding measure. The vote was 12 for and 32 against. The motion was defeated.

The *Times* roundly mocked the aldermen, charging, "Several of them, indeed, talked in a way to justify a slight suspicion that their real objection to the plan was fear of its possible efficiency." The paper went so far as to suggest that Bingham might appeal to U.S. Secretary of Labor and Commerce Oscar Straus to dispatch a squad of Secret Service agents to investigate the matter. Such a drastic step was necessary because the Sullivans and their ilk were "subservient to controlling criminal minds."

Denied by the aldermen, Bingham took his cause to the public, speaking at banquets and lectures attended by the city's wealthiest citizens. On January 12, 1909, he gave a talk to the members of the Washington Square Association, made up of the oldest and richest families in the metropolis: the Delanos, the Schermerhorns, the Rhinelanders, the Van

Rensselaers. He had new claims to make. "There was an attempt of the Black Handers in this town," he told the assembled grandees, "to make an alliance with the Anarchists of Paterson, one of them to make bombs, the others to throw them, and both to divide the spoils." This was most likely nonsense: no such conspiracy had ever been uncovered in Manhattan. But if the aldermen wouldn't support a secret police force, Bingham believed, he might be able to get the rich merchants of New York to pay for it, and to this wealthy crowd, an alliance between anarchists and Black Handers was lit dynamite.

As Bingham courted the moguls, rumors flew. After tackling the Black Hand, the *Journal* reported, Bingham intended to go after Manhattan gambling houses and even investigate corruption in the NYPD. The Sullivans must have blanched at the report. Their initial fears about Bingham were being realized.

• • •

IN LATE JANUARY 1909, AFTER A FURIOUS CAMPAIGN, BINGHAM WON his little war. A group of wealthy New Yorkers, "men of means," agreed to supply enough funds to get his secret service up and running. Bingham wouldn't name his benefactors, but he'd received a rumored $30,000 for his private police force.

Later, the New York papers tried to puzzle out the financial angle. The *Tribune* had heard that the money came from "one man, not an Italian, head of one of the great industries of the country, whose great wealth has made him the target for all sorts of letters." Two names were bandied about: Andrew Carnegie and John D. Rockefeller, both of whom had interests in industries — steelmaking, coal, railroads — that the Black Hand had attacked. Still other sources believed it was the Italian merchants of the city and their bankers who'd put up the funds.

Now that he had his money, the General went looking for his "super-sleuth" to lead the final battle with the Society. Apparently the search was more difficult than he'd foreseen. No Italian-speaking guru appeared at 300 Mulberry; in fact, it's probable that no such creature existed in the United States, apart from, perhaps, Frank Dimaio of the

Pinkerton agency and the NYPD's Joseph Petrosino. Quietly, Bingham chose the latter to lead his service. It's possible, in fact, that Bingham had engineered the whole controversy simply to get funds to send Petrosino on a covert mission. Because it soon became clear that the General had a very specific task in mind.

The project, which was finalized in the early months of 1909, bore Petrosino's fingerprints in all of its aspects. Bingham wanted the detective to go to Italy in secret and do what the federal government and the king of Italy had failed to: stop the flow of criminals from Italy to America, or as one journalist put it, "dam the noxious human stream." The mission would have three separate aims:

• To check Italian judicial records for the penal certificates of criminals who'd immigrated to the United States. If it was found that those men had in fact served time in Italy, they could be deported under the 1907 law, provided they'd been in the United States for under three years.
• To collect the names of the most dangerous criminals currently serving time in Italian jails. If these men arrived at Ellis Island after their release, they could be sent back home immediately.
• To set up a spy network of trusted local agents to continue the work after the investigator had returned to the United States. The agents would feed the NYPD the names and criminal histories of any malefactors attempting to enter the country. In theory, immigration authorities would be able to stop every Italian criminal with a penal record from coming into the United States.

It was a huge and complex effort, "probably the most ambitious intelligence operation that the NYPD had ever undertaken" before 9/11. If it worked, the history of organized crime in the United States would be altered, perhaps profoundly. To give just one example, Giuseppe Profaci was a twenty-three-year-old thief from the province of Palermo who, in 1920, went to prison for a year on theft charges. On his release, he was allowed to immigrate to the United States, where he would go on to found the Colombo crime syndicate, one of the Five Families that dominated organized crime from the 1930s onward. Under Bingham's plan, Profaci would never have made it to America.

But most important to the General and Petrosino, the mission would strike a powerful blow against the Black Hand. It would deprive the Society of its most promising recruits and cut through the ranks of the current membership with a sharp scythe.

In January 1909, Joseph Petrosino was forty-eight years old. He'd been on the force for twenty-six years. His life had changed from the days when he slept on his desk in the squad office and hustled the streets for sixteen hours a day. He and his wife had a baby girl now, a home life that was by all reports peaceful and loving. It would have been perfectly reasonable to ask if it wasn't time for Petrosino to make way for a younger man to lead the fight against the Society. But after speaking with Bingham, Petrosino agreed to go to Italy. If he could make the trip a success, if he could really cut away the roots of the Black Hand and strike at its leaders, it would be the culmination of his life's work. How, in good faith, could he refuse?

• • •

IN THE EARLY MONTHS OF 1909, AS PETROSINO BEGAN TO PREPARE for the trip, members of the Italian Squad sought him out and offered what advice they had. It mostly took the form of warning him to be careful once he reached Italy. "Joe, you may be safe and all right up in the North," Lieutenant Vachris told him, "but look out for yourself as you never did before when you get down in the South. You know who is there." (He meant the Mafia.) Petrosino was tetchy. "I'm no fool, Tony," he responded, "and I'll be ready for anything that happens." The U.S. ambassador offered similar advice. "Perhaps a thousand criminals know you there," he said. "They hate you and may stab you." Petrosino's response is not recorded.

Just before his departure, the detective went to St. Patrick's Cathedral, where he'd been married and his daughter had been baptized, to meet with one of the priests there. "Do not go to Italy," the cleric begged him, "because I am afraid you will not return alive." This time, Petrosino's answer was taken down. "Probably not," Petrosino replied. "But it is my duty, and I am going." Clubber Williams, his early mentor, ran across the detective two days before his departure and reported finding him in a less pessimistic mood. "I told him to take care of himself, as he would be in constant danger, but he replied, with a laugh, that he was not afraid."

The detective took time out of his preparations to make a trip to his lawyer's office, where he signed over power of attorney to Adelina. It would allow her, in the event of his death, to collect his remaining salary. But perhaps the most intriguing report of his state of mind during this time came from his niece. One afternoon, she was out walking the Petrosinos' baby to give her aunt some rest. She pushed the stroller along the sidewalks of Little Italy, avoiding the crowds while she and little Adelina took in the fresh air. At one point she saw the familiar shape of Petrosino approaching in his black coat and black derby hat.

"Uncle Joe!" she called out to him. "Look, I have the baby."

Petrosino, stone-faced, passed her by without a glance. The young woman was confused by the detective's reaction. She finished the walk, wheeled the stroller back to 233 Lafayette, and carried the baby up to the couple's rooms. Petrosino was waiting for her, his face flushed with anger.

"Don't you *ever*," he said in a fury, "recognize me on the street when you have the child."

The young woman was taken aback. Later, she realized that Petrosino was terrified that, if his enemies knew the baby was his, they would find a way to harm her. From that point on, she never greeted him on her strolls around Little Italy, but passed him as if he were a stranger.

• • •

THE FIRST AGENT OF THE NEW YORK CITY SECRET SERVICE WAS scheduled to sail for Italy aboard the 475-foot steamship *Duca di Genova* on February 9, 1909. Extraordinary precautions had been taken for his mission. The first-class ticket was booked under the name Simone Velletri; his cover story was that he was an Italian Jewish merchant traveling to the Continent on business. A few days before his departure, detectives began spreading the news throughout the NYPD that Petrosino had fallen sick and his doctors had advised him to stop working in order to recover fully. It was implied that he'd left town to start his rest cure. Apart from Petrosino's family, the only people who knew his true whereabouts were Commissioner Bingham and a few trusted police officials.

Petrosino packed two large yellow leather suitcases and tucked his .38 Smith & Wesson revolver into one of them. He also packed letters of introduction to the minister of the interior in Rome and the head of the Italian police, as well as a notebook filled with the names of one thousand Italian criminals whose true status within the justice system he would investigate. The letters stated that his work was a simple fact-finding mission, but Petrosino knew the truth. "He had the key," one writer said, "that could have closed the gates . . . to the immigration of Italian criminals virtually in his pocket."

But the elaborate secrecy and the promise of high-level cooperation didn't cheer Petrosino. He knew how perilous the mission was, and even before he left he must have been missing his wife and infant daughter. Lieutenant Vachris, the head of the Brooklyn Italian Squad, came to see him off at the pier; during their farewells, the detective was "in the worst of moods."

At four o'clock on the frigid afternoon of February 9, horns sounded and the harbor workers tossed the dock lines to sailors aboard the *Duca di Genova*. Black smoke poured from its two funnels, while beneath the slate-gray surface of the water its twin screws began to spin. The ship powered out into the middle of the Hudson and slipped through the cold water toward the Upper Bay. The other passengers stood at the railing and waved vigorously at the diminishing figures on the pier, then hurried down to their staterooms. But Petrosino lingered, gazing on the tiny figures. He was one of the last passengers to descend.

• • •

AROUND THIS TIME, IN THE SMALL TOWN OF HIGHLAND, NEW YORK, a team of counterfeiters was working in a farmhouse on a run of Canadian currency. Every day they inked the plates of fake Canadian $2 and $5 bills and ran the paper through the press, then stacked the phony currency against a wall. It would sit there until someone arrived to pick up a bundle and transport it to New York City and beyond.

One of the men was Antonio Comito, a printer from Calabria who'd come to New York in June 1907. At a meeting of the Order of the Sons of Italy, he'd met a printer from Philadelphia and had been hired — not, as it turned out, to work in the man's Pennsylvania shop, but to travel to the small upstate town to become a counterfeiter. The young Comito, practically penniless, had little choice and accepted the offer. He was given the name "Comito the Sheep" — he was, apparently, a passive type — and was given the job of operating the presses.

One night, Comito and the other men were upstairs in their beds sleeping after a long day's work. Around 2 a.m., he heard a sound from downstairs: someone was knocking on the farmhouse door. One of the other counterfeiters, Giuseppe "Uncle Vincent" Palermo, got up and took a rifle in his hands. "He turned deadly pale," Comito recalled. The farmhouse was isolated, and none of the townspeople knew what the Italians were doing. A visit from anyone in the middle of the night was an unwelcome and worrying event.

Two of the other counterfeiters grabbed their revolvers. They told Comito to go downstairs and answer the door. Comito resisted, but the men spoke forcefully. The young Italian felt his way down the stairway to the front door — he didn't stop to light a candle — and stood before it in the darkness.

"Who is there?" he asked.

"We," came the answer. The voice was high and sounded almost feminine.

"Who are you?"

"Open, Professor."

As Comito was debating what to do, Uncle Vincent came down the stairs and passed him, saying only, "Ignazio has come."

When the door was opened, a group of men walked in, led by a smooth-featured young man dressed in an expensive fur coat. It was Ignazio "the Wolf" Lupo, the urbane gang leader whom Petrosino had run out of New York with a beating after Lupo had publicly threatened him. The men greeted each other with kisses on both cheeks, in the Italian fashion. Comito realized that he was "about to meet the brains of the whole scheme," the men who'd planned and financed the counterfeiting operation, which was producing thousands of fake Canadian dollars every week. Lupo, especially, seemed cut from a different cloth, "a man of polished manners and much etiquette."

The men had brought Italian delicacies from New York — packages of sausage and other meat — and they woke the cook to prepare a feast. They'd also brought two larger packages; opened up, they were found to contain military machine guns and a few pistols, along with ammunition. Lupo passed the guns around and showed the men how to work them; the bullets, whose noses were hatched with a cross, "would spread and tear nasty holes instead of neatly boring in or through." Satisfied with the new weapons, the men sat down for their meal, with Comito waiting on them.

"What news do you bring, Ignazio?" Uncle Vincent asked after the Italians had seated themselves around the table.

Lupo turned to the older man.

"You know all that I know," he said, "except perhaps that Petrosino has gone to Italy."

14

THE GENTLEMAN

THE *DUCA DI GENOVA* STEAMED EASTWARD AT SIXTEEN KNOTS, ITS twin funnels sending spouts of black smoke high into the crisp Atlantic air. Each day brought Petrosino closer to Italy and his eventual destination, the island of Sicily. After the detective left the Atlantic seaboard behind and fell into the rhythms of life aboard the ship, his mood had improved and he was proving quite sociable. "We spent so many sympathetic hours together," wrote one passenger to Petrosino's wife, Adelina, "that it seemed as if we had known each other a long time . . . Your husband constantly talked of America and hoped his mission to Europe would be brief. I was tremendously impressed with his love for the United States."

Sicily wasn't just the place where the real work of the mission would occur; it was also populated by scores of men whom Petrosino had deported from America. One of them, Vito Cascio Ferro, the suspect from the 1903 Barrel Murder case who'd escaped prosecution and vowed vengeance on the American detective, had risen in the Sicilian underworld since his arrival back in his native land. After his exile from America, he'd returned to his home province of Palermo and quickly moved up the ranks of Mafia leaders. Sicily was fertile ground for a sharp mind like Cascio Ferro's. In the years since his arrival, Cascio Ferro had proved himself, much like Petrosino, to be a brilliant innovator. Switching an innocent man for a killer during the investigation of the Barrel Murder had turned out to be an early glimpse of how he approached his vocation.

Sicily had been a place apart for centuries. In Roman times, the island served as a granary for the empire, with large estates worked by *strumenti vocali,* or slaves. Even the family names that survived from the era bore the marks of that history: Schiavo (slave), Loschiavo, Nigro, Lo Nigro. In the time of the Normans, the provincial authorities had fought bands of Arab-Berber bandits — practitioners of Islam — and forced them into the central regions of western Sicily, which are now covered by the provinces of Palermo, Trapani, and Agrigento. Those areas formed a kind of sanctuary for the persecuted Muslims, as well as escaped slaves and wanted criminals. "Their importance to the formation of the character of the region which they inhabited should not be underestimated," wrote historian Henner Hess. "They handed down certain norms and values which stemmed from the fugitive and asylum character of their political existence . . . A strong feature is a strong anarchist dislike of any State system of law or coercion." The leaders of the Five Families of the American Mafia — Bonanno, Lucchese, Colombo, Genovese, and Gambino — all came from the central part of western Sicily. The murder rate there at the time of Petrosino's journey was approximately fifty times that of mainland Italy.

As a young man, Cascio Ferro had begun his career as a politician. He was the son of struggling peasants and quite naturally found the concepts of socialism and anarchism to his liking. He preached revolution in the Sicilian countryside, where poor farmers were often victimized by the landowning elite. When he returned from America, Cascio Ferro abandoned his first career for crime, but not the rhetoric;

he made speeches during political rallies and was by all accounts a rousing orator who often used the refrain "Property is theft!" to excite the peasant crowd. When Cascio Ferro started a company that delivered mail and packages, he was taken to court for refusing to pay his bills. His defense was that he was an anarchist and didn't believe in property rights.

Even in the beginning of his criminal career, before the trip to America, Cascio Ferro had the idea of transforming crime into something else. One of his first offenses, which occurred in 1898, was the kidnapping of Baroness Clorinda Peritelli di Valpetroso. Only nineteen, the baroness was being driven in her carriage through Palermo when she was accosted by three men. The bandits, or whoever they were, treated the woman gently, drove her deep into the countryside, and deposited their victim at a house, where an old woman watched over her. Everyone was very kind, especially the handsome, charming leader of the band, who didn't bother to cover his face. The baroness was released the next day, none the worse for wear. It was assumed that her father paid a handsome sum for her freedom.

The police soon arrested Vito Cascio Ferro and two associates and charged them with kidnapping. But Cascio Ferro had a novel defense. He freely admitted he and the others had taken the baroness, but claimed that this wasn't a crime committed to earn money. On the contrary: it had been an act of love. One of his fellow suspects, a student named Campisi, was infatuated with the baroness but didn't believe he had a chance to win her heart. Stealing a few hours of the rich girl's time had allowed Campisi to lay out his case for marriage. Which had, regrettably, not been accepted.

Remarkably, the Italian police, who were notoriously harsh, at least on Mafia suspects, accepted Cascio Ferro's explanation. He was convicted of the crime but received only a suspended sentence. Cascio Ferro walked away from the courthouse a free man. To be arrested and then freed was actually a mark of distinction for a budding mafioso like Cascio Ferro. It showed his power and influence. And his stratagem — representing an old crime as something new — was validated.

This conceit was essential to Cascio Ferro's rise. When he returned from America, he began an extortion racket that was similar to many others in Italy at the time: merchants paid a small fee every week or month, and their shops and businesses went unmolested. But instead of threatening the merchants, as most extortionists did, Cascio Ferro coached his underlings to speak softly and with respect, to make it appear they were good men who wanted to protect the merchants from bad men. It wasn't extortion; it was a kind of gallantry. His new method was so successful that, after a few months, some of Cascio Ferro's victims actually sought him out and thanked him for taking their money.

Call it sleight of hand, call it cheek. Cascio Ferro was dressing the Mafia in new clothes.

Cascio Ferro's second innovation was to make crime into an actual business. Every nefarious activity in his zone of influence was organized, rationalized, and regulated. Beggars, whom no one had thought to bother with before, were given specific spots to work. Robbers who stole from alms boxes were assigned to particular churches and charged a cut of their takings. Cascio Ferro even organized chicken thieves, pickpockets, and blackmailers into a kind of corporation. "Don Vito," said one writer, using the honorific that Cascio Ferro was now addressed with, "was the first to adopt the Mafia's archaic and pastoral systems of the 20th century to the complex life of a modern city." This is perhaps overstating the case. The entity we now call the Mafia had always been a modern organization that exploited the changes in Sicilian political and economic culture of the late 1800s and early 1900s. But Cascio Ferro was thinking hard about how to weave his business so closely into the fabric of Sicilian life that the two could not be picked apart.

As his fortunes rose, Cascio Ferro walked the streets of rural Sicily like an *uomo di rispetto,* taking the air, dressed in suits made to order in the English style by the famous Bustarino's of Via Maqueda in Palermo. He smoked a long, elegant pipe and rubbed elbows with politicians and the gentry at the theater and the opera. True, he was still illiterate (even though he'd married a schoolteacher), and when he needed to calculate a sum, he often reached down to a wide leather belt that he

wore underneath his vest. The belt had rows cut into it, a crude count-
ing device which helped Cascio Ferro determine what his take in any
deal would be. The description of another mafioso given by the Italian
author Carlo Levi hews closely to what we know of Cascio Ferro at this
point in his life:

> His face was impassive and inscrutable, and yet at the same time it
> was enlivened by grimaces expressing feelings different from those
> we are accustomed to perceiving, a mixture of cunning, extreme mis-
> trust, mingled confidence and fear, arrogance and violence and even,
> perhaps, a certain wit: and yet all these elements seemed to be fused
> in that face in a way that was distant and alien to us, as if the tone
> of the emotions, and the very appearance of the face, belonged to
> another era, of which we have nothing more than an archaic, hered-
> itary recollection. I had the distinct impression of being in the pres-
> ence of a rare representative of a lost race.

Cascio Ferro murdered people, too, ordering a hundred or more kill-
ings over his career, according to authorities. "His behavior is bold,"
said one police report, "violent and full of outspoken incitements to
destruction." His dossier with the Palermo police included a wide
range of crimes: arson, murder, extortion, kidnapping, "outrage," and
racketeering. His ambition was boundless. The other great power in
rural Sicily was the Catholic Church. Cascio Ferro was jealous of the
priests' hold over their parishioners, so he persuaded the women of
his district to "stop going to Holy Communion and make their confes-
sions to him." Petrosino's Italian biographer referred to this as "a thing
that seems incredible" in the deeply Catholic countryside of Sicily. And
indeed it was.

Petrosino, as he walked the decks of the *Duca di Genova,* had probably not thought of Vito Cascio Ferro for years. He had many other
names and faces in his mind, and a bout of mid-journey seasickness
forced him to his cabin and his bed, making his life a torment. After
his sickness passed, Petrosino seems to have recovered his spirits. Part
of this change, ironically for a man on a secret mission, was the result

of being recognized by the ship's purser. "I know who you are," this individual told the detective. "I've seen your picture in the papers. But you can rely on my discretion." Instead of being horrified by this breach of his anonymity, Petrosino seemed flattered. He fell into conversation with the purser and even revealed he was going to Italy for an important project. The object of which, at least, he kept to himself.

Other gaffes followed. Petrosino either forgot his cover name or invented a new one on the fly; in any case, he introduced himself to other passengers as Guglielmo Simone, which was a different name from the one he'd started the voyage with. When a steerage passenger kept sneaking into the second-class passage and annoying people, instead of letting the ship's crew handle the matter, Petrosino took the man aside and had a few (probably ominous) words with him. The man never repeated the offense, but the intervention could only have served to draw attention to the detective.

Why did Petrosino not guard his identity more closely? Why did he not take more care to preserve the anonymity that protected him? And why hadn't the NYPD allowed him to bring along another detective to watch his back?

A clue came later in the journey when Petrosino remarked to a fellow passenger that he was headed to Sicily (another slipup: the ship was bound for Genoa). "Be careful not to look at the women," the man joked. "Otherwise they'll kill you down there."

Petrosino's pride blazed up. "I'm not afraid of anybody!" he cried.

Why was Petrosino so cavalier with his safety? He had for so many years depended on a cloak of invulnerability that seemed draped around his shoulders; to admit fear would be to lose that protection. And besides, he was a proud man. As one young immigrant said after being asked why he spent money on clothes instead of food: "You know the Italian people. You gotta starve but your honor is first."

• • •

AFTER A STORMY PASSAGE, PETROSINO STEPPED OFF THE GANG-plank in Genoa at 8:20 p.m. on February 21 and made his way to Rome to present his credentials and begin his work. He was still recovering from the voyage and confessed he was feeling ill. Rome was celebrating Carnival, and most of the public offices were closed anyway. With no other business at hand, Petrosino was cut adrift and walked the streets, taking in the old city.

The Italian capital utterly bewitched him. He wrote to Adelina (in Italian) to describe as best he could the glories of Rome:

I've seen St. Peter's, the Sistine Chapel and Michelangelo's Galleries, which are the wonders of the world. At the sight of St. Peter's, I was spellbound. It is beyond human imagination. What a huge, magnificent place! The church could easily hold a hundred and fifty thousand people. But how can I give you any idea of it? . . . In spite of everything I am sad, and I must say that when it comes to comfort, I prefer dear old New York . . . In any case, it seems as if it's a thousand years before I go home . . . Kiss my dear little girl for me and remember me to all our friends and relatives.

A kiss from your affectionate husband.

Petrosino, lonely and frustrated by the delay in his work, was still entranced by the physical signs of Italy's splendors. Here, under a winter sun, was evidence of the Italy he'd spent two and a half decades defending. Americans called Italians a mongrel race descended from the Asiatic hordes, but everything the detective saw in the old city disproved this. The hours he spent as a tourist must have filled Petrosino with a deep sense of his culture's worth.

That first day, the detective managed to see the U.S. ambassador to Italy, Lloyd Griscom, a Quaker and career diplomat from New Jersey, who assured Petrosino that he was working on getting him in to see the Italian interior minister and the chief of the national police. Petrosino then returned to his hotel and slept. The next day, he finally began his work. He went to see the chief of the Italian police, Francesco Leonardi, announcing as he walked in, "My name is Petrosino."

Leonardi smiled. Although he knew Petrosino by reputation, he had the feeling that the detective thought he was far more famous in Italy than he actually was. Petrosino handed Leonardi a letter of introduction from Bingham and sketched out the official reason for his visit. He didn't reveal Bingham's plan for seeding Italy with intelligence agents who would report back to the NYPD; that could come later.

Two days later, Petrosino wrote Bingham his first letter (later he would use encrypted telegrams), informing him:

> I was able to meet the Minister of the Interior, the Honorable Mr. Peano, with whom I had a discussion on the subject of Italian criminals and their activities in the U.S.A. He was so much interested in this matter that he gave instructions to the Head of Police, His Excellency Francesco Leonardi, to issue definitive orders to the Prefects, Sub-Prefects and Mayors of the entire kingdom not to issue passports to Italian criminals heading for the U.S.A. He also gave me a letter addressed to all the police commissioners in Sicily, Calabria and Naples with instructions to assist me in every way in the performance of my mission . . . Wishing you and Mr. Woods a long and happy life, I remain
>
> Your very devoted,
> Joseph Petrosino

It's questionable whether he really believed that Leonardi's command would be obeyed. This was, after all, Italy. But it was a beginning.

One day as Petrosino walked through Rome, two newspapermen from New York recognized him on the street. Then, in Palermo, an old family friend named Cianfarra ran into the detective at the post office. They were chatting when Petrosino spotted a man walking by. "I know that face," he said in a low voice. "I know it." Cianfarra turned to see a badly dressed stranger who seemed to be glancing at them while trying to avoid being spotted. Petrosino passed his hand in front of his face as if he were attempting to brush away a veil obscuring his memory. His friend protested that Petrosino knew thousands of people, and so it was inevitable that he should run into one or two of them in Palermo. But the detective exhibited signs of "extreme worry and perplexity."

Petrosino and his friend watched as the man calmly passed them by, then walked into the post office to send a telegram. That night, over dinner, the detective was quiet, but at one point he confided to Cianfarra. "Here I am totally alone," he told his friend. "I know no one and have no friends. In New York it's different; I have friends and collaborators on every street corner, and policemen who will help me in an emergency."

"Italian cities are safer than New York," Cianfarra protested with a smile. But Petrosino wouldn't be comforted. He began to speak quietly, as if to himself. "I would pay one thousand dollars to know where he lives." And then, "But I have to go and whatever happens, happens." Petrosino felt he was being watched, and there was one individual in particular who was worrying him. Who that was has never been revealed. But Petrosino was full of misgivings. There were dozens if not hundreds of men and a few women in Italy who had a vendetta against the American. Even the Sicilian police commissioner admitted as much. "It was sufficient only to hear Petrosino's name," he said later, "to hear oaths of vengeance."

Petrosino in Italy is a figure that grows less recognizable by the day. In New York, he braved assassins with icy composure; in Italy, he is confused. In New York, his memory was photographic; in Italy, he struggles to remember a familiar face. It's almost as if our snapshots of him on the streets of Italy are slowly obscured by some shadow that creeps in bit by bit from the margin of the photograph.

• • •

THE NEXT MORNING, PETROSINO CABLED HIS BROTHER VINCENZO in Padula to tell him he was taking a train that would arrive there at 1:53 the next afternoon. His bill at the Hotel Inghilterra was thirty lire. He paid it, made his way to the railroad station, and boarded the train.

He hadn't seen his younger brother in decades. Vincenzo was waiting at the station with their second cousin. Petrosino embraced his brother, glanced at the other man, then asked Vincenzo why he hadn't come alone.

"But this is our cousin, Vincenzo Arato," his brother exclaimed, "the son of our sainted mother's sister!"

"You know my trip is secret," Petrosino said. "Nobody's supposed to know."

Vincenzo had bad news on that very score. He pulled a newspaper out of his pocket, *Il Pungolo* (The Goad). It contained an article about Petrosino's supposedly secret mission. There was even a quote from General Bingham, who'd been asked about the detective's absence from New York. "Why, he may be on his way to Italy, for all I know!" the General had replied.

Petrosino uttered a curse under his breath. The article laid out the details of Petrosino's trip and even tied it to the mission of defeating the Black Hand. His cover had been blown by his own commissioner.

The day was ruined. Vincenzo's friends lined up outside the family home to greet the famous detective, but he stayed inside a bedroom, furious. How could Bingham do this? Petrosino had hundreds of enemies in Italy, and here the commissioner had revealed his plans to the entire nation. It was an inconceivable blunder.

Bingham was prone to such gaffes, of course; he'd insulted Jews and Italians in his first days in office and shot off his mouth at the most inconvenient times. It's impossible to say exactly what the General was trying to achieve when he granted the interview. He was certainly under pressure to reduce Italian outrages: 1909 was another election year, and William Randolph Hearst was again gearing up to attack Tammany on its crime-fighting record. What better evidence could there be of the NYPD's commitment to fighting the Society than the fact that the world's greatest Italian detective was at that very moment headed to Sicily to cut off the supply of thugs once and for all? Bingham's ambitions for higher office might explain the gaffe, but its recklessness is still almost incomprehensible. Would the commissioner have exposed his best Irish detective in such a rash and ham-handed way?

The next morning at seven, Petrosino cut his visit short and boarded the train to Naples. From there he would take the mail boat to Palermo, where most of the criminals who plagued his life had originated. Sicily awaited him.

His old suspiciousness had returned. When his brother asked him where he was headed, Petrosino equivocated. "Maybe I'll go to Messina," he said. "On the way back I'll stop and see you again." Clearly, he now felt that no one in Italy — not even his own brother — could be fully trusted.

Petrosino boarded the train. As his car clicked over the rails as it headed northwest to the seaport of Naples, Petrosino ate the home-cooked meal that Vincenzo's wife had prepared for him. There was another man in the compartment, one Valentino di Montesano, a captain of the *carabinieri*. He recognized Petrosino but said nothing.

15

IN SICILY

PETROSINO REACHED PALERMO AND CHECKED INTO THE HOTEL de France, using yet another fake identity: Simone Valenti di Giudea. His first stop was the office of the American consul, William A. Bishop, where he presented his plans and revealed that he had informers in the city who would be helping him with his secretive work. Petrosino settled in for a long stay, opening a bank account at the Banca Commerciale and depositing two thousand lire for his future use. Any incoming mail would be directed to the bank. He later rented a Remington typewriter, this time under the name Salvatore Basilico. (*Basilico* is Italian for sweet basil, as *petrosino* is slang for parsley, so perhaps the detective was amusing himself by switching one herb-inspired name for another.) The intent was clear: he didn't want to leave any trail in Sicily that could connect one false identity with the next.

His preparations complete, Petrosino met a local man, most likely one of his old informants from New York who'd returned to Sicily.

Together they headed to the courthouse in Palermo and began going through the files of penal certificates. Petrosino spent hours checking the names on the documents against the list of criminals in his notebook. If it occurred to him how odd this mission was — after years of violent combat, he was now endeavoring to defeat the Society through what amounted to paperwork — he never expressed it. Indeed, it was a heady moment. The evidence the New York police needed to stop the Black Hand was laid out before Petrosino's eyes. His work in Italy had truly begun.

But something was bothering him mightily. On February 28, he wrote Adelina:

> My dearest wife:
>   I have arrived in Palermo. I am completely confused and it seems a thousand years until I come home. I don't like anything about Italy at all which I'll explain to you when I come home. God, God, what misery! I was sick for five days. It was influenza and I had to stay in Rome, but now I feel all right . . . Kiss cousin Arturo for me and also my brother-in-law Antonio and his family . . . Greet your sister and her husband, to my dear Baby and to you thousands and thousands of kisses.

What exactly had disturbed him in Palermo he never spelled out. Had he recognized the face of an old enemy on the street? Had he been threatened?

Despite his depressed mood, Petrosino was making progress. The next day he sat in his hotel room typing out copies of the penal certificates he'd found in the Palermo courthouse. When he was done, he packaged them up and sent them to Bingham in New York, along with a letter:

> Dear Sir:
>   Following my cablegram, I enclose the penal certificates of Gioacchino Candela and others . . . I will explain everything to you

in full in my next letter. There is nothing in the penal files dealing
with Manatteri, Pericò, and Matranga. Maybe I will find something
about them later.

Faithfully,
Joseph Petrosino

With the certificates, Bingham could begin tracking down criminals
and deporting them. Everything was going according to plan.

For the next five days, Petrosino attempted to keep a low profile. He
ate his meals at the Café Oreto, met with his informers, visited Bishop
daily, and burrowed deep into the criminal archives. He changed his
cover names constantly. No one seemed to bother him. On March 5, he
told Bishop that he had scheduled a meeting with the police commissioner of Palermo, Baldassare Ceola. He expressed misgivings about
the conference. Bishop assured Petrosino that the commissioner wasn't
cut from the same cloth as the rest of the Sicilian police bureaucracy; he
was a cultivated man who'd spent ten years working in the northern city
of Milan, where he'd led the investigation into the assassination of King
Umberto I. Ceola's task in Palermo was to root out Mafia infiltration.
The country's leaders in Rome obviously trusted Ceola, and Bishop
encouraged the detective to do so as well.

Petrosino met with Ceola the next day. The commissioner felt a
twitch of class consciousness when first sizing up this legend from
America. "I saw at once," he said, "that Lieutenant Petrosino, to his dis-
advantage, was not a man of excessive education." Petrosino was blunt
that day. He told Ceola that the U.S. government had sent him to find
out whether criminals were entering the country with papers falsely
stating they'd never committed any offenses in Italy.

Ceola protested. No documents issued by his office had been altered
or falsified.

Petrosino had apparently had enough of the protestations of Italian
officials. He brushed aside the commissioner's answer. "Then why is it
that many of the criminals I have arrested showed perfectly clean penal
certificates even though they had been convicted here?"

"Perhaps because they had been rehabilitated," Ceola replied. The commissioner was being rather slippery. There was, in fact, an official process called "rehabilitation" in Italy, but it often involved nothing more than deleting any mention of a man's crimes just as he set off for Ellis Island. Ceola was defending his department, but he must have known that Petrosino was essentially correct.

There was another matter the commissioner had to discuss with Petrosino: his safety. Bishop had already told the detective he needed protection in Sicily; the island was just too dangerous for him to travel from neighborhood to neighborhood unguarded. Ceola agreed and volunteered to supply the American with a bodyguard. The last thing he wanted was a prominent American being assaulted or even murdered in his city.

Petrosino declined. "Thank you, but I don't want a bodyguard."

"But it will be too dangerous for you to wander alone around Palermo!" Ceola protested. "You're too well known . . . No one knows how many enemies you have in this city."

Petrosino's answer was enigmatic. "I also have friends in Palermo, Commissioner. They will be enough to protect me."

An irritated Ceola called in a Lieutenant Poli, the head of the mobile brigade, and introduced him to the American detective. Poli would be his contact in the police bureaucracy. Then Ceola wrapped up the meeting. Petrosino's lack of trust in the Italian police had obviously grated on the commissioner. The detective had even declined to reveal where he was staying in Palermo. Whatever Petrosino had learned in the past week, hinted at in his letter to Adelina, had destroyed his trust in Ceola and his men. But pride certainly played a part as well in his refusal to accept protection. How would it look if Petrosino had to be escorted around town by a Sicilian cop?

Even if the American wouldn't accept a bodyguard or let the Palermo police know what he was doing and whom he was doing it with, Ceola intended to keep close watch over him. Poli and Petrosino met several times in the next few days, with the detective reporting on what records he was looking at and what documents he needed next. Poli, too, had

informants who spotted Petrosino around the city, and he reported to
Ceola that the detective was visiting "the most dangerous underworld
areas," even at night, taking notes and having secret meetings with informants and high-ranking officials. How the police got this information,
whether through tailing Petrosino or through informants, is unknown.
But the Palermo police were anything but trusting of Petrosino; one
report even tried to paint his natural caution as suspicious. "In every
way," it said, "he adhered to the custom of those among the Sicilians
who believe that they get the best protection when, instead of turning to
the Authorities and the forces of Law and Order, they put their trust in
some notorious and dreaded criminal who has authority and influence
in the underworld."

Petrosino had found a godfather of his own. Such was the impli-
cation of the harsh report. In reality, the detective was taking precautions: he was using false names and perhaps even disguises. Certainly,
Petrosino's self-confidence was apparent in his actions, but he wasn't
behaving recklessly. He didn't, however, trust Ceola, and that clearly
stung.

But it was also clear, at least to Poli, that Petrosino was making significant headway. He "saw at once that his American colleague must
indeed have a certain number of informers at his disposal, and that
some of these must be persons in high places." The documents that
Petrosino was looking at could have come to him only from "persons
who had legitimate access to judicial circles."

Did Petrosino have a secret mission in Sicily? Later, reports would
surface that, as well as targeting the backgrounds of known criminals,
the detective was working on other, even more confidential missions.
President Theodore Roosevelt was scheduled to visit Italy later in 1909,
and one American journalist subsequently claimed that members of the
Black Hand planned to assassinate him on Italian soil. But Petrosino's
mission was kept secret in New York, at least until Bingham's interview, and it's unlikely that the Secret Service knew beforehand that he
was making the journey. And what motive did they have to assassinate

Roosevelt? The vast majority of Black Hand members were convicted in state and city courts; the president had no power over them anyway.

• • •

IN THE FOLLOWING DAYS, THE DETECTIVE HURRIED FROM MEETING to meeting. None of the people he spoke with about the Black Hand ever came forward afterward, so we don't know much about whom he spoke to or what he learned. Even more so than in Little Italy, the detective moved amid rumors and conspiracies, veiled threats, inchoate rage. His name was on a thousand lips, whispered in several dialects. He was confronting a centuries-old culture that he'd once thought he understood but now found inscrutable. It's hard not to see him in those days as remarkably American: alone by choice and conviction, mission oriented, a bit arrogant, courageous, and naïve.

Giuseppe Petrosino was truly at the heart of the sprawling thing he'd come to end.

On March 11, as he strode through the streets of Palermo, Petrosino passed two men standing near the migration office. One of the men watched the detective step into a coach and drive off; he turned to his friend and said, "This man is Petrosino, who came to die in Palermo." The speaker was later identified as Paolo Palazzotto. This was the same man, arrested in New York for his involvement in a prostitution ring, who had been deported after receiving a beating from Petrosino. Palazzotto had arrived back in Italy on March 2. That night, as the detective ate at the Café Oreto, the young man and a friend named Ernesto Militano (whom the police described as "an incorrigible robber of prostitutes") watched Petrosino from the bar, where the pair sipped wine and "looked threateningly" at the American. Two more friends joined them, Francesco Nono and Salvatore Seminara. The latter was another one of Petrosino's many "victims." He'd been forced to leave the United States after the detective arrested him.

Down the bar from the four men, who were drinking and laughing, was a man named Volpe, quietly eating his dinner. Volpe was a police informant, and he eavesdropped on the conversation of the four men, who were speaking in a local dialect. What he heard was fascinating:

NONO (laughing): But you know parsley [*petrosino*] gives you diarrhea!

SEMINARA: If I die, they'll bury me, but if I get over it, I'll kill him.

NONO: You haven't got the guts.

SEMINARA: You don't know the Seminaras.

It sounded ominous, but in reality there were many such bad actors walking the streets of Sicily's capital. In Via Salvatore Vico lived a man named Angelo Caruso, who nursed a lingering bitterness toward the detective after Petrosino had treated him roughly during his arrest for possession of a sword-cane and an unlicensed pistol. Caruso despised Petrosino so much he'd named his dog after him. Another informant told of seeing a small boy who lived at 9 Via Lungarini following Petrosino for days, tracking him from place to place, without being spotted by the detective. It was said the boy was being paid by a pair of unnamed women.

Two suspects from the 1903 Barrel Murder case were also circulating in Palermo in early March, including Giovanni Pecoraro, who'd impersonated the killer in court. The two men went to visit a third suspect in the murder — Vito Cascio Ferro — at his home. Afterwards Pecoraro sent a mysterious coded telegram back to New York: "I Lo Baido work Fontana." The meaning remains unclear.

The swirling motives for wishing Petrosino harm extended back in time and across an ocean. *Petrosino arrested me, Petrosino showed no respect, Petrosino broke my jaw in two places, Petrosino betrayed the Sicilians.* They also projected into the future. Whom was Petrosino building cases against? Was he trying to stir up trouble with the Italian police? Or was he, as it was rumored, shutting off forever the escape routes to New York that so many gangsters had utilized when times got tough in Palermo? The ships to Ellis Island had become a vital pressure valve for criminals of all types. To cut it off would be to sentence many of them to poverty or prison. Certainly many criminals looked on Petrosino as the "enemy of the Sicilians" who'd come to Italy to take food out of their families' mouths.

The fear reached across the Atlantic. Police in Chicago later reported that secret societies in New Orleans, Chicago, and New York were plotting a coordinated strike on their enemies in law enforcement. Assassins in each of those cities would target the three leading opponents of the Black Hand. The second name on the list was Detective Gabriele Longobardi, known as "the Petrosino of Chicago." The third name was John D'Antonio of New Orleans. The first was Petrosino.

And what of Vito Cascio Ferro, the peasant genius who carried around the photo of Petrosino in his wallet? By March 10, he was staying in the small town of Burgio, about thirty-five miles south of Palermo. He was the guest of a prominent politician, Domenico De Michele Ferrantelli, who later claimed Cascio Ferro was helping with a political campaign Ferrantelli was mounting. But it was difficult to get information on Cascio Ferro's whereabouts, the police commander in Burgio admitted, because of "the absolute silence . . . the fear of Vito Cascio Ferro inspires." He believed Cascio Ferro had slipped away from Burgio on March 11, even though Ferrantelli swore publicly that Cascio Ferro never left his house.

On the evening of March 11, Petrosino made a hasty notation on his list of criminals: "Vito Ferro . . . dreaded criminal." The list contained suspects in America who might have entered the country illegally. But Cascio Ferro had lived in Italy since 1903. Why did Petrosino suddenly write his name, six years after he'd encountered him? Did he see him on the street that day, watching him? Or was Cascio Ferro one of the informants Petrosino had scheduled to meet? The handwritten note sits there in Petrosino's notebook, without context.

. . .

ON THE MORNING OF MARCH 12, PETROSINO JOURNEYED TO THE small Sicilian town of Caltanissetta to check more penal certificates. He spent a great deal of time that day speaking with the chief court chancellor, then met with Leonardi, the chief of police in Palermo, whom he told about two appointments he had that afternoon in the city. While in Caltanissetta, the detective confided to an unnamed person that he also had a meeting that evening "which he could not miss [for] any reason."

That afternoon, a Palermo street vendor would later testify, he sold some postcards to a slim, handsome gentleman who bore a startling resemblance to Vito Cascio Ferro. Another individual spotted the *capo* that same day in Piazza Marina, the old city square, near the waterfront. According to this witness, Cascio Ferro was speaking with a man named Pasquale Enea, a well-known crime figure in the city. Enea had spent years in New York, where he owned a grocery store that had doubled as a meeting spot for criminals. Commissioner Bingham would later reveal that Enea had been known to the department as a "person of confidence." In other words, an informant.

After he'd finished his work in Caltanissetta, the detective returned to his hotel on the east side of the Piazza Marina. The square was a small park bordered by a spiked wrought-iron fence set in the heart of the historic district in Palermo, not far from the sea. Around the fence were wide sidewalks where locals liked to stroll. In medieval times, when the piazza was nothing more than vacant wasteland, it was here that heretics were brought from their prisons and executed by agents of the Inquisition.

The detective went up to his room, where he remained through the late afternoon. Dusk fell around 6 p.m., and a storm front moved over the city. Lightning flashed and thunder sounded; rain pounded down on the piazza and ran in small rivulets toward the gutter, leaving puddles in its wake. The showers had stopped by 7:30 p.m., when Petrosino emerged from the hotel carrying an umbrella and walked along one side of the square toward the Café Oreto for dinner.

The piazza's gaslights glowed steadily as the sky grew dark. Arriving at the near-empty restaurant, Petrosino sat at his usual corner table, his back to the wall. He studied the menu and ordered pasta with marinara sauce, fish, fried potatoes, cheese, peppers, and fruit. To wash the meal down, he chose a half liter of local wine. The waiters recalled that Petrosino wasn't alone as he dined that night, but spent the evening talking to two men they were unable to identify who sat with the detective at his table. After dinner, Petrosino paid his bill, stood up, said farewell to the men, and left the restaurant alone.

He strode across the Piazza Marina, but took a different route from the one he would normally have followed to get back to his hotel. Perhaps he was on his way to the meeting he couldn't miss for any reason. With his umbrella in hand, he disappeared into the gloom.

At around 8:45 p.m., a man was walking down Via Vittorio Emanuele, a street one block from the piazza on its northern side. Suddenly, two shots—powerful ones the man described as "detonations"—sounded in the night. The noise was so loud that the man thought fishermen had exploded a pair of mines in the harbor. In the seconds after the shots, the pedestrian was amazed to see two guards standing in front of the nearby customs house talking with another man, as if nothing had happened. Four more shots rang out.

Men and women rushed toward the sounds, which appeared to have come from a spot about a hundred feet from the local tram station. (At the same time, other people were seen running *away* from the noises.) A sailor from the ship *Calabria,* which was docked in the port of Palermo, saw two men fleeing into the park at the heart of the piazza, then heard a carriage speed off in the darkness. The seaman ran along with the others toward the point where the gunfire had erupted. There he saw the body of a thickset man with strong features, well dressed in black clothes, with the appearance of a foreigner, lying on the pavement, an umbrella at his side. A large revolver lay on the ground a few feet from the body, which was "dripping blood." A black derby hat had been flung to the base of a nearby pedestal.

Bystanders knelt around the body. Suddenly, the gaslights that illuminated the four sides of the square flickered and went out. The piazza was cast into darkness. More locals came running with candles, and the body was lit by flickering flames held by nervous hands.

Detective Joseph Petrosino was dead.

• • •

IT TOOK FIFTEEN MINUTES FOR THE FIRST POLICEMEN TO ARRIVE, and when they finally came on the scene, they began going through the dead man's belongings. They didn't yet know the victim's name, but found in his pockets thirty business cards, which identified the man as a detective from New York. Petrosino was wearing a black suit and a charcoal gray overcoat, a brown silk tie, and a gold watch. In his pockets were letters of introduction to various officials such as the mayor of Palermo and the captain of the port, as well as the notebook containing the names of Italian American criminals, seventy lire in banknotes, an NYPD badge (number 285), a scrap of paper with "6824" written on it, various notes on things Petrosino needed to do, plus a postcard of Palermo with Adelina's address in New York written on it, along with the message "A kiss for you and my little girl, who has spent months far from her daddy."

Policemen spread out across the square and to the nearby trolley station, interviewing everyone they found. The sailor told them about the two men he'd seen fleeing the scene. One had "a hard hat," meaning a derby, which to one eyewitness indicated a man who'd recently returned from America, and the other a round one, perhaps a homburg. A ticket collector on the nearby tram told investigators that he'd seen the man who shot Petrosino, and that the detective had ducked to avoid the bullets but had been caught by the fusillade. The conductor of the tram overheard the conversation and quickly told his fellow employee to be quiet. The man provided no further details.

Commissioner Ceola was at the theater that night, the new Teatro Biondo, taking in a play. In the middle of the performance, an aide came up to his seat, leaned over, and whispered the news into his ear. Ceola left at once and rushed to the scene. By the time he arrived, the men and women who'd reported seeing the fleeing men were already retracting their stories. No one, it turned out, had witnessed anything definitive. More remarkably, several people on the scene denied even having *heard* anything, although a number of loud gunshots from a large-caliber gun (the murder weapon was left lying on the pavement near the umbrella) had torn through a night with almost no ambient noise to disguise the sound.

At 10 a.m. on March 13, a telegram arrived at police headquarters in New York City. It was from William Bishop, the consul who had sympathized with Petrosino over the strange folkways of the Italians. It read: PETROSINO KILLED REVOLVER CENTER CITY TONIGHT. KILLERS UNKNOWN. MARTYR'S DEATH.

16

BLACK HORSES

ON MARCH 13, TEDDY ROOSEVELT HAD BEEN A PRIVATE CITIZEN for all of nine days. After completing his second term as president, he'd left Washington, D.C., for New York City. He was already planning a yearlong safari to Africa, both to hunt and to avoid the impression that he was secretly running the country, despite the installation of William Howard Taft in the White House. Roosevelt had traveled to New York to attend a breakfast at his aunt's house and was walking down the steps of her town house at 110 West 31st Street when he spotted a gaggle of reporters moving toward him along the sidewalk. The ex-president was used to such groups clamoring for his reactions to the day's political news and he cried out to them good-naturedly, "No, I cannot say anything about anybody or thing."

"Cannot you say something," a voice called back, "about the assassination of Lt. Petrosino?"

"What's that?" Roosevelt said in a shocked voice.

A reporter filled Roosevelt in as he stood silently on the town house steps and listened, his expression somber. "I can't say anything but to express my deepest regrets," he replied when he'd heard all the details. "Petrosino was a great man and a good man. I knew him for years and he did not know the name of fear. He was a man worth while. I regret most sincerely the death of such a man as Joe Petrosino."

The news spread quickly through the city that morning. In Little Italy, crowds stood in front of newspaper offices, waiting for employees to bring out the cables arriving from Italy; when the employees emerged, the crowds would pack around them to hear the latest news on the killing. Those who'd learned English read the stories from the newspapers to little groups of immigrants that formed on the sidewalks and in cafés. Once they'd absorbed the news, people gathered in the doorways of the tenement buildings and the little shops and repeated the same words: *"È morto, il povero Petrosino"* (He's dead, poor Petrosino). Newsboys cried out the news on Broadway and up and down Seventh Avenue, yelling, "Huxtry! Huxtry!" (Extra! Extra!), holding up papers emblazoned with headlines about the murder. Members of the Italian Squad, who'd been out on their usual rounds or trailing suspects and interviewing Black Hand victims, broke away from their assignments and spoke among themselves, their voices low. One member wouldn't hear the news for weeks: Rocco Cavone was onboard a ship bringing a murder suspect back from Buenos Aires and would have to wait another sixteen days to learn that his mentor was dead.

Even those cops who'd once hated Petrosino, called him "wop" and "guinea," now mourned his passing. "The news . . . was recited at first with scoffing," noted one reporter out on the street, "then amazement, and then anger. Not only at headquarters, but among the policemen all over the city, the same bitter anger and resentment was shown, for Petrosino was a great favorite among his brothers." Petrosino still had enemies within the NYPD; there were those who had never accepted Italians on the force. But he'd earned the respect of many of those who'd once despised him.

Not everyone was saddened. When a ship called the *Europa* carrying four hundred Neapolitans approached the 34th Street pier just after the news reached Manhattan, small boats filled with friends of the passengers went out to greet the newcomers, and the men called up to the passengers that Petrosino was dead in Sicily. "Bravo!" many of the Neapolitans cried in response. "The news that the foremost enemy of the Black Hand had been slain … acted like a stimulant on the immigrants."

Commissioner Bingham read about the assassination while eating his breakfast and perusing the *Herald.* He locked himself in his room while he considered the ramifications, then emerged to give a very Binghamesque statement to the ranks of cops at 300 Mulberry: "I feel deeply the death of Petrosino," he told the men. "He died like a soldier in action, a grand way for any man to die … Let it be an incentive to every man to exert himself to the utmost to the end, that he may do his duty and carry out the orders of his superiors as a courageous man should." There was no mention of responsibility for his death. But the commissioner swore that the killers would pay. "I'll avenge him," he told reporters. The mayor ordered flags at City Hall to be flown at half-mast, where they would remain for four days.

The detective's widow, Adelina, was at home at 233 Lafayette Street when a reporter from the *New York Herald* knocked on her door and asked her if she'd heard the news. When she responded in the negative, the journalist explained what had happened. Her sister and brother-in-law, who lived in the apartment above the Petrosinos', heard her cries and hurried down to comfort Adelina. But the new widow was inconsolable. "He was always … gentle and affectionate with us," Adelina said, "as if the world was populated by angels." One can easily forgive the falsehood — Petrosino saw enemies everywhere, and rightly so — in a woman who'd lost a second and, by all appearances, beloved husband.

The news shot along telegraph wires from coast to coast, and papers around the country announced it in martial tones: "WAR TO THE DEATH ON THE BLACK HAND," proclaimed the *Atlanta Constitution.* "The Black Hand have no more right to live than mad dogs," declared the *New York Sun.* "They are enemies of society and should be exterminated at

all hazards." The *Washington Post* again called for an end to all immigration from southern Italy. In a confidential cable, Consul Bishop in
Palermo agreed. "It is time the words of warning were spoken," he
wrote the Department of State. If nothing was done, "it seems but a
question of a short time when the U.S. will be submerged by a veritable
inundation of alien elements that will render its fine type of civilized
development but a mockery and chaos."

The city was in shock, alternating between bewildered sorrow and
signs of "collective hysteria." The "human butchers" who had killed
Petrosino, argued the *New York Times,* "owe their continued existence
to a radical fault in the character of many Italians—their aversion to
naming the cutthroats as public enemies." Gino Speranza, the head of
the Society for the Protection of Immigrants, who fought for the rights
of Italians, advocated "warfare" on the Black Hand and endorsed the
call for a private force to find and kill its members. "Let us not be so sen-
timentally afraid of a 'secret police,'" he wrote. "The underworld works
in the dark and we must fight it in the dark." To calm the fears that
percolated throughout the city, Mayor McClellan and Commissioner
Bingham huddled for a conference. When they emerged, they asked
the Board of Aldermen to approve a reward for information leading to
the capture of Petrosino's killer. The sum was eventually set at $3,000.
The pair requested an additional $50,000 for Bingham's secret service,
to complete the work that Petrosino had begun. The *New York World*
endorsed the idea. "It is not too late," its editorial board urged, "for
the Aldermen to recede from their position as protectors of dangerous
criminals." Bingham and the mayor, ironically, also called on the U.S.
Secret Service to help in the investigation of Petrosino's murder; the
agency immediately dispatched agents into the field to find the killers.

Even the Board of Aldermen voiced its anger in a March 17 resolution.
Little Tim Sullivan, who had blocked the detective's work at every turn,
expressed along with his peers the desire "that [Petrosino's] cowardly
assassins may be speedily brought to justice." That same day, the board
passed a new ordinance ordering all gun and knife merchants to keep
records of the names, addresses, and physical descriptions of people

purchasing "guns, revolvers, pistols or other firearms, or dirks, daggers or dangerous knives." Dealers had to register their business with the city, and each weapon sold had to bear an identifying mark. It was one of the first gun control measures ever adopted in New York City. The state, too, promised action. In Albany, Louis Cuvillier, a Spanish-American War veteran and a member of the New York State Assembly, announced that he was drawing up a bill to make bomb throwing a capital crime, along with other common Black Hand offenses. Under the proposed law, anyone convicted of dynamiting a building or kidnapping a child would go to the electric chair.

In death, Petrosino's honesty was proven one last time. After twenty-six years on the force, he had almost no savings to leave his family. In a gracious gesture, Little Tim Sullivan introduced a bill to grant Adelina a special widow's pension of $2,000. As for the $50,000 for the secret service, Sullivan and his allies vetoed the request.

The *New York American* started a Hero's Fund to help Adelina pay her bills. William Randolph Hearst pledged $500, and he was joined by justices of the New York State Supreme Court, New York City aldermen, borough presidents, the president of Columbia University, and the Jewish banker and philanthropist Jacob Henry Schiff. Enrico Caruso, Petrosino's old friend, pledged $100 in honor of Petrosino's "splendid service, not only for America, but for Italy."

A backlash against Italians quickly gathered force. The men of the Italian Squad swept into action and did themselves no credit. They marched downtown and raided businesses in the Italian quarter, including a tavern on Monroe Street and a billiard room at 164 Watt Street, arresting twenty-seven Italians and charging them with disorderly conduct, even though the men had simply been socializing. The arrests continued night after night: a dance hall on Thompson Street, a barbershop on First Avenue. "The raids," reported the *Sun,* "were said to be a part of a plan to discourage the meeting of large numbers of Italians." The arrested men were released in court, and no viable information as to Petrosino's killer was gathered. In reality, the squad was simply lashing out. A similar raid in Brooklyn on March 15 resulted in the arrest of everyone in one establishment; the men were accused of "knowledge of the recent assassination of a detective of world-wide repute." These charges, too, were later dropped.

It wasn't just New York. Petrosino's death was "calamitous for Italian-Americans," spurring "a plague of vilification and persecution," wrote the historian Richard Gambino. The police in major cities conducted sweeps of Italians with no justification, netting 194 people in just one such raid in Chicago. Italians grew tired of the constant harassment. In May, two Irish policemen hurried to the scene of an accident in an Italian section of Hoboken, New Jersey. The sight of the bluecoats after a spring of persecution enraged the residents. Men leaned out of windows in the tenements, firing guns at arriving cops. A full-scale riot broke out, and the cops narrowly avoided being killed in the streets.

. . .

THE STORY FLASHED ACROSS THE HEADLINES IN LONDON, Manchester, Berlin, even Bombay. In Berlin, the chief of the Criminal Investigations Department told reporters: "I wish to pay tribute to the ability and extraordinary courage of Petrosino . . . I have often wished we had a man of such fearlessness and striking talent." In Italy, there was shame and mortification. Americans had donated $4 million for the victims of a devastating earthquake in Sicily and Calabria that struck on December 28, 1908, which took the lives of up to 200,000 people, and now the nation was sending back one of America's most famous sons in a coffin. "SICILY RISES AGAINST MAFIA," reported the *New York Globe,* telling its readers of mass meetings planned to help find the killers. Italians donated $2,000 to a fund for the capture of the assassins; the Italian government advertised a separate reward of $3,000 ("a large sum here," noted the *Post*); and officials floated the idea of opening foreign bureaus to watch over emigrants in foreign lands.

King Victor Emmanuel III of Italy met with J. Pierpont Morgan, the American financier, and laid out a new plan for defeating the scourge of Italian crime: a chain of night schools. "The king believes that ignorance is the principal cause of criminality among Italian emigrants," reported the *Washington Post*. The monarch reportedly wrote letters to John D. Rockefeller and Andrew Carnegie, as well as the Astors, the Vanderbilts, and the Goulds, seeking funds to start his classes. The scheme went nowhere. And though he acknowledged that criminals were making it to America, even at this late date the king refused to admit that such a thing as the Society existed. "The Black Hand, whatever that may be," he said, rejecting the very notion, "is an atmosphere, an intangible and an indefinable something." This from the leader of the country where Petrosino had been executed.

• • •

IN PALERMO, THE AMERICAN CONSUL, WILLIAM BISHOP, UNDER-took the mournful duty of arranging for the return of Petrosino's remains. He reached an agreement with a steamship company to ship the body on one of its vessels. But with the sailing date approaching, the consul received a call from the company's agent. His life had been threatened because he'd involved himself in the Petrosino affair; he was breaking the contract. The consul scrambled for a replacement and finally found another ship leaving for America that would take Petrosino home. The body was placed in a walnut coffin lined with zinc and guarded, rather ironically, by eighty Italian policemen on its journey to the pier. The coffin was then brought to the Palermo city center for a farewell, followed by a long train of notables and local politicians as spectators crowded on balconies to get a look. "I had the impression," said one onlooker, "the armed police accompanied the corpse, being afraid that, if Petrosino was resurrected, he would cry the guilt of having left him to be murdered."

The procession was eerily silent. No one called out a blessing; no women were heard to cry over the coffin. As the hearse passed, many men refused to take off their hats, the sign of respect for the dead.

Amid threats that the ship carrying the body wouldn't be allowed to sail, Bishop draped the coffin in an American flag and watched as it was put aboard the steamship *Slavonia,* which would become famous months later for wrecking in the Azores and sending out the world's first SOS message. The consul must have breathed a deep sigh of relief when the vessel steamed out of the port without incident.

Bishop would soon follow Petrosino home to America. His life was threatened in a letter sent to his home, while another note was sent to police detailing what a citizen had heard near a chemist's shop in Via Maqueda. "If the U.S. consul took an interest in Petrosino," a black-haired man had said within hearing of the letter writer, "I would kill him, and so he would also arrive dead in America." Bishop remarked bitterly that the chief of police in Palermo had told him confidentially that the circumstances of Petrosino's murder made little difference: if the detective had been executed at high noon in the city's main square, with a hundred or a thousand people watching, nobody would have been found to testify as to who killed him. Bishop boarded a steamship for America and followed Petrosino's coffin across the Atlantic. President Taft had requested that, on his arrival in New York, Bishop take a train to Washington in order to update him on the assassination. The consul readily agreed.

• • •

AFTER AN UNEVENTFUL VOYAGE, THE *SLAVONIA* WAS FINALLY SIGHTED in New York Harbor. The coffin, which had been damaged en route, was unloaded and brought to Pier A on the West Side. On the wooden casket was perched a wreath from the king of Italy, as well as garlands from the Baltimore Police Department and the police of other cities. Thousands of men and women had spontaneously appeared on the streets of Manhattan, their heads uncovered, and they lined the sidewalks as the body passed on its way from the pier to Petrosino's home, where Adelina was waiting. Accompanied by prominent Italian Americans, the procession arrived at 233 Lafayette and was met by the NYPD police band, which played a funereal piece. "As the last notes of the music died away," one newspaper reported, "a hush fell over the great crowd before the house and in the silence the shrill sound of women's wailing voices came from the windows above." A cart brought the damaged coffin to a garage behind the home, and the body was transferred to a new one.

Adelina was frantic. A physician was called to attend her, but she was inconsolable. She kept asking to see her husband, but the funeral director, Rocco Marasco, gently told her it was impossible. What he didn't mention was that when his men had opened the coffin, they'd found that the body was deteriorating rapidly. It was later discovered that Professor Giacento Vetere of the University of Naples had been hired by the Italian government to travel to Palermo to prepare the body for shipment. Vetere was an expert in such matters and assured officials that when he was done, the body would be preserved for a hundred years. The professor traveled to Palermo, but there he met one obstacle after another. He wasn't allowed even to see the body; for four days he implored officials in the city to let him do his job, but because of "insidious influences," he was prevented from carrying out his work. When the body arrived in New York, it was found that no embalmment had been performed, and that Petrosino's naked body had traveled across the ocean in the same filthy sheet on which it had lain during the autopsy. It was taken as a final insult to the detective and his family from the Palermo underworld.

The body, in its new casket, was then transported to the headquarters of the Republican League, where it lay in state in a room draped with purple curtains, watched over by an honor guard in white gloves. Candles burned around the casket, and flower tributes were heaped behind it. The next morning, thousands of mourners waited patiently outside for their chance to view the casket, in lines that snaked around the corner and up a nearby street. When the mourners entered the room, some of them stepped out of line and dropped to their knees in prayer. One elderly Italian woman prostrated herself before the coffin, then beat her head on the floor and cried, "He must be avenged!" A group of Catholic attendees chanted the litany for the dead, while two officers of the traffic squad stood at the head and the foot of the bier, "motionless like statues." Adelina came early in the morning but was unable to stand the sight of the coffin among the low-burning candles and fled, "sobbing passionately." On the roof of the building, armed detectives scanned the crowds for Black Handers, as Inspector James McCafferty, head of the detective bureau, was worried that someone might dynamite the building. Other armed officers kept watch over the Petrosinos' apartment.

One of the thousands who came to pay tribute to the fallen detective was an elderly African American man. It turned out to be William Farraday, who had been beaten by white thugs twenty years before on the Manhattan piers when Petrosino intervened. "Joe saved my life many years ago," he told a lieutenant standing guard. "I never forgot him for that. I owe my life to him." An emotional Farraday approached the coffin and knelt beside an Italian woman whose head was bent in prayer. He was crying when he left the room. A Chinese American man arrived hours later, telling mourners that Petrosino had walked in on a robbery at his shop years before and broken it up. "I'd be a dead man but for Joe," said the immigrant. "He a fine man." There were others, including the grown children of Meyer Weisbard, who had been murdered and dismembered in the Mulberry Street tenements years before in the notorious Trunk Murder. Petrosino had spent weeks of his own personal time tracking down the Jewish peddler's killers. "Petrosino," declared the *American Israelite* at the time of the arrests, "has accomplished what forty detectives, the stars of the New York force, failed to do." The family arrived to pay their respects.

An Italian artist from Naples was commissioned to create a bust of Petrosino to sit atop a pedestal, and Enrico Caruso pledged the money for a bronze wreath to be placed at the monument. George M. Cohan, the Broadway impresario and original Yankee Doodle Boy, organized a concert to raise money for the detective's family, and many of the top vaudeville stars of the day agreed to perform. Dances, bake sales, and charity auctions were held; eventually, $10,000 would be presented to Adelina. Postcards were printed bearing the detective's likeness, with the caption "HE WARNED PRESIDENT MCKINLEY. NOW HE IS A MARTYR." The newspapers attempted to outdo one another in their praise. "It is hard to have a man go out of life as this brave, courageous, heroic Italian went out of life," lamented the *Catholic Times,* "leaving little behind him but his good name . . . God give sweet peace to his soul."

Adelina received visits from wealthy Italian women and dozens of condolence letters. A member of Congress wrote to praise her husband's "manly gravitas and fearless bravery." Many of the messages were florid. "Think of how much He must have loved your dear husband to let him die as a martyr," wrote a Mrs. Jacolucci. "The time is not very distant at which we are to deposit in the same cement our sorrows and suffering bodies and to ascend in essence to an everlasting meeting with our dear ones." Some of the letters were addressed simply "To the Martyr's Widow and Orphan." A reporter who'd covered Petrosino for one of the dailies sent the condolences of Park Row and reminded Adelina of a bitter truth: there were families in Manhattan at that moment living under a Black Hand death sentence, and others who'd hoped Petrosino would recover their stolen children, and they grieved her husband's death just as deeply as she did. "While you weep for the loss of your loved one," he wrote, "you must remember that in many another home who once looked to him as a protector, his loss is keenly felt."

• • •

ON THE DAY OF THE FUNERAL, APRIL 12, MAYOR McCLELLAN declared a public holiday. City offices were closed. A large crowd was expected to send Petrosino to his rest.

The day dawned crisp and clear. Just after 10 a.m., a phalanx of mounted policemen appeared on Grand Street, their horses' hooves thundering on the cobblestones. They turned onto Lafayette Street and swept back and forth, pressing back the masses of people who had gathered on the sidewalks and clearing a path from Grand Street to Houston, a total of five city blocks. Reporters from every major newspaper and some foreign correspondents were part of the jostling crowds. "Then the scene became most impressive," wrote one. "In every factory, in every office building, as far as the eye could see up Lafayette

Street, windows, balconies of the fire escapes and roofs were filled to overflowing with bare-headed shirt-sleeved workers. There was not a sound except that made by the carriages as they took up their places and the horses of the mounted squad. The girls in the paper-box factories, the cigar-makers, those who manufacture 'pants' for so much the dozen pair—all of them could find enough time to spare to pay tribute to this man."

The lower portion of the city came to a standstill. The Italian flag fluttered from hundreds of buildings in the silence. The police band marched into place and faced 233 Lafayette, the door Petrosino had last walked through to board the *Duca di Genova* to Italy. The pallbearers —members of Traffic Squad A, all strapping six-footers who looked splendid and rosy-cheeked in their blue wool uniforms—waited, sun glinting off the gold bars on their collars. One after another, men emerged from the house carrying bouquets of flowers sent to Adelina by well-wishers. Carriages pulled up, and the men heaped the flowers inside. After a few minutes, eight victoria coaches had been filled to overflowing.

The turnout exceeded the wildest predictions. Some 250,000 people thronged the streets of New York waiting to honor the detective, more than had gathered for President McKinley's funeral. Never before in the history of New York or any other American city had such a crowd turned out for a man of the class to which Petrosino belonged, a humble police lieutenant. Eighteen years later, the funeral of Rudolph Valentino, the most famous actor in the world, would attract 100,000 mourners in Manhattan, even though the city had added a million people by then. Many onlookers in 1909 were reminded of the gigantic processions for Ulysses S. Grant and General William Tecumseh Sherman following their deaths. A movie crew aimed its cameras at the faces in the crowd, collecting footage for a documentary film that would play in theaters weeks later.

At the stroke of 10 a.m., the pallbearers entered the house. They soon emerged bearing the coffin, which had been brought back from the Republican League headquarters. As they carried the coffin down and prepared to load it onto the hearse, a flock of pigeons shot from a nearby rooftop and wheeled overhead before flying off. Adelina, on the arm of her brother, followed the coffin, along with members of her family and friends, and stepped into a black coach. When all was in readiness, the hearse began to clatter up the street toward St. Patrick's, pulled by six coal-black horses draped in white silk netting. When it passed by 243 Lafayette, firefighters from Engine 20 pulled their truck onto the street and rang the bells. There were so many policemen that the sun flashing on their brass buttons "dazzled the eye."

The procession approached Mott, where Inspector McCafferty waited in front of ranks of bluecoats backed up to the brick buildings that lined the street. As the hearse approached, the policemen presented their batons in salute, the blue tassels swinging with the motion, the white tassels hanging straight down. The weathered brown stone of St. Patrick's Cathedral was ahead, the mullioned windows of the church sunk deep into the masonry, presenting an air of cloistered solitude. The procession arrived at the front door, and the pallbearers lifted the coffin to their shoulders while a schoolboy choir burst into a rendition of "Raise Me, Jesus, to Thy Bosom from This World of Sinborn Care." At the sound of the choir, the orphans at the Children's Aid Society, who lived in a building across the street from the church, abandoned their chores, went to the windows, and pressed their faces against the glass to watch. The coffin bobbled slightly as it approached the door of St. Patrick's, where cassocked priests and an overflowing crowd were waiting. Flowers covered every available space inside the church, and so many were piled on the coffin that the polished wood was barely visible. On the roof, detectives scanned the streets for provocateurs, while a hundred undercover cops mingled with the crowd, studying the faces of suspicious men, looking for "crack-brained anarchists" or "desperate Black Handers."

Inside, Italians crowded into the pews on the right side, and policemen took up the seats on the left. Adelina entered, heavily veiled and still leaning on the arm of her brother, and took her place in a pew near the front of the church, sitting next to a young choirboy. She wept hysterically throughout the ceremony, her head bowed. The priests began to chant the Latin mass. The church was deathly quiet except for the voices of the priests and Adelina's sobs. The priests chanted out the liturgy and were answered by the high voices of the choirboys. Many mourners wept openly.

For his text, the monsignor had chosen the story of Herod's revenge: how, just after the birth of Jesus, Joseph saw in a dream that he was to take the infant to Egypt to prevent him from being killed by the Romans. But Herod, on hearing that the child had escaped, sent an order to his soldiers to kill every male child in Bethlehem and the surrounding countryside under the age of two. Matthew 2:18 was the focus: "A cry was heard in Ramah — weeping and great mourning. Rachel weeps for her children, refusing to be comforted, for they are dead." Outside the church, mourners who'd been unable to get a ticket to the funeral mass — seats inside were assigned by lottery, owing to the enormous demand — listened to the liturgy; some knelt on the cobblestone streets, their lips moving in cadence with the priest's. The monsignor, aware of the intense anger the killing had provoked, moved on to the sermon and spoke passionately of the need to heal the city's divisions. "I hope and pray that the death of this faithful, true, large-hearted, devoted, and beloved man," he said, "may be the means of inspiring self-respect among his countrymen, so that no mere handful of criminals shall longer degrade their race. May it teach to the rest of the people the debt and the love that we owe to these strangers on our shores, so that we may not wrongly discriminate. Let us make every one as welcome in our hearts as they are under our flag."

When the mass ended, the pallbearers carried the coffin to the hearse for the procession to the graveyard, in Woodside, Queens, which lay seven miles away, across the 59th Street Bridge. Some 3,200 members of the NYPD bowed their heads to the sound of muffled drums as the six horses bore the hearse away from St. Patrick's. The procession wound its way down Houston, turned onto Mulberry, and went past police headquarters. As the mourners made their way uptown, the police band played Verdi's Requiem on trumpet, trombone, tuba, clarinet, flute, and drums. Whenever the band crossed an intersection, the music flowed outward and down the side streets, mingling farther into the city with the sounds of streetcars and the calls of pushcart men. Except for the music, the city was unnaturally still, its business postponed. The windows of the office buildings along Fifth Avenue were crowded with faces, the sidewalks jammed with people; no car could make its way forward. Many of the mansions of the rich and the leather goods stores and boutiques of Fifth Avenue wore emblems of mourning: crepe or black cloth, company and family flags flown at half-mast. "If Petrosino had died a President or Emperor," the *Times* proclaimed, "no deeper or truer feeling could have been manifested."

As the hearse made its way slowly, detectives walked alongside. At the intersections, members of the traffic squad snapped to attention. Men and women in the crowd wept, and the men took off their hats in respect. Many mourners knelt in prayer on the sidewalks. The faces in the crowd represented every nationality, "from Chinese to Turk."

The whole city was mindful of what was happening along Broadway, but the spirit of the newspaper eulogies was paired with more tough-minded thinking in distant boroughs. In a criminal courtroom in Brooklyn, as the cortege headed toward Queens, a Judge Dike was sentencing an Italian named Frank Truglio to a year in the penitentiary for assault. "We are burying a good Italian today," he said bitterly to the defendant. "You, I am inclined to believe, are a bad Italian. You belong to the class which was not wanted on the other side and which is not wanted here."

The procession moved north. Children emerged from the crowd and threw flower petals to the cobblestones before the horses clopped past to the sounds of Verdi. Church bells tolled as the casket passed, and the great hotels of midtown, the St. Regis and the Waldorf-Astoria included, lowered their flags out of respect. Sixty Italian societies, including the United Bootblack Protective League — honoring one of its own — and veterans of the Italian War of Independence in their bright red shirts, scarlet jackets, and blue Zouave trousers, accompanied the body. Dr. Sellaro, the activist and Black Hand target, marched with the men of the Sons of Italy. Whether he'd continued to resist the Society or paid up after the bombing at his Grand Street building was known only to him and his persecutors.

The procession crossed the 59th Street Bridge, to the sound of thousands of footfalls treading on the steel grates, then followed along Newtown Creek until it reached the entrance of Calvary Cemetery, which had been carved out of the Alsop family farm in 1845 and which had grown along with the city that lay to its west. The cemetery had been split into four divisions, each of which bore the title of a different Roman catacomb. The procession made its way to the third division, named after Saint Sebastian, the Gaul who'd been accused of betrayal and shot with arrows before becoming the patron of archers and holy Christian death. When the mourners had gathered around the open grave, members of the mounted police presented arms as Adelina stepped from her carriage, nearly collapsing before her brother caught her. "Joe, Joe," she cried, "my Giuseppe, come back to me! My God, can't I have my Giuseppe again?"

The mounted horsemen saluted the coffin as it was lowered down. Five and a half hours after the procession set out from St. Patrick's, "Taps" was played. A captain called out, "Fours right! Trot!" and the mounted officers pulled their steeds away from the grave and toward the cemetery exit. The Patriotic Garibaldi, the Sons of Italy, the police brass, and the political notables turned and followed, and a new procession made its way toward the bridge and the city. It had been a long and tiring day.

As the crowd of mourners trudged toward the cemetery's exit, they could hear Adelina's screams behind them.

17

GOATVILLE

Even with Petrosino buried, Manhattanites found it difficult to move on. Wild rumors flew about the city: The detective had been wearing a coat of armor in Sicily that had somehow been breached by the fatal bullets. Or he'd been posing as a British lord, wearing a blond wig, "Dundreary side whiskers," and a monocle. "SLAYERS OF PETROSINO ARRESTED," read a headline in the *New York Journal.* The killer was supposedly an Italian miner who had been located in Mount Kisco, New York. The arrested man, however, was soon set free.

One of the more popular conspiracy theories, especially in the colonies, was that Petrosino's enemies at the NYPD had sent him into a trap, hoping he would be killed. Why, many Italians wanted to know, had Bingham ordered Petrosino to Sicily, that nest of vipers, completely alone and unguarded? Why had he revealed Petrosino's mission when it was supposed to be secret? "He went into a den of lions," said Frank Frugone, publisher of the *Bollettino della Sera* and the president of the defunct protection league. "He had no chance." Italians would be blamed, but many felt that other forces were at work and would inevitably escape punishment.

Petrosino's family embraced another theory: the detective hadn't really died at all. According to this rumor, the murder had been staged so that Petrosino could disappear and continue to work undercover. The theory became so entrenched in New York that Deputy Commissioner Woods was forced to refute it publicly. "I only wish it were true," he told journalists. "And while you might not expect me to tell you if it were, it really is not true. Petrosino is dead."

As the weeks passed, Commissioner Bingham grew defensive about his part in the tragedy. "He was eager to go," the General said of Petrosino, "and looked upon it as a great opportunity. He had no fear." The commissioner wrote to Secretary of State Philander Chase Knox, asking him to push for new laws, including one that would require all immigrants to carry identification cards, to register with the police in the cities where they lived, and to notify authorities of any change of address. This was followed by a newspaper interview in which Bingham spoke of the risks Petrosino had run; in it, he managed, not for the first time, to sound like a callous idiot. "All of those men [in the Italian Squad] take big chances and they know it," he told the journalist. "It's a wonder they haven't all been wiped out before this." The distancing — "those men," "wiped out" — made Petrosino seem like a stranger, and the General's expression of wonderment at the survival of any member of the Italian Squad was unfortunate. By now, Petrosino's belief that the Italians finally had a commissioner they could trust looked terribly naïve. Bingham's own role in the murder went unmentioned in the interview.

In Italy, police arrested hundreds of men, mostly known Mafia members. Dozens and dozens of tips and letters poured in, but they contained a welter of contradictory "clues." There were plenty of rumors but few or no witnesses willing to come forward. Before long, officials in Sicily began sending out worrying signals. "The police in Palermo," noted the *Washington Post,* "seem to have reached the conclusion that neither the Mafia nor the Black Hand had anything to do with the crime. 'Bad characters from America' were responsible." The report turned the stomachs of many Americans. Francis Corrao, the dashing young prosecutor in Brooklyn, fired back, telling reporters, "There is no question that the officials in Sicily are in league with the Mafia." American newspapers began to snipe at Sicilians and their representatives: the island was "a land of shame, where a conspiracy of silence protects assassins." Bingham sent three telegrams to the Palermo police demanding to know what progress they'd made, but heard nothing back. After that, he too began to accuse the Italians of complicity.

Little was said of American responsibility for the assassination. Bingham's baffling decision to send Petrosino alone, the revelation of his mission, the years of neglect that had allowed the Black Hand to grow: all were mostly passed over or forgotten. The journalist Frank Marshall White, the fiercest denouncer of Black Hand policies in New York, was one of the few who criticized the government. "Had Congress done its plain duty in checking the inroads of foreign criminals when that sinister visitation began," he wrote in the *Times*, "Joseph Petrosino would not have been sent to his death in Sicily." But it was a rare broadside; American anger was largely focused abroad.

In Palermo, Vito Cascio Ferro was arrested on suspicion of the murder of Petrosino, along with Paolo Palazzotto and thirteen others. But the case soon fell apart in the courtroom and all the defendants were acquitted. As Commissioner Ceola had predicted, not a single eyewitness came forward to testify as to who had killed the American. The very thing that Petrosino had decried during his lifetime ensured that his murderers would never be brought to justice.

Tips and anonymous letters would continue to pour into the offices of the Palermo police for decades. In February 2013, Italian police were conducting a long-running drug sting, code-named "Apocalypse," aimed at the Mafia in Palermo. As they listened in to their taps, the investigators were startled to hear one suspect, Domenico Palazzotto, begin to brag about the murder. "Petrosino?" the twenty-eight-year-old asked some compatriots. "He was killed by my father's uncle. I'll even show you the books. Our family has been *Mafiosi* for a hundred years." Why was Petrosino murdered, according to this rising young mafioso? "He dropped in from America, to stir shit up here, to investigate the Mafia." To be descended from the man who killed Petrosino would have been a mark of great pride for the young thug, but unfortunately for him, his facts were a bit confused. Italian police don't believe that Domenico is related to the Palazzotto who was arrested for the murder. They're convinced that this was simply a case of a man trying to burnish his credentials by claiming credit for a murder his clan had nothing to do with.

For Italians, the murder can be compared, in some ways, to the JFK assassination for Americans: each a notorious execution with dozens of theories floating around as to who truly pulled the trigger. But there is one key difference. The motives of the various suspects in the JFK murder couldn't be more different: the Mob, the CIA, the Cubans, the Russians. According to the conspiracy theorists, each group had a competing, and even contradictory, reason for wanting Kennedy dead.

That isn't the case with Petrosino's death. There are many rumors as to who did it, but all of the suspects share only one motive: Petrosino's work against the Black Hand and the Italian underworld. There are no competing theories. In this sense, it's irrelevant who actually pulled the trigger that night in Palermo. Any of a thousand men could have done it, and their reasons would all have been nearly identical. Petrosino's murder was that rare thing, a truly collective crime.

• • •

IN NEW YORK, THE CARVERS FINISHED THE MONUMENT TO Petrosino, complete with a marble bust, and it was dedicated at Calvary Cemetery in Queens. Father Chadwick, the NYPD's chaplain, gave the benediction: "The man who sleeps here was a true son of the people," he told the gathered bluecoats. "There is an irresistible conflict now going on between the forces of darkness, anarchy, and riot, and the forces of light, law, and order." A speech by Chief Captain Richard Enright was more personal and lyrical: "Sleep on, brave Petrosino, noblest of the city's dead. Sleep here in the bosom of a grateful city, within sight of its busy life, within sound of its manifold voices, enshrined in the hearts of a people you gave your all to save."

Other plans were being altered. The New York assemblyman who had intended to introduce a bill making bomb throwing a death penalty crime announced that, after further consideration, he'd decided to withdraw it. "I live in a Black Hand district," he told reporters, "and I know what these fellows are capable of doing. On second thought, I will leave the bill to some of the upstate members to introduce." The proposed law never came before the Assembly.

Fear of the Black Hand lived on. Detective Salvatore Santoro of the Brooklyn Italian Squad returned home two weeks after Petrosino's death to find a notice of eviction from his landlord. Santoro and his wife and children were ordered to leave the premises by April 1. When he asked the landlord why he was being evicted, the man admitted that the Petrosino assassination had caused him to fear that his home would be blown up by the Society because it housed a member of the Italian Squad. Santoro was forced to find another place to live.

The raids on suspected Society hangouts continued, and the mayor, worried about reprisals, told Commissioner Bingham that it might be best if he took a vacation "until the agitation over the Black Hand war had come to an end." Bingham refused. One night, the commissioner was driving toward his office at 300 Mulberry Street when he passed a dark alleyway. A single shot rang out. The bullet "passed so close to [Bingham] that it was regarded as marvelous that he was not shot down." The projectile lodged in the woodwork of a building across from the alleyway; policemen swarmed the area looking for clues.

A deluxe benefit for Adelina was scheduled at the Academy of Music, featuring thirty-five famous actors and vaudeville stars. But the organizers ran into difficulties. "We received every assurance that the theater, although one of the biggest in the city, would be sold out," said George M. Cohan, who was producing the event. "At the last minute it began to be mysteriously whispered about that dire calamity would follow anyone having anything to do with the enterprise." Performers received menacing letters; many canceled. On the night of the show, there was a slew of empty seats. Officials who'd reserved tickets failed to show up, costing the organizers thousands of dollars. Even Mayor McClellan, who'd arranged for several seats, sent his regrets. A humiliated Cohan told the press that the benefit raised only half of what it was supposed to.

The response of the federal government, after much chest-beating about a new war on the Black Hand, was muted. The single concrete action came when government officials asked the post office to be on the lookout for Society letters. The suggestions in Bingham's letter to the secretary of state were never implemented and were probably not seriously considered.

• • •

MEANWHILE, THE SOCIETY CONTINUED ITS WORK AS IF NOTHING had happened. In 1911 an Italian grocer with a shop on Spring Street received a letter with the usual demand for money. "Petrosino is dead," it read, "but the Black Hand lives on." He brought the letter to the police station. Soon after, the tenement where he lived was set on fire. Trapped residents ran to the rooftop to escape the flames. "The screams of women and children and the noise of the fireballs," wrote a journalist at the scene, "awoke most everyone living on the block." Men and women jumped off the roof to escape the blaze, dying as they struck the pavement below. Others were found dead at the foot of a ladder leading to the roof. Nine people perished in the flames, including six children, among them two infants, both one year old. The outrages, and Petrosino's murder, cemented an image of the Italian that still persists today. "The killing," wrote two historians, "more than any other single happening, convinced the American people that organized crime in America was a major import from Italy."

Adelina, brokenhearted, found she could no longer stay at 233 Lafayette. It wasn't considered safe for her to live there alone; already there was a guard posted outside her door day and night. She decided to move to Brooklyn. She carried with her every scrap of paper relating to her husband, every article about his life, his service gun, the gold watch sent by King Victor Emmanuel III, every possession of Petrosino's, every condolence letter. Adelina had internalized the anxiety over her husband's death. Years later, when her daughter married a policeman — and an Irishman at that — Adelina was terrified. "She felt that history could repeat itself," says her granddaughter. "She was against the marriage from the beginning."

The NYPD continued to take the threat against her seriously. More than fifty years after Petrosino's death, long after every criminal he'd fought was either dead or approaching senility, *Pay or Die,* the 1960 film about his life, premiered, with Ernest Borgnine in the lead role. Family members arrived on the red carpet with a full police guard; a detective sat near them in the theater as the film played. Gene Kelly had beaten Borgnine to the screen with a Society feature; ten years before, he'd portrayed a character vaguely based on Petrosino in a film called *Black Hand,* his first non-singing, non-dancing role. The movie was undistinguished, but Kelly's performance received glowing reviews.

• • •

IF THERE WAS ONE MAN ABOVE ANY OTHER WHO WANTED TO AVENGE the death of Joseph Petrosino, it was his friend Anthony Vachris, the head of the Brooklyn Italian Squad. He was willing to go to Sicily to find the killers. "Vachris is a bull-necked, hard-knuckled man . . . who does not know what fear is," declared the *Brooklyn Eagle,* echoing Roosevelt's comments about Petrosino. "He has been threatened over and again with violence in many shapes, and he has been told that he may be found some day in a bag or a barrel, but he laughs all the threateners to scorn, for he would like to find any gosh-blamed, dog-gasted Dago who would do him."

Days after his friend's assassination, Vachris stood before reporters and asked that the commissioner send him to Italy. "I feel certain that I can land the gang responsible for the death of Petrosino," he insisted. "I know of nothing that would suit me better than to be sent over there with a squad of secret service men. That is what must be done to avenge the death of our comrade, and I shall ask leave to go." Bingham, who could hardly refuse any offer to catch Petrosino's killer, gave his permission. Vachris grew a beard and acquired documents identifying him as John Simon, a Jewish businessman. He boarded a ship headed for Liverpool, along with Detective Joseph Crowley, an Irish detective who'd learned Italian while patrolling the Brooklyn colony. The NYPD didn't want to make the same mistake they had with Petrosino; the two detectives would watch out for each other while abroad. The pair sailed for Europe on April 12, 1909.

The secrecy of the mission was preserved. "John Simon" and his partner arrived safely in England, then boarded a ship for Italy. Once installed in the capital, they removed fresh disguises from their suitcases. From now on, they would go about Italy dressed as peasants. The pair began their investigation, visiting Rome, Genoa, and Naples, and interviewing anyone they could find with a connection to the case. The Italian police warned them that their lives were in danger, but they carried on regardless. Agents of the Italian secret service stood guard while the Americans sat in court offices poring over criminal records. But as with Ceola and his investigators, Vachris made little headway into solving the murder itself.

Vachris felt that the answers to the killing lay in Sicily, but when he told his Italian keepers that he intended to visit the island, they were aghast. "They said it was madness," he recalled, "and meant certain death." Vachris and Crowley argued with police officials, but to no avail. So the two returned to their rooms one afternoon, changed out of their disguises into new outfits, and snuck past their guards out of the hotel. Consul Bishop, who was readying for his return to America, helped smuggle the pair into Sicily. In Palermo, they made their way to the Piazza Marina and had their picture taken at the spot where Petrosino had been gunned down.

They also took up Petrosino's unfinished work and began gathering more penal certificates. Here, Vachris and Crowley made significant progress. They collected more than 350 documents pertaining to men who were living illegally in New York. Italian officials promised that they would comb through the files and send hundreds more.

But in the middle of their Sicilian investigation, a telegram arrived at their hotel in Sicily. Commissioner Bingham had been fired and a new regime had assumed control at the NYPD. The detectives were ordered back to Manhattan immediately. The two hurriedly packed their bags and caught the next steamship for America, the *Regina d'Italia*. It landed in Jersey City on August 11.

Bingham's firing is cloaked in mystery. It was rumored that he'd done the unthinkable and raided the taverns and Tammany strongholds in the "Sullivan wards" of Manhattan. In fact, this is exactly what happened: Bingham had ordered his men to close down a dive at 6 Mott Street owned by Paddy Mullin, a friend and ally of Big Tim. When asked by a politician if Big Tim had approved the move, Bingham scoffed. "The Sullivans! They can't even get the time of the day from the department." Mayor McClellan relieved the commissioner of his duties soon after.

Bingham, being Bingham, didn't go quietly. He accused the mayor and his Tammany bosses of "waste, rascality, and general cussedness" and stumped for the opposition fusion ticket in the next election. "Oh, the Mayor made a great mistake when he fired me," Bingham told crowds at one anti-Tammany rally. "Not because it was Bingham, but because he could have done it like a white man, asking for my resignation, and thereby effectively shutting my mouth. Now, I'll admit, my policy is to drive him into the ground good and hard and break him off good and short." Despite his bluster, the General's career in government was over; his reputation had never recovered from the Petrosino affair.

Despite their early departure, Vachris and Crowley could be well satisfied with their Italian trip. They hadn't uncovered the identity of their friend's assassin, but they'd completed his mission. They had hundreds of penal certificates packed away in their luggage, and Vachris was convinced that the Italians would cooperate in sending many more. Scores of Society men would be deported and many leading gangs crippled. It could spell the end of the Black Hand terror in Manhattan.

When they arrived in New York, the two detectives were ushered into a meeting with Commissioner William F. Baker, the new chief of police. Afterwards Baker, who'd been raised from a lowly clerk to the very top of the department for no discernible reason apart from his loyalty to Tammany, gave a public announcement welcoming the two back: "Lieutenants Vachris and Crowley report as a result of their visit to Italy that they have brought back much information in regard to Italian criminals in this country," he told reporters, "which will be of great benefit." But in private, the commissioner ordered Vachris and Crowley not to talk to reporters or fellow policemen about their mission. Instead of being allowed to arrest the men named in the penal certificates and begin deportation proceedings, Vachris was told to sit at a desk and translate the documents. Crowley, meanwhile, was demoted from acting lieutenant to the rank of sergeant, relieved of his detective duties, and sent to the Bronx, where he was to walk a beat on St. Nicholas Avenue, nowhere near the Italian colonies. He'd been exiled to "Goatville."

Vachris spent his days working on the certificates. New ones, along with mug shots of Italian criminals who'd escaped to America, were constantly arriving from Italy, where the authorities were apparently taking the matter more seriously than they had in the past. The number of certificates climbed to over seven hundred. Something very close to the permanent tracking system for Italian criminals that Petrosino had envisioned was now in place. Still, Vachris was concerned. Each of the cases raised by the penal certificates had an expiration date: once the criminal passed his three-year mark in the United States, he could no longer be deported. But days and weeks passed, and nothing happened. No one came to retrieve the certificates, no orders were given to arrest the culprits, and no deportations occurred.

When he'd finished with all the certificates, Vachris placed the originals and their translations in a file cabinet for safekeeping. Then, like Crowley, Vachris was taken off his detective duties and ordered to walk a beat, this time on City Island. It was, in the Byzantine symbology of the

NYPD, a ticket to the gulag. His new assignment required a four-hour trip each way from his home in Bay Ridge, Brooklyn, and his shift ran from 5 p.m. to 1 a.m. He wasn't allowed, because of NYPD regulations, to leave until 8 a.m. So he often slept in the precinct house, cooking his own meals and separated from his family for days at a time. Someone had clearly decided that Lieutenant Vachris needed to be punished.

What could the two detectives do? Some profound yet mysterious change had occurred in the department. If they spoke to reporters, they'd be crossing their new commissioner. Arthur Woods, the former Groton instructor who'd come to the NYPD and grown close to Petrosino, now served at the pleasure of Baker and appeared powerless to reverse the decision. The department wanted no part of the investigation into the Black Hand that had cost Petrosino his life. Meanwhile, the bombings and kidnappings continued.

"It is probable," reported one magazine, "that the Black Hand would have been extirpated before the end of 1910" had Vachris's files been utilized. It was a distinct possibility. Arresting and deporting seven hundred Society members would have been a major victory that could have led to a waning of the attacks and sent a signal that the price for participating in Society crimes had risen dramatically. "As it was," the article continued, "the evil grew and thrived." A special code that Petrosino had established with officials in the Italian government, by which they could inform New York police about criminals who were believed to be headed to New York, was never even used.

But why had this happened? Who had given the orders to quash Vachris's mission?

All signs pointed toward City Hall. "The certificates were suppressed at police headquarters," charged *New Outlook* magazine, "under orders of Mayor McClellan." The affair seemed to be proof of what Bingham and Petrosino had attested to before the mission to Palermo: that criminals, including Black Hand criminals, were being shielded from prosecution by officials high up in city government. The cover-up "gave these exotic desperadoes assurance of the power of American political leaders to protect them."

There is, as Salvatore LaGumina has pointed out, one other possible explanation. General Bingham had been at the forefront of the fight against the Black Hand and had green-lighted the Vachris trip. Any success it reaped would be seen as his accomplishment. For McClellan, who had publicly fired Bingham in a power struggle, to then turn around and finish the project that the General had set in motion would have given Bingham a tremendous political boost. It would have brought into question McClellan's reasons for firing Bingham, and perhaps even given the General a platform from which to seek higher office — including the office of mayor. There were excellent tactical reasons for burying the results of Vachris's trip, and Petrosino's, too.

Whichever theory was true, it was a shameful affair. Petrosino had died carrying out his mission, and now its fruits were lying in an index card file at police headquarters. Criminals had been given their freedom. "The acceptance of either theory," wrote LaGumina, "convicts McClellan of a crime against civilization and makes him more than any other one man responsible for the fearful carnage since wrought by these exotic desperadoes." The language is overblown, but it's difficult to argue with the conclusion. In the first sixteen and a half months following Petrosino's death, one hundred Italians died violently, with many of the murders directly linked to the Black Hand, including the deaths of fifteen victims who perished in fires set by the Society and two kidnapped children who were killed because their parents couldn't pay the ransom. Many of those deaths could have been prevented. In the same period, the conviction rate for Black Hand crimes plunged to less than 10 percent.

In 1910, a new advocacy group, the Italian-American Civic League, sent a letter to John Purroy Mitchel, the idealistic, aloof politician who was serving as acting mayor after the elected mayor, William Gaynor, was shot during an assassination attempt. The letter recounted the success of the Italian Squad and decried the explosion of violence and the unrelenting terror that had followed Petrosino's death. "How utterly unjust this state of things is you will certainly appreciate," the league members wrote. They wished to transform "a great civically inert mass of half a million Italians into an active and organic part of the city's life," but first they needed to be freed from the oppression of the Society. The league wanted action.

Mitchel ignored the plea, as did Gaynor after his recovery. On November 17, the Italian Squad was disbanded. Petrosino's life's work was fading into obscurity.

Meanwhile, in Italy, Vito Cascio Ferro resumed his rise to become arguably the greatest and most influential Mafia boss of his era. Over the years, Cascio Ferro's record with law enforcement was enviable: sixty-nine felony arrests, zero convictions. In the black-is-white world of Sicily, being accused of killing Petrosino had made him even more famous and powerful. "As he grew older," wrote Petrosino's biographer Arrigo Pettaco, "he assumed an almost royal manner, and he was actually a kind of king."

. . .

IN 1914 THE U.S. SECRET SERVICE, WHICH HAD BEEN ON THE TRAIL of the Lupo-Morello counterfeiting operation, arrested Antonio Comito, who'd overheard the conversation about Petrosino in an upstate New York farmhouse five years earlier. During the long interrogation that followed, an agent got the Italian to talk about what had happened the night Ignazio Lupo came to visit and announced that Petrosino had left for Italy.

Comito recalled that the men had been stunned by the news. The man he knew as Uncle Vincent smiled. "Then he has gone to a good place," he said, "for he will be killed."

Another man, Cito, chimed in. "I only hope the plan may be successful."

This was the first that Comito had heard of a plan to kill Petrosino. He listened closely to what followed. Lupo spoke with bitterness, no doubt remembering his confrontation with the detective four months before.

"He has ruined many," Lupo said. "You all know that he would have himself locked up in the Tombs as though detained and there listen to conversations and make arrests upon the strength of what he eaves-dropped for."

"Many are the mother's children he has ruined," Uncle Vincent said, "and he still has many crying."

Lupo made a reference to a Calabrian he had sent back to Italy, a man named Michele. Was this a messenger? An assassin? The men didn't elaborate.

"You have done well," said one of the counterfeiters, a man named Cecala, who winked at Lupo and picked up his glass to toast the visitor. "Here's a drink to our success here and a hope of death to him. To hell with that *carogna* [piece of carrion]."

Lupo raised his glass and drank some wine. "'Tis a pity," he said, after setting the glass back down. "'Tis a pity it must be done stealthily — that he cannot first be made to suffer as he has made so many others. But he guards his hide so well it will have to be done quickly."

After the men had eaten, they sat and listened as Lupo sang in Italian, most likely the folksongs they knew from their youth. Lupo was in good voice and sang "like a happy man." Everything was in readiness.

If we can believe Comito, and there's no reason not to (the Secret Service agent certainly did), the plan to kill Petrosino had been set in motion in America. Lupo and Morello were likely the plotters behind it, and their friend Vito Cascio Ferro is the leading suspect as the man who arranged the details in Palermo, even if he didn't pull the trigger. Comito's confession is the closest thing we have to a blueprint of what happened to Joseph Petrosino that night in the Piazza Marina.

18

A RETURN

IN APRIL 1914, "A TALL, DARK, PLEASANT MAN" CLIMBED THE
stairs of the new NYPD headquarters located at 240 Centre Street,
greeting policemen warmly as he headed inside the sturdy, gleaming
white Beaux Arts building. It was Arthur Woods, the former Groton
teacher who'd joined the New York police years before. A new reform
mayor, John Purroy Mitchel, had been swept into office, and he had
named Woods his choice for commissioner.

When he arrived that first day, Woods had plans, known only to
him, to change the very mission of the NYPD. He wasn't just another
reformer; he bordered on being a wild-eyed radical intent on blowing
up the police force from the inside. Woods had new and drastic ideas
on how to engage the people his men watched over, and how to turn
the NYPD from a head-breaking army of overweight, graft-loving Gaels
to something almost cerebral and benevolent. One of his earliest ideas
was to require all detectives to take classes in applied psychology at

local colleges. Eventually he changed his mind, but it was an indication of Woods's mindset. He would become perhaps the most progressive head of the NYPD in history.

The new commissioner began his term with a slew of changes. He ordered cops to slim down and undergo military-style physical training. "The fat policeman," proclaimed one journalist, "shirking behind a political pull has gone forever." He demanded that precise crime statistics be kept for every neighborhood, a preview of the CompStat program developed in the 1990s. Trained chemists, members of the first forensic teams in the country, now hurried to crime scenes with detectives and analyzed bloodstains and clothing, collecting dust, fabric, hair, wood, metal, and other clue-bearing materials from the scene. Professor L. E. Bisch of Columbia University opened the "Psychopathic Library" inside an NYPD facility, where he and his staff gave criminals tests to measure their reasoning and personality types. Bisch's work became one of the first large-scale studies of the criminal mind. New York even got its first aquatic police station, an NYPD office that floated on the East River, complete with sleeping quarters, a "desk room," a wireless, and a lounging cabin. There were regular film classes; detectives sat in a darkened room at police headquarters and studied motion pictures of theater performers acting out various crimes so they could better learn the telltale signs of felonies and misdemeanors.

In August 1914, Woods even ordered his men *not* to enforce certain kinds of laws, especially city ordinances. Instead, he wanted them to show the violators how to avoid breaking the law. Detectives watching over anarchist rallies, who once would have waded into the crowd with nightsticks flying, were now ordered to smile, "radiate good nature," and spread an air of calm and peacefulness. The cop, to Woods, was a friend and mentor. "He becomes a teacher of cleanliness, an educator of good habits . . . He plays the part rather of a helpful friend and guide than of avenging, implacable autocrat." Captains were given tickets that they could hand out to a father or mother in distress; with them, the needy could buy milk or bread, coal for their fire, or a hot meal in a local restaurant. At Christmas, precinct houses were fitted out with balsams and Douglas firs, and poor children found gifts under the trees. Woods suggested that cops should be known as "the People's Friends." It was said that Woods had turned the police department into a "branch of Social Service."

The effects were immediate. Instances of serious crime dropped from 31,759 in the first half of 1915 to 24,267 the next year, with murders dipping from 116 to 94. Woods was invited to Sing Sing to address inmates, then to Harvard. He brought thirty ex-convicts to the prestigious Collegiate Club at Columbia University and sat down to dinner with them.

But one artifact of the past remained. The city on the eve of World War I was infested with violent gangs that were a law unto themselves. There were blocks in the city that were considered off limits to civilians and even policemen. In the neighborhood along the East River from 96th Street upward (known as the Car Barn District), you could find a sign hanging on a black lamppost: "NOTICE: COPS KEEP OUT. No policemen will hereafter be allowed in this block. By order of the Car Barn Gang." Policemen who ignored the sign and entered the block were regularly attacked and beaten. Gangsters had seemingly lost their fear of the officer in uniform. "Murder can be done cheaper in New York," according to the *World*, "than in the wildest parts of Arizona."

And then there was the Black Hand.

The Society continued to kill, maim, bomb, and extort its victims in New York, and indeed across America. After Petrosino, other cops had been attacked. Detective Gabriele Longobardi, "the Petrosino of Chicago," was nearly killed only months after his namesake's execution; and an attempt was made on the life of John D'Antonio, head of the Italian detectives in New Orleans. Three years before, in Kansas City, a cop named Joseph Raimo was sitting in a saloon when a man talking to a group of Italians at a table named the killer of Paulina Pizano, a grocery store owner slain by the Black Hand with a shotgun blast in December 1910. As the gunman's name was mentioned, one of the gang looked up and saw Raimo listening. The cop was shaken. "I know who killed Paulina Pizano," he told a friend. "And they know I know it. Some day they will get me." Weeks later, Raimo was walking home after a card game at a neighborhood bar when a man stepped in front of him with a shotgun. There were two loud reports and Raimo fell to the ground, dead. At his funeral, his wife, the mother of their four children, fell on the coffin, crying, *"Mio compagno! Mio carissimo compagno!"* (My life's companion! My dearest companion!). She was later sent to a mental institution, her grief having unbalanced her mind.

The Society had even effected a kind of institutional change within criminal culture. Many Manhattan gangs, even ones run by Jewish or Irish bosses, had adopted the methods of the Society. Extortion was rife among the small businesses of the city, which were regularly threatened by "bandmen," or gang members. The business owner "was their favorite prey, because they could so terrorize him that he would not even appeal to the police," reported the *Herald.* "The bandmen would go to him and demand that he pay so much toward their upkeep weekly or else they would kill his horses, beat his drivers, or in some cases . . . murder would be threatened." Dopey Benny's gang ran the Lower East Side; the Hudson Dusters managed the West Side and the piers. The Italian sections below 14th Street were ruled by the Jack Sirocco gang and the "Chick Triggers." Some of these gangs were descendants of the notorious Five Points outfits. But others followed a model that had been pioneered by the Society.

And what might be called the classic Black Hand was still terrorizing the city. Five kidnapped children were murdered between 1909 and 1914. Bombs still went off with regularity in lower Manhattan, and kidnappings continued unabated. But other stories and themes now captured the attention of the public. "[The Society] had perpetrated so many sanguinary outrages in New York and the country," wrote Frank Marshall White, still on the case, "that the narration of their crimes in the newspapers had almost ceased to interest, much less to horrify, the average citizen." As some officials had feared, the Black Hand had become a permanent feature of life in a number of major cities, including New York. Arthur Woods arrived in a city that had largely capitulated to the Society.

When it came to most crimes, Woods preached a gospel of compassion. When it came to the Black Hand, he read from a different prayer book, one heavily influenced by Joseph Petrosino. The case that came to exemplify Woods's approach to the Society began on Wednesday, May 13, 1915.

That afternoon, in her home above the family bakery on Bleecker Street, near Washington Square, a Mrs. Longo waited for her son Francesco to come home from Public School 3, as she did every weekday. Her "bright and pretty" child, six years old, had left that morning with a nickel in his pocket to buy a sandwich for lunch. At 3:00 p.m., when he usually came sauntering through the front door, there was no sign of the boy, nor at 4:00 p.m. or 5:00. Mrs. Longo began to feel anxious. Her husband, a "big and brawny man," told her not to worry, that the boy was out playing and would be home soon. The father, a baker also named Francesco, was combative by nature. One writer said that the motto of Scotland — *Nemo me impune lacessit,* or "No one provokes me with impunity" — could have been tattooed across his brow, so imposing was his expression. The Black Hand had never threatened him.

But two years before, Longo's four-year-old nephew had been kidnapped by the Society. Longo had encouraged the boy's father, Felippo di Fiore, to report the crime to the police, and had argued with him vociferously when di Fiore resisted. Longo had always suspected that his brother-in-law had paid a ransom for his boy, which in the world of the Black Hand also endangered the victim's relatives. Di Fiore refused to say what had happened, and had never told his brother-in-law the names of the men involved in the crime, although he knew them well.

As dusk began to fall, Mrs. Longo left her house and began knocking on the doors of Francesco's classmates. Had Francesco come home with them? she asked. The boys and girls shook their heads. When had they last seen him? The children all recalled having spotted Francesco at their morning classes, but no one could remember running into him after the lunch recess. Mrs. Longo thanked them, then rushed to the school and caught the janitor before he left for the day. He'd seen nothing. With dusk falling, she tried the homes of Francesco's teachers. No one could remember having come across Francesco after noon. Mrs. Longo left the house of the last teacher and walked home, "her lips continuously moving in silent prayer to Santa Lucia," the patron saint of small children.

Like most boys, Francesco loved toys and candy, so on her way home, Mrs. Longo dashed into each small store along the path from the school to her home on Bleecker, even inquiring at the Italian fruit stands. Had Francesco stopped that day? The owners shook their heads. When she emerged from the last one, her eyes swept the street. "There were hundreds of children playing in the streets of the populous neighborhood," wrote one reporter, "and every few moments the signora's heart came into her throat when she caught sight of a boy who looked in the distance like Francesco." At this moment, Mrs. Longo would envision boxing her son's ears and sending him to bed hungry. But when each boy turned out be someone else's child and not her own, "she would bitterly reproach herself for her cruel thought, promising herself that when he got home, as of course he would before dark, he should have *ravioli* and frosted cake for his evening repast, and that then she would hold him close in her arms until his bedtime."

At 8:00 p.m., instead of the figure of Francesco appearing, a letter was slipped under the door. It was in a special delivery envelope and had been postmarked Brooklyn at 5:30 p.m. It read: "Dear Friend: Beware not to seek your son Francesco. He will be found in good hands, and we want the sum of $5000 . . . If this comes to the attention of the police, you will receive the body of your son by parcel post." Francesco had been kidnapped by the Society.

Immediately after reading the note, Francesco's father rushed to his brother-in-law's house and burst through the front door. "Had it not been for your cowardice," he shouted at di Fiore, "my son would not have been stolen from me today." He was convinced the same gang had targeted his boy, and demanded the names of the men who'd kidnapped his nephew two years before. "You say that the Black Hand will take your life if you do [tell me]," he said. "Well, I will take your life if you do *not.*" Still, di Fiore held back the names of his kidnappers: as ferocious as his brother-in-law was, he feared the Black Hand even more.

Di Fiore nevertheless accompanied his brother-in-law to the MacDougal Street police station, where they asked to speak to the detective on duty. A man emerged from the back: Rocco Cavone. Cavone had continued working Black Hand cases even after his mentor, Petrosino, had been killed.

That evening, Commissioner Woods was told of the case. It was the first Black Hand kidnapping under his administration. He called a captain, who was in charge of the bomb squad and was familiar with Society cases, to his office. "Take the matter in charge yourself," he said, "and drop everything else until you get the boy. Use every member of the detective bureau, if you find it necessary. Spare no time or effort in fastening the crime upon its perpetrators, so that we may infallibly prove it upon them in court." Woods told the officer that he didn't want just the bagmen and the underlings of the gang but the principals as well. Time, money, man-hours: they were all irrelevant. The detectives would stay on the kidnapping until they built an airtight case. Petrosino had never enjoyed such a mandate. Woods was determined to use the Longo case to crush the Society once and for all.

Meanwhile, Longo again ordered his brother-in-law to name the kidnappers of his son. Cavone, too, worked on di Fiore. Finally, the man blurted out the names: Nicolo Rotolo, a baker on Bedford Street, near the Longo home, and the Zarcone brothers, from Islip, Long Island. Fifteen minutes later, detectives set up surveillance near Longo's bread shop and Rotolo's store and kept both locations under constant watch. Others went to Islip and found that the Zarcones had moved, their whereabouts unknown.

The police rented rooms across from the two bakery shops. They would maintain twenty-four-hour surveillance of both businesses for the next forty-eight days. And they developed an elaborate system for observing every man or woman seen entering the shop or lingering nearby. The movements of the suspects were logged, and any suspicious characters they encountered were followed as well. The Black Hand knew to look for solo detectives tailing them, so Woods assigned a team of four investigators to each person. If a suspect noticed the first detective, he would stroll past and the next man would take his place. The tails were dressed in different disguises every day: streetcar conductors, ditchdiggers, motormen, chauffeurs, firemen. The same team was never allowed to tail the same man twice. If two suspects seen at one of the stores individually came into contact later, this was noted. Suspects were tailed to all the boroughs, and to Long Island, to Westchester, to Perth Amboy, New Jersey, and to Bridgeport, Connecticut.

When a suspect entered a home, it was soon visited by a mailman, a deliveryman, or some other service worker. In reality, all these people were NYPD detectives in disguise. If the suspect was unwilling to answer ordinary questions about his house, a second detective would soon arrive, dressed as an inspector from the local health department. Using an imaginary gas leak as a pretext, the inspector would go through every room in the house and ensure that Francesco wasn't present.

Two weeks went by, and Cavone's men built up a large database of people connected with Rotolo and all their associates. The notes kept by the surveillance teams turned up an anomaly: two men who had been tailed from the two shops had both separately entered another store, a grocery owned by one Francesco Macaluso on East 76th Street. Macaluso, as it turned out, was known to the NYPD: he'd been a longtime associate of none other than Giuseppe Morello and Ignazio Lupo. The pair had been convicted of counterfeiting (in the same case that led to the confession of Antonio Comito) and were imprisoned at the federal penitentiary in Atlanta, but Macaluso, the detectives believed, was still an active criminal. He'd been a suspect in other kidnapping cases, but police had never been able to collect enough evidence to convict him.

The investigation expanded yet again. The NYPD rented an apartment across from Macaluso's store and began to log every visitor. A few aroused the curiosity of the investigators: One Antonio Siragossa was "known to the police," and Longo had once done business with him. The Milone brothers, also known to the police, were seen at both

Siragossa's place and the grocery; each got his own surveillance team. A Nunzio Paladino haunted taverns that were known to be Black Hand hangouts. He, too, was put under a twenty-four-hour watch.

Cavone met regularly with the father of the kidnapped boy to exchange information. After a few weeks, he began noticing something odd: the same three or four men kept appearing near the places where he talked to Longo. Cavone came to the conclusion that the Society had turned the tables on the NYPD and was now following the father of the victim. He knew that if he was seen in Longo's presence, it could mean the death of Francesco. To avoid this, he instituted a new protocol. Instead of meeting Longo on the street, Cavone began slipping into the apartment building of one or another of Longo's regular customers on his bread delivery route. When Longo showed up at the door, Cavone would be waiting in the hallway, out of sight of anyone watching from the street. The two would talk briefly, then Longo would exit and continue on his way. Taking no chances, Cavone would ascend to the top of the stairs within the building, open the skylight, then escape across the rooftops. He would then enter the skylight of another building. The Black Hand tails never spotted him walking down the stairs and out the front door of an apartment building down the block, so his meetings with Longo remained secret.

The outlines of a kidnapping gang were emerging, but the members were clearly wary. Three more letters arrived at the Longo house, but none contained a drop-off address for the ransom. Perhaps the gang suspected something. Perhaps there was a leak in the investigation. More time went by.

Finally, Cavone decided on a plan to force the Society's hand. He told Longo to go to Siragossa and tell him about the kidnapping, and ask what he should do. In effect, Cavone was planning to turn the Society's own psychological strategy — the use of a connected "friend" — against itself. If he could get Siragossa to trust Longo, he might lead the police to the boy. Longo agreed. The next day, he walked into Siragossa's store and poured out the story of his missing son, leaving out the parts about contacting the police. Siragossa listened attentively and tried to comfort

Longo. Then he suggested that the baker see a friend of his who might be able to help: Macaluso.

Now Cavone knew he had the kidnappers within reach. He told Longo to open the negotiations. Longo went to see Macaluso, who professed to be stricken by the news of the crime and promised to act as an intermediary. The bargaining went on for days. Longo would tell Macaluso a price that he could pay, and the mediator would take his offer to the kidnappers (in reality, his associates). Then he would come back with a higher figure. The tension rose. Cavone still had no idea where the boy was being kept. The two sides remained far apart.

Eventually, Macaluso came to Longo with a final offer: $700 and he would get the boy back. Longo went to the bank, got the money, and met up with Cavone on one of his deliveries. He handed over the bundle of money, then turned and walked out the front door. Cavone took the money, hustled up the stairs to the skylight, and popped out the front door of a building down the street. The next day, the process worked in reverse: Cavone climbed down through the skylight with the package of bills, now secretly marked by the NYPD, and handed it off to Longo, who hid it in a bread bag. When Macaluso accepted the cash, he told Longo to expect the boy at his shop within the next few days.

Cavone had essentially reverse-engineered the Society blueprint. The "intermediary" usually protected the Society from detection by acting as a buffer between the gang and their victim. But Woods and his men, by dedicating unlimited resources to the surveillance of suspects, had been able to tap into the Society's pipeline and inject marked bills into the process. Now the NYPD sent surveillance teams to watch the homes of all the suspects, a list that had expanded to twenty individuals. They'd already documented the ransom money going to the kidnappers. Now they needed the boy. Then they could spring their trap.

At six o'clock that night, Francesco Longo walked through the door of his parents' home into his mother's arms. Within an hour, detectives began swooping down on the homes of the suspects. All were arrested, many pulled out of their beds and handcuffed. Not one had suspected that the NYPD was watching them.

Each member of the gang was charged according to his role in the plot. Vincenzo Acena and his wife had kept the boy in their home; he was charged, tried, and convicted, and received fifty years in the penitentiary. Pasquale Milone had kidnapped the boy off the street and delivered him to the Acenas; he received thirty years. Macaluso took a plea and got twenty-five. Siragossa couldn't be tied to the plot and escaped, but four other members of the gang were held on other Black Hand charges.

The long sentences, and the extraordinary investigation, utilizing dozens of detectives and thousands of man-hours, was a stunning reversal of the laissez-faire attitude the NYPD had maintained for so many years. "It came as a bolt from the blue to the Black Hand," wrote Frank Marshall White. "It ended kidnapping in the Italian settlements in New York, and was the beginning of the end of Black Hand crime."

Not quite. Some elements of the Society remained. But Woods had one last tactic up his sleeve.

The commissioner quickly adopted another of Petrosino's methods, one that went directly against his reform platform. His men began to trail known Black Hand suspects and "brace" them, throwing them up against a wall and questioning them closely about their activities, just as the Italian Squad had done years before. Essentially, it was targeted harassment. "The incorrigible criminals among the Italians," wrote White, "began to discover that what they considered to be their constitutional rights were not being respected by police." Accustomed to swaggering down the streets, with women crossing themselves whenever their eyes met, Black Hand suspects were now harassed, humiliated, belittled in front of the neighborhood locals. Detectives knocked on their door, sometimes in the middle of the night, brushed past the Society member, and tossed the place, looking for stolen property. (Often, of course, the "stolen property" didn't exist.) If the men protested, they were slapped around. If a Black Hander left his home and walked down the street, he was often greeted by a bluecoat, who informed him he was guilty of disorderly conduct and if he didn't move, he'd be arrested. If the Black Hander moved to the next corner, the same cop would approach him again and tell him that he was violating the loitering ordinance. Move or take a beating. If the Black Hander got tired of this and told the cop, "Fine, arrest me," the bluecoat would take him in, book him, and alert the district attorney. Black Hand crimes were moved to the top of the D.A.'s priority list, and the offenders were prosecuted to the fullest extent of the law.

The unit that specialized in the Society and other gangs became known as the Strong Arm Squad, then the Massage Squad, for their skill in deploying their blackjacks. "Commissioner Woods," observed the *Washington Post*, "is a firm believer in handling the blackmailer, the bomb thrower, and the gunman without gloves and with stout locust sticks in the grip of husky policemen." For the rest of the population, the commissioner wanted scientific policing, infused with a healthy dose of mercy. But for the Black Hand? "Relentless warfare."

The pressure became relentless indeed. Woods had made it clear that the full force of the department and the New York justice system was now behind the war. He had turned Petrosino's own habit of targeting Black Handers with rough treatment into a vertically integrated campaign against the Society. And it worked. "The result of these indignities constantly practiced upon them," wrote White, "was that hundreds of the Black-Handers shook the dust of New York from their feet within a year after Woods became police commissioner."

It was all, of course, completely unconstitutional. But Woods was determined to break the Society in New York once and for all. And he did.

Why, one must ask in the name of the dead Petrosino and the thousands of Italians who'd fled New York or seen their dreams aborted, couldn't this have been done years before? There's no single answer. It was prejudice and it was money. It was Tammany Hall. It was McAdoo's conservatism and Bingham's blind aggression. It was the opacity of Italian culture to the outsider. It was disgust and fear of what Americans did not understand. It was the "o" at the end of Petrosino's name. Had he been an American without the hyphen, had he been a pedigreed Yankee like Arthur Woods, a WASP and a blueblood, he would most likely have been allowed to destroy the Society in much the same way the commissioner did. But a dozen years earlier.

A number of other factors also contributed to the demise of the Society: Prohibition, which lured many Italian criminals into the profitable world of bootlegging; the gradual breakup of the Italian colonies as members of the second generation moved to the suburbs; the increasing sophistication and Americanization of that generation, which insulated them from Old World superstitions; and, finally, several prominent cases brought by federal prosecutors and tried in federal court.

But Woods and his men led the way. They broke the spell by putting two hundred gangsters, Black Hand and otherwise, in jail and running hundreds of others off into the wilds of New Jersey. This "perfect example of detective work" broke the terror wave in New York, and it followed the blueprint that Petrosino had laid out years before. That blueprint was beautifully executed, but what really made Woods's push so unusual was its dedication. Woods hadn't treated the crime as an Italian problem. He'd gone after it as a threat to the American way of life.

• • •

THE SOCIETY LINGERED ON FOR DECADES, REDUCED AND SCATtered, a remnant from the past, like typhus or the Charleston. In the 1930s, in tiny Wellsville, Ohio, a young Matthew Monte watched a group of Black Hand men move purposefully down his block. "They would walk from house to house and knock on doors," he remembered, "visiting all the Italian families in the neighborhood." The Society's tactics had evolved; these men offered protection and money to pay off debts. Monte's father turned them away, but they returned each month. When one Carlos Marcello of New Orleans was deported from the country in 1953, he was identified as the "alleged leader" of the Black Hand. But it was really meant as a synonym for the Mafia. The true Black Hand was a relic by then.

The man who remains the most likely suspect in Petrosino's killing, Vito Cascio Ferro, prospered for another fifteen years after the assassination. When his fall from grace came, it wasn't because of a police investigator but because of a dictator. Mussolini came to power around 1924, and the Mafia's influence rapidly declined. Cascio Ferro was abandoned by his political friends and, in May 1925, was arrested for killing two men who had refused to pay extortion money. Cascio Ferro managed to post bail and remained free for another five years, but during that time Mussolini appointed a new prefect for Sicily, an experienced Mafia fighter named Cesare Mori, who launched an all-out war against the secret society and its allies. By 1930, when Cascio Ferro was convicted of murder and sent to prison to serve nine years in solitary confinement, the Mafia had been defanged in Sicily.

Those who'd spent time in the gloomy Pozzuoli prison and met Cascio Ferro recalled that he often spoke of the detective from New York. "In my entire life," he told them, "I have only killed one person. Petrosino was a courageous enemy; he did not deserve a dirty death at the hands of just any hired killer." This slippery-worded "confession," like every part of the Petrosino assassination story, has been argued and re-argued for decades. Cascio Ferro never came out directly and said he was the triggerman in the Piazza Marina, and, as many argue, it could be a case of wanting to take credit for something he didn't actually do.

The *capo* would never see freedom again. Though he requested clemency, he was kept in prison past the nine years of his sentence. In the summer of 1943, as Allied forces swept across Sicily after the launch of Operation Husky, the Italian defenses in the area of the prison crumbled, and the authorities evacuated the cells before the American bombers could reach it. Vito Cascio Ferro was an old man by this time, and his great fame had long since been forgotten. Somehow, in the rush to flee the prison, the guards forgot about the elderly prisoner and Cascio Ferro was left behind. Abandoned, the sole prisoner of Pozzuoli, he died in his cell of thirst, "like the villain in some old serial story."

• • •

As for petrosino's legacy, it's difficult to locate. there's a park in lower Manhattan called Petrosino Square, not too far from the streets of Little Italy the detective once walked, a Little Italy that has largely evaporated and given way to a polyglot neighborhood beyond the detective's wildest imaginings. The park's name is somewhat ironic: it was originally called Kenmare Square, after Kenmare Street, itself named by Big Tim Sullivan after the town in County Kerry where his mother was born. The Irish arrived in New York too late to name many places; the square was what was left to them after the Dutch and English had given names to the important things. So the park received an Irish name, and then the Italian name of Petrosino followed, on land that was claimed by a tribe of Manhattoes when the Dutch ships of Henry Hudson sailed into the bay in 1609.

There's a small Petrosino museum in Padula, his birthplace, run by a relative. There's a grandnephew who, inspired by the detective, worked as a Brooklyn district attorney for many years, and his son, who now serves as a cop in Queens. But little else that you can see or touch. Petrosino lived at a time of racing terror and alienation for his people in America, and stories about what he'd done on the street were told and retold in the minutes and hours afterward by barbers and housewives and young girls who were under the threat of death themselves. No statue or plaque can re-create that electric, almost unbearable atmosphere of their lives or tell what Petrosino meant to his fellow Italian Americans in the dark days of 1908.

What remained after his death were the people he fought for, fought against, moved, and bewildered. He was the most American of all of them, and yet he died in a style that was quite Italian and even traditional. Perhaps the way life was lived in the small villages of Sicily and the way it was lived in America turned out to be so incompatible that a person had to be found to act out the violence of the passage from x to y, and Petrosino became that man.

He certainly changed the way Italians were seen in America. At the time of his assassination, the beginning of World War I, with its spasm of anti-Italian sentiment and its new restrictions on Italian immigration, was five years away. The executions of Sacco and Vanzetti were nearly twenty years in the future. The hatred of Italians didn't come to an end in 1909, but Petrosino's death had established a precedent that was widely recognized and understood.

On the day of the detective's funeral, the anonymous reporter from Hearst's *New York American* watched the cortege pass on its way to Queens. He spent some time observing the crowds — perhaps he even spoke to a few of the mourners — before returning to the newspaper's office to write his story, the same kind of story that every editor in New York had assigned to his reporters. His turned out to be the clearest on the larger meaning of what had happened in Palermo. "Men live and die, and New York seems not to care," the journalist wrote.

> But a day comes when a man dies under circumstances so striking and dramatic that the brooding soul of the city is touched and its distracted attention riveted . . . Then it matters not that the man was lowly born and not high placed, the spirit of the world's great democratic city rises up, collected and intent, to do him honor. Who shall say — in the presence of this august demonstration — that the foreign-born men who have poured into the gates of the city are not at home here? The Italian citizens of New York entered yesterday into a new sense of fellowship in the all-embracing household of the civic life.

ACKNOWLEDGMENTS

Many thanks to Anthony Giacchino, whose deep research into Petrosino's life made this a better book. To Susan Burke, for her gracious cooperation in this project. To Vince Petrosino and his daughter Courteney for their invaluable and generous help with the family's history. To Andrew Eisenmann for his generosity and sharp eye. To Bruce Nichols and Ben Hyman at HMH for improving its prose. And to Scott Waxman, who saw where the road led.

A NOTE ON SOURCES

The Petrosino family kept a large collection of newspaper clippings, articles, family documents, and condolence letters that arrived after the detective's death. This is referred to throughout the notes as the Petrosino archive. The newspaper clippings often don't include any reference to the papers they came from or the dates when they were published. I'm grateful to Susan Burke and Anthony Giacchino for allowing me access to the archive. "Comito confession" refers to the statements given by Antonio Comito to the Secret Service after his arrest, which are now kept at the Herbert Hoover Presidential Library and Museum, as part of the Lawrence Richey Papers, 1900–1957, in the folder "Black Hand Confession, 1910." The quoted material is from the document "Comito's Confession," a 109-page typescript of his original statements.

NOTES

PROLOGUE: "A GREAT AND CONSUMING TERROR"

page

xi   *On the afternoon of September 21:* For the kidnapping of Willie Labarbera, see the *Brooklyn Eagle,* October 9 and October 10, 1906.

xii *"that fiendish":* Washington Post, June 28, 1914.

"a record of crime": Frank Marshall White, "How the United States Fosters the Black Hand," *Outlook,* October 30, 1909.

xiii *"From the bottom":* Pittsburgh Post, September 4, 1904.

"Your son is among us": Quoted in the *New York Times,* December 15, 1906.

"There was a popular belief": Wayne Moquin, *A Documentary History of the Italian-Americans* (New York: Praeger, 1974), p. 169.

that it was a myth: This was a running theme with the ambassador, Baron Edmondo Mayor des Planches, in his public statements on the Society. See, for example, "Is the Black Hand a Myth or a Terrible Reality?" *New York Times,* March 3, 1907, in which Mayor des Planches is quoted as saying, "A few men . . . spread the Black Hand story as a means of playing upon the fears of their victims."

"Its sole existence": Frances J. Oppenheimer, "The Truth About the Black Hand" pamphlet, *National Liberal Immigration League,* January 7, 1909,

p. 2, quoting Dr. G. E. Di Palma Castiglione, head of the Labor Information Center for Italians in New York.

xiv *which some described as:* For gray eyes, see the *New York Times,* March 14, 1909. For black eyes, see the *New York Sun,* February 12, 1908: "a big, strapping man with flashing coal-black eyes and a melodious voice." Arthur Train also refers to "the occasional flash from his black eyes" in his book *Courts and Criminals* (New York: McKinlay, Stone & Mackenzie, 1912), p. 109.

"muscles like steel cords": New York Tribune, March 13, 1909.

"could make a fiddle talk": Undated clipping, *New York Sun,* Petrosino newspaper archive.

"the greatest Italian detective": New York Times, April 30, 1905.

the *"Italian Sherlock Holmes":* Giorgio Bertellini, *Italy in Early American Cinema: Race, Landscape, and the Picturesque* (Bloomington: Indiana University Press, 2009), p. 342. An Italian publisher printed a novelized version of Petrosino's life called *Giuseppe Petrosino: Il Sherlock Holmes d'Italia.*

"a career as thrilling": New York Tribune, March 14, 1909.

adept with disguises: See the *Evening World,* April 29, 1927: "He disguised himself as a hod carrier; he pushed an organ and led a monkey. He would black boots on a ferryboat or drive a truck." See also Edward Radin, "Detective in a Derby Hat," *New York Times,* March 12, 1944; and Arrigo Pettaco, *Joe Petrosino* (New York: Macmillan, 1974), p. 40.

possessed a photographic memory: See Pettaco, *Joe Petrosino,* p. 127: "Petrosino boasted he could recognize 3,000 Italians on sight." See also the *New York World,* March 13, 1909: "He knew by sight every Italian and Anarchist lawbreaker in the East." And see chapter 2 for the incident in which Petrosino recognized the murderer Sineni four years after glimpsing his photo in a Chicago police circular.

He hummed operettas: New York Tribune, March 14, 1909: "Joseph Petrosino would be the perfect model of the jolly friar . . . he hummed snatches of opera."

his customary black suit: Pettaco, *Joe Petrosino,* p. 40. Photographs of Petrosino in plainclothes show him dressed in dark suits and a black derby hat.

"nearly crazed with grief": Unattributed clipping, Petrosino newspaper archive.

He had a vast network: Pettaco, *Joe Petrosino,* p. 60, among other sources.

xv   *This man had heard: Brooklyn Eagle,* October 10, 1906.

xvi   *(two cents for the unsterilized):* Paul Collins, *The Murder of the Century* (New York: Crown, 2011), p. 3.

    men patrolled: See the case of Giovanni Laberry, *New York Tribune,* July 9, 1905. Tenement landlord Salvatore Spinella was also reported in various newspaper articles to be patrolling in front of his buildings with a loaded shotgun (see chapter 6).

    "society of darkness": Pittsburgh Post, March 26, 1907.

xvii   *"nervous prostration": Cleveland Plain Dealer,* January 31, 1906.

    "Conditions here intolerable": Austin Statesman, September 30, 1908.

    was said to be: Cincinnati Enquirer, February 5, 1906.

    an expensive gold watch: Interview with Susan Burke. The watch is still in the possession of the Petrosino family.

    "The Italian has a natural love": "Petrosini [sic], Detective and Sociologist," *New York Times,* December 30, 1906.

xviii   *"vampires": Chicago Daily Tribune,* January 1, 1908.

    "could not by any stretch": H. P. Lovecraft to Frank Belknap, March 21, 1924, quoted in Maurice Levy, *Lovecraft: A Study in the Fantastic* (Detroit: Wayne State University Press, 1988), p. 28.

xix   *it was his habit: New York Evening World,* April 29, 1927: "When worried by a big problem or wearied, he went home and played the Di Provenza from *Traviata* on his violin, incessantly."

1. "THIS CAPITAL OF HALF A WORLD"

1   *On January 5, 1855:* Michael L. Kurtz, "Organized Crime in Louisiana History: Myth and Reality," *Louisiana History: The Journal of the Louisiana Historical Association* 24, no. 4 (Autumn 1983): 355–76.

2   *His father, Prospero:* For Petrosino's family history, see Pettaco, *Joe Petrosino,* pp. 34–37; and Ercole Joseph Gaudioso, "The Detective in the Derby," documents of the Order of the Sons of Italy, https://www.osia.org/documents/Giuseppe_Petrosino.pdf.

    "He never smiled": Arthur Train, who knew Petrosino, writes in *Courts and Criminals,* p. 109, that he "rarely" smiled. Radin, "Detective in a Derby Hat," also says that "he rarely smiled and almost never laughed aloud."

3   *In 1888 a series:* The illustration ran in the *New Orleans Mascot.* It can be
viewed at http://ecflabs.org/lab/borders/regarding-italian-population.

At one flashpoint: Paul Moses, *An Unlikely Union: The Love-Hate Story of
New York's Irish and Italians* (New York: New York University Press, 2015),
p. 44. The anecdote is recounted by Dr. Rafaele Asselta.

4   *Young Joe Petrosino: New York Herald,* July 5, 1914.

"Petrosino was a big": For Anthony Marria's memories of Petrosino, see the
New York World, March 14, 1909.

"Shine your shoes?": For a fictional portrayal, see Horatio Alger, *Tom Turner's
Legacy* (New York: A. L. Burt, 1902), p. 196.

required to shine: Richard Zacks, *Island of Vice: Theodore Roosevelt's Quest
to Clean Up Sin-Loving New York* (New York: Anchor, 2012), p. 54.

"He was irresponsible": Interview with Vincent Petrosino, December 22,
2014.

"He was bent": Ibid.

6   *"Pazienza does not involve":* Richard Gambino, *Blood of My Blood: The
Dilemma of the Italian-Americans* (New York: Doubleday, 1974), p. 120.

One day Anthony and Joseph: New York World, March 14, 1909.

7   *He tried a succession:* The list of Petrosino's early jobs comes from A. R.
Parkhurst Jr., "The Perils of Petrosino," part 1 of a five-part series in the
Washington Post, July–August 1914.

He even toured the country: New York Herald, July 5, 1914; *New York Tribune,*
March 14, 1909.

"I am so well known": M. R. Werner, *Tammany Hall* (New York: Doubleday,
1928), p. 361.

One day, wanting to impress: Moses, *An Unlikely Union,* p. 119.

8   *"Japanese real estate":* David Goeway, *Crash Out: The True Tale of a Hell's
Kitchen Kid and the Bloodiest Escape in Sing Sing History* (New York:
Crown, 2006), p. 30.

The 150,000 horses: Eric Morris, "From Horse Power to Horsepower" (master's thesis, UCLA, 2006).

"most magnificent": Maury Klein, *The Life and Legend of Jay Gould*
(Baltimore: Johns Hopkins University Press, 1986), p. 318.

9   *Electric light began to replace:* Mike Dash, *Satan's Circus: Murder, Vice,*

Police Corruption, and New York's Trial of the Century (New York: Crown, 2007), p. 24.

"Wall Street supplied the country": Ibid., p. 26.

("this capital of half a world"): William McAdoo, *Guarding a Great City* (New York: Harpers, 1906), p. 350.

"The outline of the city": Henry Adams, *The Education of Henry Adams: An Autobiography* (New York: Houghton Mifflin, 1918), p. 499.

10　*"Why don't you join?":* *New York Times,* March 14, 1909.

11　*"insults and obscenities":* Pettaco, *Joe Petrosino,* p. 38.

"The government is a huge": Henner Hess, *Mafia and Mafiosi: The Structure of Power* (Lexington, Mass.: Saxon House, 1970), p. 27.

Even the church: Ibid., p. 26.

He "was contadino-*born":* Gambino, *Blood of My Blood,* p. 260.

12　*"Parsley will make":* Pettaco, *Joe Petrosino,* p. 38.

13　*His first arrest:* *New York Times,* April 16, 1894.

As he strode along: For the Farraday incident, see the *New York Times,* April 11, 1909.

"The Tenderloin Negro": Quoted in Thomas Reppetto and James Lardner, *NYPD: A City and Its Police* (New York: Henry Holt, 2000), p. 141.

Abruzzese, Neapolitan, Sicilian: Anna Maria Corradini, *Joe Petrosino: 20th Century Hero* (Palermo: Provincia Regionale di Palermo, 2009), p. 25.

14　*veteran cops often gave:* Arthur Carey, *Memoirs of a Murder Man* (New York: Doubleday, 1930), p. 6.

"Every hand . . . was turned": Parkhurst, "The Perils of Petrosino," part 5.

2. HUNTER OF MEN

15　*"the one golden chance":* Quoted in Sylvia Morris, *Edith Kermit Roosevelt: Portrait of a First Lady* (New York: Random House, 2009), p. 153.

16　*"No man ever helped":* Jacob August Riis, *The Making of an American* (New York: Macmillan, 1901), p. 328.

"Sing, heavenly muse": Quoted in Zacks, *Island of Vice,* p. 79.

"He didn't know": *New York Times,* March 14, 1909.

His dizzying array: For references to some of the disguises he used, see Pettaco, *Joe Petrosino,* p. 40.

17 *"It was one of":* *New York Tribune,* March 14, 1909.

"He is a master": Pettaco, *Joe Petrosino,* p. 41.

"in his hat": "Why Petrosino Gets a New Office," *New York Tribune,* October 4, 1905.

One evening: The anecdote is from "Caught After Four Years," *New York Times,* August 17, 1903.

18 *"resurrection insurance":* Frank Marshall White, "New York's Secret Police," *Harper's Weekly,* March 9, 1907.

He uncovered a scheme: Gaudioso, "The Detective in the Derby," p. 8.

Petrosino won seventeen: White, "New York's Secret Police."

Petrosino became so famous: The story comes from John Dickie, *Cosa Nostra: A History of the Sicilian Mafia* (New York: Palgrave, 2004), p. 172.

"Petrosino seemed to epitomize": Humbert Nelli, *The Business of Crime: Italians and Syndicate Crime in the United States* (New York: Oxford University Press, 1976), p. 95.

19 *The young Italian was drinking:* Many of the details of the Carbone case come from the trial transcript, records of the New York Court of General Sessions, 1883–1927, microfilm, Lloyd Sealey Library, New York.

20 *"I didn't kill him":* Pettaco, *Joe Petrosino,* p. 43. (Pettaco refers to the prisoner as "Carboni," but court records give his name as "Carbone.")

Finding nothing: For Petrosino's travels on the Carbone case and his arrest of Ceramello, see ibid., p. 44.

22 *"BALTIMORE – ALLESANDRO CIAROMELLO":* Unattributed clipping, Petrosino newspaper archive; spelling as in the source.

"Be at ease": Ibid.

Carbone never fully enjoyed: Moses, *An Unlikely Union,* p. 126.

"In every crime": "The Italian White Hand Society: Studies, Actions and Results," pamphlet, Petrosino archive.

23 *"Petrosino was no":* *New York Evening World,* April 29, 1927.

"the most thrilling evening": The anecdote is from Train, *Courts and Criminals,* p. 108.

"A big, strapping man": *New York Sun,* February 12, 1908.

"his dark restless eyes": Radin, "Detective in a Derby Hat."

"My name is Petrosino": There are numerous examples of Petrosino saying this, from Pettaco, *Joe Petrosino,* pp. 60 and 70, to various accounts of the Carbone case.

24 *"The police department":* Unattributed clipping, Petrosino newspaper archive.

"If he talked music": Undated clipping from the *New York Sun,* Petrosino newspaper archive.

"His reputation was": Michael Fiaschetti, *You Gotta Be Rough: The Adventures of Detective Fiaschetti of the Italian Squad* (New York: A. L. Burt, 1931), p. 19.

25 *a myth began to grow:* The legend is included in the Wikipedia article on Petrosino.

Soon after daybreak: The account of the Barrel Murder is taken from various sources, including Dash, *The First Family,* chapter 1; and Dickie, *Cosa Nostra,* pp. 165–70.

26 *"My name is Giovanni Pecoraro":* Pettaco, *Joe Petrosino,* p. 13.

27 *"Something was changing":* Ibid., p. 29.

"in unlimited esteem": Ibid., p. 57.

28 *"I who have never":* Ibid., p. 90. Pettaco believed that the quote was a fake but didn't provide any source for this conclusion.

"the Sicilian wolves": Unattributed clipping, Petrosino newspaper archive.

"that mysterious": Mercantile and Financial Times, April 8, 1908.

3. "IN MORTAL DREAD"

30 *"Scores of Italian murderers":* Parkhurst, "The Perils of Petrosino," part 2. Parkhurst dates the diary entry to around the time of the so-called Trunk Murder, the Black Hand slaying of a Jewish peddler, Meyer Weisbard, in January 1901.

A letter was dropped: Unless otherwise noted, this account of the Cappiello case is taken from the *New York Herald,* September 13, 1903, and subsequent articles in the paper.

"If you don't meet us": Quoted in Dickie, *Cosa Nostra,* p. 171.

31 *"mysterious stranger":* New York Herald, September 13, 1903.

"We are in mortal dread": Ibid.

On August 2: This account of the Mannino case is drawn from news reports in the *New York Times,* August 11, August 13, and August 16, 1904; *Los Angeles Times,* August 14, 1904; *Chicago Daily Tribune,* August 18, 1904; *New York Tribune,* August 18 and August 20, 1904.

32 *"Go out and make arrests":* New York Times, August 13, 1904.

"Evidently," wrote one journalist: Unattributed clipping, Petrosino newspaper archive.

"pulling little Italian boys": Ibid.

33 *"Stop chasing us": New York Tribune,* August 18, 1904.

"The Mannino kidnapping case": Undated clipping, Petrosino newspaper archive.

"Five hundred frenzied men": Brooklyn Eagle, October 8, 1904.

"The 'Black Hand' gang": Unidentified clipping, Petrosino newspaper archive.

"We will not kill": Ibid.

34 *as many as thirty-five:* "Is the Black Hand a Myth or a Terrible Reality?" *New York Times,* March 3, 1907.

The Black Hand burned: New York Tribune, August 21, 1904.

A bomb exploded on 151st Street: Ibid.

Five girls in East Harlem: Pittsburgh Post, June 6, 1904.

one of their bodies was found: Sidney Reid, "The Death Sign," *The Independent,* April 6, 1911.

35 *"cried most of the time": Washington Post,* September 20, 1907.

36 *On August 22:* "'Black Hand' in Murder," *New York Times,* August 29, 1904.

A bomb blew up: "Record of the Nefarious Work of the Black Hand," *New York Evening World,* August 11, 1904.

a wealthy Bronx contractor: Unattributed clipping, Petrosino newspaper archive.

"to remember the fate": Nashville American, October 7, 1904.

"The kidnapping of young Mannino": Quoted in the *Los Angeles Times,* August 14, 1904.

37 *"the sound American doctrine":* Quoted in the *New York Mail,* October 17, 1904.

"Newspapers," it declared: Nashville American, October 17, 1904.

"He was laughed at": Parkhurst, "The Perils of Petrosino," part 5.

38 *"The ramifications"*: *Pittsburgh Post,* September 4, 1904.

    "Imagine the captain": McAdoo, *Guarding a Great City,* pp. 43, 50.

39 *At the turn:* Terry Galway, *Machine Made: Tammany Hall and the Creation of Modern American Politics* (New York: Liveright, 2014), p. 161.

40 *"The trouble now"*: Quoted in Moses, *An Unlikely Union,* p. 133.

    "The sight of a uniform": Arthur Train, "Imported Crime: The Story of the Camorra in America," *McClure's* 39 (May 1912).

    "Do you know": Pettaco, *Joe Petrosino,* p. 32.

41 *In Franklin Park:* *Pittsburgh Post,* October 23, 1906.

    "Of other crimes": White, "How the United States Fosters the Black Hand."

    "Petrosino could expect": Parkhurst, "The Perils of Petrosino," part 5.

    "When murder and blackmail": *New York Times,* December 30, 1906.

42 *"He endeavored"*: Parkhurst, "The Perils of Petrosino," part 2.

    "The problem with my people": *Austin Statesman,* September 22, 1905.

    He *"called the victims"*: Quoted in Corradini, *Joe Petrosino,* p. 63.

43 *"The endless frustration"*: Pettaco, *Joe Petrosino,* p. 31.

    "At present," he said: "New York Is Full of Italian Brigands," *New York Times,* October 15, 1905.

    "He felt abandoned": Quoted in Pettaco, *Joe Petrosino,* p. 41.

4. THE MYSTERIOUS SIX

44 *"They finally granted"*: Pettaco, *Joe Petrosino,* p. 59.

45 *"The honest Italian"*: *New York Times,* September 4, 1904.

    The last recruit: Pettaco, *Joe Petrosino,* p. 59.

46 *"the mysterious six"*: *New York Evening World,* April 29, 1907.

    "They had no office": Ibid.

47 *"forlorn"*: Ibid.

    "to deal with": Thomas M. Pitkin, *The Black Hand: A Chapter in Ethnic Crime* (New York: Rowman and Littlefield, 1977), p. 56.

    193,296 Italian men: The statistics are taken from a table, "Italian Immigration to the United States by Years," compiled by the Bureau of the Census, published in *Historical Statistics of the U.S., Colonial Times to 1957* (Washington, D.C.: U.S. Department of Commerce, 1960), pp. 56–57.

    "There are thousands": *New York Times,* October 15, 1905.

between 35,000 and 40,000: The numbers come from George E. Pozzetta, "The Italians in New York City, 1890–1914" (Ph.D. diss., University of North Carolina at Chapel Hill, 1971), p. 211.

He estimated that 95 percent: Frank Marshall White, "The Passing of the Black Hand," *Century,* January 1918.

"The Black Hand": Frank Marshall White, "The Black Hand in Control in Italian New York," *Outlook,* August 16, 1913.

48   *"It seemed like":* Moses, *An Unlikely Union,* p. 133.

49   *"The eyes are":* Quotations are from the *New York Times,* December 30, 1906.

50   *Three policemen were guarding: New York Tribune,* September 17, 1905.

"If you don't pay": Washington Post, September 11, 1905.

"Our society is composed": New York Times, September 11, 1905.

One evening, the baker: Washington Post, September 11, 1905.

51   *"I'll go to jail": New York Times,* September 11, 1905.

"Black Hand Is Now the Rage": This account is from the *Pittsburgh Post,* September 2, 1904.

In nearby Westfield: Washington Post, October 8, 1905.

52   *When the steamship* Sibiria: *New York Times,* November 9, 1905.

53   *"I swear by the God": Washington Post,* February 16, 1908.

One judge in Baltimore: Baltimore Sun, March 5, 1908.

5. A GENERAL REBELLION

54   *When a butcher: New York Times,* October 18, 1905.

55   *In a later case:* The case is detailed in the *New York Times,* September 4, 1907.

"See here," it began: Austin Statesman, September 26, 1905.

56   *"You know what to expect":* Ibid., September 22, 1905.

"Please, papa": Unattributed clipping, Petrosino newspaper archive.

finally unraveled the scheme: Petrosino laid out the scheme in an interview with the *New York Times,* March 3, 1907.

57   *Petrosino soon discovered: Cincinnati Enquirer,* October 19, 1905.

$120 million in property: The figures are from White, "How the United States Fosters the Black Hand."

"tilted rakishly": Dash, *The First Family,* pp. 100, 98.

58   *One such merchant:* For Manzella's story, see the *New York Times,* March 17, 1909.

    "Theirs is a secret": Pittsburgh Post, September 4, 1904.

    On one occasion: The hunchback story is told by an anonymous author in "The Black Hand Scourge," *Cosmopolitan,* June 1909.

59   *one gang rented a mailbox:* See the case of the banker Angelo Cuneo, reported in the *New York Times,* December 19, 1905.

    When the squad found a few scrawled words: Fiaschetti, *You Gotta Be Rough,* p. 100.

    It was composed: New York Times, September 12, 1905.

60   *"Screams of 'Black Hand!' ": New York Times,* September 29, 1905.

    Adolph Horowitz, the president: Detroit Free Press, October 1, 1905.

    "Up in Westchester County": Washington Post, September 16, 1906.

61   *plummeted by 50 percent:* Pettaco, *Joe Petrosino,* p. 70.

    "a calmness that is certainly curious": Pozzetta, "The Italians in New York City, 1890–1914," p. 206.

    "a homeless, drifting little band": Parkhurst, "The Perils of Petrosino," part 5.

62   *"That little band of zealots":* Ibid.

    "He had shown capacity": Cavone's story is from "Joe Petrosino's Men Served City Loyally," a clipping in the Petrosino newspaper archive from the *New York Evening World* dated "Saturday, April" with no date or year visible.

64   *"Every possible handicap":* Parkhurst, "The Perils of Petrosino," part 5.

    the officers in charge: Ibid.

    "young and ambitious" roundsman: This account is taken from the *New York Times,* October 18, 1905.

66   *"rusticating in Greenpoint": New York Tribune,* October 4, 1905.

    "'The Dago' had become": Moses, *An Unlikely Union,* p. 136.

6. EXPLOSION

67   *owned by the Gimavalvo brothers:* For the story of the Gimavalvos and Petrosino's other open cases, see the *New York Times,* October 18, 1905.

    "My name is Salvatore Spinella": Spinella's story was widely reported in

the press of the day. See the *New York Times,* July 25, 1908; Parkhurst, "The Perils of Petrosino," part 6; and White, "The Black Hand in Control."

68 *"who say they are not afraid":* New York Times, October 18, 1905. The story of the fruit peddler is from the same source.

"was unanimous for murder": New York Times, October 19, 1905.

69 *"The Italians pay their taxes":* Quoted in Pitkin, *The Black Hand,* p. 114.

"If the police had been paid": Reid, "The Death Sign," p. 711.

70 *a "terrific explosion":* This account is from the *New York Times,* October 18, 1905.

71 *"They are getting bolder":* This interview appeared in the *New York Times,* October 18, 1905.

73 *"This country":* Frank H. Nichols, "The Anarchists in America," *New Outlook,* August 10, 1901, p. 859.

"Panic reigned in Washington": Parkhurst, "The Perils of Petrosino," part 1.

"I have just the man": Pettaco, *Joe Petrosino,* p. 50.

Petrosino walked back: The details of Petrosino's investigation of the anarchists are taken from ibid., pp. 48–55; Radin, "Detective in a Derby Hat"; and Parkhurst, "The Perils of Petrosino," part 1.

75 *"as copiously and hysterically":* Parkhurst, "The Perils of Petrosino," part 1.

76 *"No native-born American":* White, "How the United States Fosters the Black Hand."

"I warned him!": Pettaco, *Joe Petrosino,* p. 53.

On a hot August day: The details of the Marx affair are from the *New York Tribune,* August 21, 1904.

78 *"You may think":* Brooklyn Eagle, October 19, 1905.

"If Detective Prosini": New York Times, October 21, 1905.

7. WAVE

80 *brightly colored hand-drawn portraits:* McAdoo, *Guarding a Great City,* p. 149.

Delivery wagons trundled down: This description of the scene is based on Dash, *The First Family,* p. 60.

81 *high wages:* Gay Talese, *Unto the Sons* (New York: Knopf, 2006), Kindle edition.

There was even one poster: Elizabeth Ewen, *Immigrant Women in the Land of Dollars: Life and Culture on the Lower East Side, 1890–1925* (New York: Monthly Review Press, 1985), p. 55.

a ball of yarn: Salvatore Lupo, *History of the Mafia* (New York: Columbia University Press, 2009), p. 202.

82 *"Your railroads":* Quoted ibid., p. 91.

"My attention was drawn": Quoted in Moquin, *A Documentary History of the Italian-Americans,* p. 120.

the Irish and other nationalities: Lupo, *History of the Mafia,* p. 94.

83 *In October 1906, a Black Hander: New York Times,* December 29, 1907.

In Pennsylvania: Ibid., March 13, 1906.

in another village: Ibid., February 12, 1906.

Governor Samuel W. Pennypacker: Los Angeles Times, March 13, 1906.

"The murderous spirit": Ibid.

"sneered at the officers": Washington Post, January 26, 1906.

"WHOLESALE MURDERS": New York Times, August 21, 1906.

84 *composed in Latin: Baltimore Sun,* March 3, 1908. It was sent to Charles Rosenfeld of the Baldwin Detective Agency.

The affair began: For an account of the threats, see the *Cleveland Plain Dealer,* January 31, 1906. A similar campaign addressed to a private individual is recorded in the *Austin Statesman,* February 5, 1906.

That same winter: The Wesson case was widely reported in the press. This account is drawn from various newspapers, including the *St. Louis Dispatch,* August 5 and August 19, 1906; the *Boston Daily Globe,* January 28, 1906; and the *Washington Post,* August 8, 1906.

"Half a dozen": Washington Post, August 8, 1906.

a steel vault: St. Louis Dispatch, August 19, 1906.

85 *"The writer of the Black Hand": Boston Daily Globe,* January 28, 1906.

"My dear Dr. Marvin": Quoted in Claire Bond Potter, *War on Crime: Bandits, G-Men, and the Politics of Mass Culture* (New Brunswick, NJ: Rutgers University Press, 1998), p. 111.

87 *even the heir: Atlanta Constitution,* April 7, 1909.

A justice of the peace: Washington Post, February 16, 1908.

Count István Tisza: Ibid., January 9, 1905.

"A reign of murder": New York Tribune, May 27, 1906.

88   *"From the moment"*: *Cincinnati Enquirer*, September 30, 1907.

    In the tiny Pennsylvania town: Both estimates — from Hillsville and Newcastle — are from the *Pittsburgh Post*, May 9, 1907.

    Benjamin de Gilda: De Gilda's story is from the *Philadelphia North American*, August 17, 1908.

89   *On June 23, 1906: Pittsburgh Post*, June 24, 1906.

    In West Mount Vernon: New York Tribune, December 19, 1907.

    Mrs. Fiandini: Washington Post, January 28, 1908.

    John Benteregna was a barber: This account is from the *Los Angeles Times*, January 1, 1908.

91   *There were instances:* Robert E. Park, *Old World Traits Transplanted* (New York: Harper, 1921), p. 257, quoting the *Bollettino della Sera* from January 29, 1910.

    After being threatened: For the case of Vincenzo Buffardo, see the *New York Times*, May 15, 1907.

    "The far-reaching power": Parkhurst, "The Perils of Petrosino," part 2.

    "Across deserts, rivers, seas": "The Long Arm of the Black Hand," unattributed clipping, Petrosino newspaper archive.

92   Kidnapped in New York: *Nashville American*, October 25, 1908.

    The plot of A Midnight Escape: *Hartford Courant*, November 8, 1907.

    Bat Masterson: Pittsburgh Post, March 29, 1905.

93   *"the electrifying touch"*: Quoted in Pitkin, *The Black Hand*, p. 68.

    If a "master hand": New York Times, June 28, 1908.

    Every payday: Ibid., August 11, 1907.

94   *When the children:* Lawrence P. Gooley, *Lyon Mountain: The Tragedy of a Mining Town* (Rutland, Vt.: Bloated Toe, 2004), p. 242.

    "There are people": Ibid., p. 235.

    "I lived in fear": Ibid., p. 242. Testimony of Mrs. Victoria Robinson.

    Some of the Helltown thugs: Cincinnati Enquirer, July 29, 1909.

    "Use not clubs": Baltimore Sun, February 12, 1908.

    "mustered up courage enough": Baltimore Sun, May 1, 1907.

95   *In the shack: The Independent*, February 1, 1906, p. 244. See also the *Los Angeles Times*, January 24, 1906.

8. THE GENERAL

96   *One Monday:* This account comes from "Willie's Own Story of His Kidnapping," *New York Times,* October 10, 1906.

98   *"His eyes":* **Chicago Daily Tribune,** October 14, 1908.

     "a foot high": Dash, *The First Family,* p. 68.

     "I will give nothing": This account is from Reid, "The Death Sign," p. 711.

99   *around $154,000:* Michael Scott, *The Great Caruso* (London: Hamish Hamilton, 1988), p. 168.

     "a starved panther": Los Angeles Times, April 28, 1907.

     "He is a soldier": Ibid.

100   *"major domo, drum major":* Princeton (Minn.) Union, April 4, 1907.

     "friction and fire": Ibid.

     "The White House was not": Ibid.

     "It is said": Ibid.

101   *"which render it":* Ibid.

     He certainly: Pitkin, *The Black Hand,* p. 64.

     "It's going to be": Los Angeles Times, April 28, 1907.

102   *"I'll watch myself":* Ibid.

     "The people of New York": Princeton (Minn.) Union, April 4, 1907.

     "At last": Pettaco, *Joe Petrosino,* p. 69.

     He'd grown up: For Woods's background, see the *New York Times,* August 31, 1907.

103   *Before Woods accepted: Boston Daily Globe,* July 25, 1907.

     "gave a strong impression": Undated clipping from the *Christian Science Monitor,* Petrosino newspaper archive.

     "the greatest overlord": Thomas M. Henderson, *Tammany Hall and the New Immigrants: The Progressive Years* (New York: Arno Press, 1976), pp. 4, 10.

104   *"The Tammany man":* Obituary, *New York Times,* December 23, 1909.

     "Their fondness for each other": Albany Evening Journal, September 13, 1913.

     Big Tim perfumed the ballots: Werner, *Tammany Hall,* p. 439.

"He does not know enough": Pozzetta, "The Italians in New York City, 1890–1914," p. 208.

105 *"My headquarters":* Theodore Bingham, "The Organized Criminals of New York," *McClure's,* November 1909.

     Many evenings: The account of Petrosino's courtship of Adelina Saulino comes from an interview with their granddaughter Susan Burke and from Pettaco, *Joe Petrosino,* p. 71.

107 *"Waiting made him extremely nervous":* Pettaco, *Joe Petrosino,* p. 70.

9. "THE TERROR OF HURTFUL PEOPLE"

109 *Vincenzo Sellaro was afraid:* For Sellaro's story, see Pitkin, *The Black Hand,* p. 60; *New York Times,* September 2, 1905. For his background, see the website of the Order of the Sons of Italy for a biography of its founder and his *New York Times* obituary, November 30, 1932.

110 *"THE CHAMPIONS OF THE BLACK HAND":* *New York Times,* September 2, 1905.

     "It became": Undated article from the *Baltimore Sun,* Petrosino newspaper archive.

112 *"We hear a great deal":* Gino Speranza, "Solving the Immigration Problem," *Outlook* 76 (April 16, 1904): 928.

113 *"certain labor camps":* Gino Speranza, "How It Feels to Be a Problem," *Charities Magazine,* May 1904.

     The young lawyer: For Corrao's story, see the *New York Tribune,* September 4, 1908, and March 14, 1909; and Moses, *An Unlikely Union,* pp. 138–52.

114 *In March 1907:* For the story of Enrico Alfano's escape from Italy, see the *New York Times,* April 22, 1907.

115 *"The Northern Italian":* Hess, *Mafia and Mafiosi,* p. 34.

     "With the ability of a genius": Quoted ibid., p. 70.

116 *the morning of June 6, 1906:* The account of the murder and investigation is taken from Walter Littlefield, "The Neapolitan Camorra and the Great Trial at Viterbo," *Metropolitan Magazine* 34, no. 4 (July 1911): 405–19.

118 *The detective's informers:* St. Louis Post-Dispatch, April 23, 1907.

119 *"Then, on April 17":* For the account of Alfano's capture, see the *New York Evening World,* April 29, 1927.

121 *After seventeen months:* For an account of the trial, see "Camorrist Leaders Get 30-Year Terms," *New York Times,* July 9, 1912.

"the terror of hurtful people": The phrase is contained in a letter written to Commissioner Bingham, William Bishop Yale Papers, Petrosino archive.

"If the courts": Gaudioso, "The Detective in the Derby," p. 12.

"the night stick cure": Detroit Free Press, February 3, 1908.

Petrosino even disguised himself: Comito confession, p. 69.

"The gangsters who had dealings": Pettaco, *Joe Petrosino,* p. 31.

"This way you'll remember": Ibid.

123 *Before the suspect left:* Ibid., p. 120.

"Guns flashed": Carey, *Memoirs of a Murder Man,* p. 6.

"leaped on them": Lincoln Steffens, *The Autobiography of Lincoln Steffens* (New York: Heyday, 1931), p. 277.

"knocked out more teeth": James Lardner and Thomas Reppetto, *NYPD: A City and Its Police* (New York: Macmillan, 2001), p. 129.

"had scars": Corradini, *Joe Petrosino,* p. 63.

A suspect named Giamio: This account comes from an unattributed clipping in the Petrosino newspaper archive.

124 *"easily the most pretentious":* Quoted in Dash, *The First Family,* p. 99.

"attacking their credit": Parkhurst, "The Perils of Petrosino," part 2.

One afternoon: For the story of Lupo's beating, see the *New York Times,* March 17, 1909.

125 *One prominent politician:* The story is told in Pitkin, *The Black Hand,* p. 118.

10. ONCE TO BE BORN, ONCE TO DIE

127 *"more furious":* Corradini, *Joe Petrosino,* p. 63, quoting Luigi Barzini.

128 *Bozzuffi was a self-made man:* For Bozzuffi's case, see primarily the *New York Times,* March 25, 1906, but also March 8, 1906.

132 *In Brooklyn:* For Francesco Abate's story, see the *Los Angeles Times,* March 5, 1909.

133 *"blossomed forth":* "Black Hand Chief Slain by Men He Sought to Trap," *New York Evening World,* March 4, 1909.

134 *One immigrant:* Both stories in the paragraph are from unattributed clippings in the Petrosino newspaper archive.

Giovanni Barberri: This account is from the *New York Times,* May 7, 1905.

135 *Two days later:* This account is from the *Atlanta Constitution*, July 7, 1905.

a Chicago group: For Big Jim Colosimo, see Luciano Iorizzio and Salvatore Mondello, "Origins of Italian-American Criminality," *Italian Americana* 1 (Spring 1975): 219.

11. "WAR WITHOUT QUARTER"

138 *On December 28, 1907:* This account is from the *New York Times*, December 29, 1907.

140 *"independent malefactors":* Quoted in White, "How the United States Fosters the Black Hand."

"Specialists" were often imported: Nelli, *The Business of Crime*, p. 77.

"spoke sneeringly": Pitkin, *The Black Hand*, p. 73.

Their oaths were sworn: Toronto Globe, September 26, 1908.

141 *by how they killed: New York Tribune*, May 27, 1906.

A body found: White, "The Passing of the Black Hand."

If a victim: Parkhurst, "The Perils of Petrosino," part 3.

the troppa bircca: Ibid.

One Manhattan gang: New York Times, July 29, 1904.

One Society gang: Fiaschetti, *You Gotta Be Rough*, p. 18.

142 *"There was a killing": Washington Post*, January 26, 1907.

143 *In August: New York Times*, August 31, 1907.

In December: New York Times, December 29, 1907.

"New York is experiencing": Chicago Daily Tribune, July 30, 1907.

"They have no imagination": Radin, "Detective in a Derby Hat."

144 *a story he was:* The story is told in the *New York World*, March 13, 1909.

"rapid deportation of Italians": Pozzetta, "The Italians in New York City, 1890–1914," p. 210.

145 *"I want the police": New York Evening World*, August 21, 1907.

"Now don't think": Baltimore Sun, February 7, 1908.

On August 18, 1907: Chicago Daily Tribune, August 18, 1907.

146 *"filled with a feeling": Detroit Free Press*, November 24, 1908.

"The Sicilian is bloodthirsty man": New York Times, April 18, 1907.

At the appointed hour: For the formation of the White Hand, see the *Chicago Daily Tribune,* November 29, 1907, and September 24, 1908, among other reports from the era; Nelli, *The Business of Crime,* pp. 94–95; and *The Italian White Hand Society in Chicago, Illinois: Studies, Actions and Results* (Chicago: Italia, 1908).

147 *"War without truce":* Nelli, *The Business of Crime,* p. 94.

"a pack of criminals": The Italian White Hand Society in Chicago, p. 23.

148 *The two sides met: New York Times,* December 10, 1907.

In "Helltown": The best account of Frank Dimaio's operation is in the *Cincinnati Enquirer,* July 29, 1909.

149 *a "big and fiery": Chicago Daily Tribune,* February 7, 1908.

"open up": "An Impatient Correspondent," *New York Tribune,* February 24, 1908.

12. BACKLASH

150 *"You too must be":* Pettaco, *Joe Petrosino,* p. 71.

151 *"MULBERRY STREET": New York Evening Sun,* January 8, 1908.

"Joe was snowed under": Ibid.

152 *"The Bomb Zone": New York Times,* November 30, 1909.

"most of the Italians": New York Tribune, May 30, 1904.

"official roof tree": New York Times, March 2, 1908.

153 February 5: *Baltimore Sun,* February 5, 1908.

February 20: *New York Times,* February 21, 1908.

March 1: *Ibid.,* March 2, 1908.

May 23: *New York Evening Herald,* May 26, 1908.

December 9: *Boston Daily Globe,* December 10, 1908.

154 *"Inspector of Combustibles":* Unattributed clipping, April 21, 1908, Petrosino newspaper archive.

He tracked down: Washington Post, February 8, 1908.

In July: Baltimore Sun, July 15, 1908.

155 *Half the town: New York Times,* February 6, 1908.

In Rockland County, New York: New York Tribune, March 10, 1908.

In Greensburg, Pennsylvania: New York Times, January 8, 1904.

156   *A surgeon:* See the *Cincinnati Enquirer,* October 30, 1908, and the *Washington Post* of the same date.

"The supreme council": Nelli, *The Business of Crime,* p. 94.

"1,000 detectives": Chicago Daily Tribune, November 9, 1907.

Trivisonno was named: Ibid., January 1, 1908.

"Never before": Ibid., February 23, 1908.

In December: Detroit Free Press, December 14, 1908.

157   "from the 'general obloquy' ": *New York Tribune,* February 7, 1908.

the New York Tribune *weighed in:* Editorial, Ibid., March 9, 1908.

In mid-January: Washington Post, January 19, 1908.

158   *When a Black Hand member: Chicago Daily Tribune,* November 18, 1908.

"Italians are being terrorized": Washington Post, February 4, 1908.

"driven from the town": Austin Statesman, April 18, 1908.

"verging on a nervous breakdown": Atlanta Constitution, April 2, 1908.

"I am not afraid": Cincinnati Enquirer, April 13, 1908.

159   *"Praise for Mr. Rockefeller": New York Times,* January 26, 1908.

"no mercy shown": The Reverend A. H. Barr quoted in the *Detroit Free Press,* November 24, 1908.

160   *"It is sometimes wiser":* "Does the South Want Them?" *Nashville American,* May 14, 1906.

"in every possible manner": Quoted in *Hearings Before Committee on Immigration and Naturalization, House of Representatives, Sixty-First Congress* (Washington, D.C.: U.S. Government Printing Office, 1910), p. 86.

"now under way": Pittsburgh Post, November 6, 1908.

"Black Hand scrapbooks": Ibid.

161   *"Unless the Black Hand": San Francisco Call,* March 22, 1908.

"a state of mind": New York Tribune, August 23, 1908.

"The trouble all along": Detroit Free Press, February 13, 1908.

162   *"Murder, assault, and robbery of":* Quoted in Moses, *An Unlikely Union,* p. 138.

"LIVES OF 10,000": New York Evening Herald, May 26, 1908.

163   *2,500 arrests: New York Times,* July 8, 1908.

"Send him to the chair": Brooklyn Eagle, July 27, 1908.

"should be classified": Ibid., March 15, 1909.

"Let the letter 'K'": Quoted in *Current Literature,* May 1909, p. 480.

13. A SECRET SERVICE

165   *"He was so happy":* Letter from Mary March Phillips, condolences file, Petrosino archive.

     "had begun to acquire": Pettaco, *Joe Petrosino,* p. 110.

166   *"You ask me": New York Sun,* February 7, 1908.

167   *"the police force itself":* Theodore Bingham, "Foreign Criminals in New York," *North American Review* (September 1908): 383–94.

     "Thanks to the carelessness": New York Times, April 2, 1908.

     "If Mr. Bingham uses": New York Evening Journal, March 19, 1909.

168   *"The fact [is]": Nashville American,* October 18, 1908.

     "go kiss yourself goodbye": Atlanta Constitution, November 12, 1908.

     "I am the Police Commissioner": Quoted in Pettaco, *Joe Petrosino,* p. 69.

169   *"You must admit":* Ibid., p. 108.

     "There are two places": New York Times, March 5, 1908.

     "It would surprise": Pitkin, *The Black Hand,* p. 90.

170   *"This Black Hand business":* Undated article, Petrosino newspaper archive.

     "subservient to controlling": New York Times, September 2, 1908.

     "There was an attempt": Ibid., January 13, 1909.

171   *"one man, not an Italian": New York Tribune,* February 20, 1909.

172   *"dam the noxious":* White, "The Black Hand in Control."

     "probably the most ambitious": Pitkin, *The Black Hand,* p. 110.

173   *"Joe, you may be safe": New York Tribune,* March 14, 1909.

     "Do not go": New York Times, April 13, 1909.

174   *"I told him":* Ibid., March 14, 1909.

     "Uncle Joe!": Interview with Susan Burke.

175   *"He had the key":* Pettaco, *Joe Petrosino,* p. 119.

     "worst of moods": Ibid.

     Around this time: This account is drawn from Comito confession, pp. 69–71.

14. THE GENTLEMAN

178   *"We spent so many":* Condolences file, Petrosino archive.

179   *Sicily had been:* This account of the Mafia's beginnings is drawn from Hess, *Mafia and Mafiosi,* pp. 15–32; and Lupo, *History of the Mafia,* pp. ix–8.

     As a young man: Cascio Ferro's early career is drawn from Hess, *Mafia and Mafiosi,* pp. 44–48; Corradini, *Joe Petrosino,* pp. 139–44; and Pettaco, *Joe Petrosino,* pp. 90–101.

181   *"Don Vito":* Luigi Barzini, quoted in Corradini, *Joe Petrosino,* p. 143.

182   *"His face was impassive":* Carlo Levi, *Words Are Stones: Impressions of Sicily* (New York: Farrar, Straus and Cudahy, 1958), quoted in Lupo, *History of the Mafia,* p. xi.

     "His behavior is bold": Quoted in Pettaco, *Joe Petrosino,* p. 97.

     "stop going to Holy Communion": Ibid.

     "I know who you are": Ibid., p. 121.

183   *"You know the Italian people":* Ewen, *Immigrant Women in the Land of Dollars,* p. 234.

184   *"I've seen St. Peter's":* Pettaco, *Joe Petrosino,* p. 129.

     "My name is Petrosino": Ibid., p. 130.

185   *"I was able to meet":* Ibid., p. 131.

     an old family friend: This account comes from Corradini, *Joe Petrosino,* pp. 77–78.

186   *"It was sufficient":* Quoted ibid., p. 118.

     He hadn't seen his younger brother: Pettaco, *Joe Petrosino,* p. 131.

15. IN SICILY

189   *Petrosino reached Palermo:* The account of Petrosino's time in Sicily is drawn from Corradini, *Joe Petrosino;* Pettaco, *Joe Petrosino,* pp. 133–45; and the many pieces on Petrosino in the *New York Times, New York Sun,* and *New York Tribune* from March 14 to April 30, 1909.

190   *"My dearest wife":* Pettaco, *Joe Petrosino,* p. 136.

     "Dear Sir": Ibid.

191   *"I saw at once":* Ibid., p. 139.

192   *"Thank you":* Ibid., p. 140.

193   *"the most dangerous":* Ibid., p. 141.

194 *"This man is Petrosino"*: For the various reports on those who would harm Petrosino, see Corradini, *Joe Petrosino*, pp. 116–37.

195 *In Via Salvatore Vico*: Ibid., p. 152.

Another informant: From an anonymous letter quoted ibid.

"I Lo Baido": Ibid., p. 119.

196 *Assassins in each*: Ibid., p. 263.

And what of Vito Cascio Ferro: For Cascio Ferro's movements, see ibid., pp. 123–25.

"Vito Ferro . . . dreaded criminal": Pettaco, *Joe Petrosino*, p. 145.

197 *"which he could not miss"*: Corradini, *Joe Petrosino*, p. 66. The source reads "despite any reason," but this is clearly a problem with the translation.

"person of confidence": Ibid., p. 123.

198 *a pair of mines*: Ibid., p. 68.

200 PETROSINO KILLED: Pettaco, *Joe Petrosino*, p. 154.

16. BLACK HORSES

201 *"Cannot you say something"*: New York Times, March 14, 1909.

202 *"È morto"*: Ibid.

"The news": New York Tribune, March 14, 1909.

203 *"Bravo!"*: Detroit Free Press, March 19, 1909.

"I feel deeply": Unidentified clipping, Petrosino newspaper archive.

"He was always . . . gentle": Quoted in Corradini, *Joe Petrosino*, p. 76.

"The Black Hand have": New York Sun, March 15, 1909.

204 *"It is time"*: Report from Bishop to the Department of State, February 5, 1910, Petrosino archive.

"human butchers": New York Times, August 9, 1909.

"Let us not be": The Survey, April 3, 1909.

"It is not too late": "Petrosino — The Lesson," undated editorial from the *New York World*, Petrosino newspaper archive.

Bingham and the mayor: New York Sun, March 16, 1909.

immediately dispatched agents: The Secret Service would turn up various suspects but never obtained a conviction. See "Petrosino's Slayer Working as a Miner," *New York Times*, January 9, 1910.

"that [Petrosino's] cowardly assassins": New York Sun, March 17, 1909.

205   *In Albany:* Undated clipping, possibly from the *New York Herald,* Petrosino newspaper archive.

The New York American: Undated clipping, Petrosino newspaper archive.

"splendid service": Ibid.

"The raids": New York Sun, April 4, 1909.

206   *"knowledge of the recent assassination": Boston Daily Globe,* March 15, 1909.

"calamitous for Italian-Americans": Gambino, *Blood of My Blood,* p. 261.

"I wish to pay tribute": Undated clipping, Petrosino newspaper archive.

"SICILY RISES AGAINST MAFIA": New York Globe, March 19, 1909.

"The king believes": Washington Post, March 20, 1909.

In Palermo: For the story of the coffin, see the *New York World,* March 19, 1909.

The coffin was then brought: For an account of the Palermo funeral, see Corradini, *Joe Petrosino,* pp. 88–95.

208   *His life was threatened:* Ibid., p. 130.

President Taft had requested: Police Chronicle, May 8, 1909.

"As the last notes": Unattributed clipping, Petrosino newspaper archive.

209   *Professor Giacento Vetere:* Ibid.

Candles burned: The description of the wake comes mostly from the Petrosino newspaper archive, which contains dozens of articles on the proceedings, most of them without any reference to the newspaper or date.

210   *declared the* American Israelite: *American Israelite,* May 9, 1901.

George M. Cohan: New York Times, May 3, 1909.

211   *"It is hard": Catholic Times,* April 13, 1909.

"manly gravitas": All the quoted letters are from the condolences file, Petrosino archive.

On the day: The account of the funeral is taken from numerous articles in the New York dailies, including the *New York Times,* April 11 and 13, 1909; the *New York Herald, World,* and *Sun,* April 13, 1909; and in Radin, "Detective in a Derby Hat."

212   *Some 250,000 people:* Radin, "Detective in a Derby Hat."

213   *"crack-brained anarchists":* Unidentified clipping, Petrosino newspaper archive.

214   *Verdi's Requiem:* Author's email interview with Lt. Tony Giorgio, New York
      Police Band.

215   *"If Petrosino had died":* New York Times, April 13, 1909.

      In a courtroom: Unidentified clipping, Petrosino newspaper archive.

216   *Five and a half hours:* Ibid.

                              17. GOATVILLE

217   *he'd been posing: New York World,* March 15, 1909.

      "SLAYERS OF PETROSINO": New York Journal, August 7, 1909.

      "a den of lions": New York World, March 13, 1909.

218   *"I only wish":* New York Times, March 14, 1909.

      "He was eager": Clipping from the *New York Times,* March 14 or 15, 1909,
      Petrosino newspaper archive.

      "All of those men": New York Times, March 16, 1909.

      "The police in Palermo": Washington Post, March 21, 1909.

219   *"There is no question":* New York Tribune, March 14, 1909.

      "Had Congress done": Frank Marshall White, "The Increasing Menace of
      the Black Hand," *New York Times,* March 21, 1909.

      In February 2013: Barbie Latza Nadeau, "Who Really Murdered Joe
      Petrosino?" dailybeast.com, June 24, 2014.

220   *"The man who sleeps here": New York World,* March 14, 1910.

221   *"I live in":* Undated article from the *New York Evening Telegram,* Petrosino
      newspaper archive.

      Detective Salvatore Santoro: New York Sun, March 27, 1909.

      "until the agitation": Washington Post, March 20, 1909.

      "We received every assurance": New York Times, May 3, 1909.

222   *"Petrosino is dead":* Quoted in Pitkin, *The Black Hand,* p. 116.

      "The killing": Iorizzio and Mondello, "Origins of Italian-American
      Criminality."

223   *"She felt that history":* Interview with Susan Burke.

      More than fifty years: Ibid.

      "Vachris is a bull-necked": Brooklyn Eagle, October 26, 1907.

"I feel certain": Nashville American, March 14, 1909.

224 *The secrecy of the mission:* For details on Vachris's mission, see White, "The Black Hand in Control."

225 *"The Sullivans!":* This account is from Richard F. Welch, *King of the Bowery: Big Tim Sullivan, Tammany Hall, and New York City from the Gilded Age to the Progressive Era* (New York: Excelsior Editions, 2009), p. 129.

"waste, rascality": "Bingham Comes Out Against Tammany," *New York Times,* October 13, 1909.

226 *Vachris spent his days:* For Vachris's exile within the NYPD and the cover-up of his mission, see White, "The Passing of the Black Hand."

227 *"It is probable":* "The Black Hand Under Control," *New Outlook,* June 14, 1916, p. 347.

"The certificates were suppressed": Quoted ibid.

There is: Salvatore LaGumina, *Wop! A Documentary History of Anti-Italian Discrimination* (Toronto: Guernica Editions, 1999), p. 101.

228 *"The acceptance":* Ibid.

"How utterly unjust": Frank Marshall White, "Against the Black Hand," *Collier's Weekly,* September 1910, p. 49.

229 *"As he grew older":* Pettaco, *Joe Petrosino,* p. 193.

Comito recalled: Comito confession.

18. A RETURN

231 *"a tall, dark, pleasant man": New York Sun,* April 8, 1914.

One of his earliest ideas: Carey, *Memoirs of a Murder Man,* p. 133.

232 *"The fat policeman": Town Topics,* June 26, 1916.

Professor L. E. Bisch: New York Sunday World, August 27, 1916.

"radiate good nature": Quotations are from Arthur Woods, *Policeman and Public* (New York: Arno Press, 1971), pp. 75, 67.

233 *"branch of Social Service": The Churchman* 31, no. 11 (November 1917).

The effects were immediate: New York Telegram, August 25, 1916.

"NOTICE: COPS KEEP OUT": Carey, *Memoirs of a Murder Man,* p. 141.

"Murder can be done cheaper": New York World, December 2, 1914.

Three years before: Terence O'Malley, *Blackhand Strawman* (By the author, 2011), p. 3.

234 *"was their favorite prey"*: "The Nightstick and the Blackjack, Well Handled, Have Driven New York's Bandmen into Prison or Ways of Decent Living," *New York Herald,* September 2, 1917. This long article is the source for most of the account of the gangs of Woods's era.

  "[The Society] had perpetrated": White, "The Passing of the Black Hand."

235 *That afternoon:* For the account of the Longo case, see ibid.

242 *"Commissioner Woods"*: *Washington Post,* December 14, 1914.

243 *the profitable world:* See Fiaschetti, *You Gotta Be Rough,* p. 15: "The 18th Amendment endowed the Black Hand with fabulous funds and took it from isolated Italian quarters and bestowed it on the cities at large."

  "perfect example of detective work": White, "The Passing of the Black Hand."

  In the 1930s: See Charles Zappia, "Labor, Race and Ethnicity in the West Virginia Mines," *Journal of American Ethnic History* 30, no. 4 (Summer 2011): 44–50.

244 *Those who'd spent time:* For Cascio Ferro's last days, see Pettaco, *Joe Petrosino,* pp. 193–95.

246 *"Men live and die"*: *New York American,* April 13, 1909.

SELECT BIBLIOGRAPHY

Bertellini, Giorgio. *Italy in Early American Cinema: Race, Landscape, and the Picturesque*. Bloomington: Indiana University Press, 2009.

Carey, Arthur. *Memoirs of a Murder Man*. New York: Doubleday, 1930.

Collins, Paul. *The Murder of the Century: The Gilded Age Crime That Scandalized a City & Sparked the Tabloid Wars*. New York: Crown, 2011.

Corradini, Anna Maria. *Joe Petrosino, a 20th Century Hero*. Palermo: Provincia Regionale di Palermo, 2009.

Critchley, David. *The Origin of Organized Crime in America: The New York City Mafia, 1891–1931*. New York: Routledge, 2008.

Daniels, Roger. *Coming to America: A History of Immigration and Ethnicity in American Life*. New York: HarperCollins, 1990.

Dash, Mike. *The First Family: Terror, Extortion, Revenge, Murder, and the Birth of the American Mafia*. New York: Random House, 2009.

Dickie, John. *Cosa Nostra: A History of the Sicilian Mafia*. New York: Palgrave Macmillan, 2004.

Ewen, Elizabeth. *Immigrant Women in the Land of Dollars: Life and Culture on the Lower East Side, 1890–1925*. New York: Monthly Review Press, 1985.

Fiaschetti, Michael. *You Gotta Be Rough: The Adventures of Detective Fiaschetti of the Italian Squad.* New York: A. L. Burt, 1931.

Gambino, Richard. *Blood of My Blood: The Dilemma of the Italian-Americans.* New York: Doubleday, 1974.

Golway, Terry. *Machine Made: Tammany Hall and the Creation of Modern American Politics.* New York: Liveright, 2014.

Henderson, Thomas M. *Tammany Hall and the New Immigrants: The Progressive Years.* New York: Arno Press, 1976.

Hess, Henner. *Mafia and Mafiosi: The Structure of Power.* Lexington, Mass.: Saxon House, 1970.

Horan, James D. *The Pinkertons: The Detective Dynasty That Changed History.* New York: Crown, 1967.

Jackson, Kenneth T., and David S. Dunbar. *Empire City: New York Through the Centuries.* New York: Columbia University Press, 2005.

Kobler, John. *Capone: The Life and World of Al Capone.* New York: Putnam, 1971.

LaGumina, Salvatore J. *Wop! A Documentary History of Anti-Italian Discrimination.* Toronto: Guernica Editions, 1999.

Lardner, James, and Thomas Reppetto. *NYPD: A City and Its Police.* New York: Holt, 2001.

Lupo, Salvatore. *History of the Mafia.* New York: Columbia University Press, 2009.

McAdoo, William. *Guarding a Great City.* New York: Harper & Bros., 1906.

Moquin, Wayne. *A Documentary History of the Italian-Americans.* New York: Praeger, 1974.

Moses, Paul. *An Unlikely Union: The Love-Hate Story of New York's Irish and Italians.* New York: NYU Press, 2015.

Nelli, Humbert. *The Business of Crime: Italians and Syndicate Crime in the United States.* New York: Oxford University Press, 1976.

Painter, Nell Irvin. *Standing at Armageddon: A Grassroots History of the Progressive Era.* New York: W. W. Norton & Co., 2008.

Park, Robert E., and Herbert Adolphus Miller. *Old World Traits Transplanted.* New York: Harper, 1921.

Pettaco, Arrigo. *Joe Petrosino*. New York: Macmillan, 1974.

Pitkin, Thomas M. *The Black Hand: A Chapter in Ethnic Crime*. New York: Rowman and Littlefield, 1977.

Potter, Claire Bond. *War on Crime: Bandits, G-Men, and the Politics of Mass Culture*. New Brunswick, N.J.: Rutgers University Press, 1998.

Pozzetta, George E. "The Italians in New York City, 1890–1914." Ph.D. dissertation, University of North Carolina at Chapel Hill, 1971.

Riis, Jacob. *How the Other Half Lives: Studies Among the Tenements of New York*. Eastford, Conn.: Martino Fine Books, 2015.

Sante, Luc. *Low Life: Lures and Snares of Old New York*. New York: Farrar, Straus and Giroux, 2003.

Talese, Gay. *Unto the Sons*. New York: Knopf, 2006.

Tonelli, Bill. *The Italian American Reader*. New York: Harper, 2005.

Train, Arthur. *Courts and Criminals*. New York: McKinlay, Stone & Mackenzie, 1912.

Weiner, Tim. *Enemies: A History of the FBI*. New York: Random House, 2013.

Welch, Richard F. *King of the Bowery: Big Tim Sullivan, Tammany Hall, and New York City from the Gilded Age to the Progressive Era*. New York: Excelsior Editions, 2009.

Werner, M. R. *Tammany Hall*. New York: Doubleday, Doran & Co., 1928.

Woods, Arthur. *Crime Prevention*. Princeton, N.J.: Princeton University Press, 1918.

———. *Policeman and Public*. New York: Arno Press, 1971.

Yochelson, Bonnie, and Daniel Czitrom. *Rediscovering Jacob Riis: Exposure Journalism and Photography in Turn-of-the-Century New York*. New York: New Press, 2008.

Zacks, Richard. *Island of Vice: Theodore Roosevelt's Quest to Clean Up Sin-Loving New York*. New York: Anchor, 2012.

Zolberg, Aristide R. *A Nation by Design: Immigration Policy in the Fashioning of America*. Cambridge, Mass.: Harvard University Press, 2006.

INDEX

Abate, Francesco, 132–34

Acena, Vincenzo, 241

Adams, Henry, 9–10

African Americans, 160

Agnone, Italy, 105

Alabama, 160–61

Albany Evening Journal, 104

Alfano, Enrico, 115–16, 118–21

Alger, Horatio, 6

American Israelite, 210

anarchism, 179–80, 213, 232

Anarchists of Paterson, 171

Arato, Vincenzo, 186–87

Asheville, North Carolina, 160–61

Atlanta Constitution, 203

Bagnato, Joe, 93

Baker, William F., 226, 227

Balstieri, Giuseppe. *See* Alfano, Enrico

Baltimore, Maryland, 21–22, 32, 53, 94, 147

Baltimore Sun, 110

Bananno, Nicolò, 138–40

Barberri, Giovanni, 134–35

Barrel Murder, 25–27, 57, 76, 178–79, 195

Barroncini, Antonio and Mrs., 36

Barzini, Luigi, 42–43

baseball, 145–46

"Bat Masterson Library" (newspaper serial), 92–93

Benteregna, John, 90–91

Berlin, Germany, 206

Big Pietro, 135

Bingham, Theodore A.
  appointed as NYPD
    commissioner, 99–102,
    104–5
  assassination attempt, 221
  blind aggression of, 242
  call for vigilantes and, 164
  criticism of, 162
  firing of, 225, 228
  intelligence operation planned
    by, 172–73, 185
  Italian Squad and, 145
  letter to secretary of state, 218,
    222
  official roof tree of, 152
  Pasquale Enea and, 197
  Petrosino's assassination and,
    203, 204, 217, 218, 219
  Petrosino's cover blown by, 187,
    193
  Petrosino's letter to, 190–91
  at Petrosino's wedding, 151
  secret service of, 166–75, 204
  Vachris and, 224, 228
Birmingham, Alabama, 160
Bisch, L. E., 232
Bishop, William A., 189, 191, 192,
  200, 204, 207–8, 224
Black Hand. *See* Society of the
  Black Hand
Black Hand (film), 223
Bonanno, Frank, 119, 145
Bonaventura, Pronzola, 154–55

Bonaventure, Max, 89
Bonnoil, Maurice, 45
bootblacks, 5, 6
Borgnine, Ernest, 223
Boston Daily Globe, 85
Bozzuffi, Antonio, 120–32, 128
Bozzuffi, John, 128–32
"bracing" suspects, 121–22
Bresci, Gaetano, 72–73, 74, 95
Brogno, Natale, 19, 20, 22
Brooklyn, New York, 96–97
  Abate in, 132–34
  Adelina's move to, 222–23
  Black Hand crimes and
    criminals in, 34, 47, 50, 52
  fear in, 152
  Francis Corrao as lawyer in, 113
  horse manure in, 8
  Italian immigrants in, 81
  obstacles to fighting Society in,
    162
  Petrosino in, 123
  police officers threatened in,
    59
  Society's public debut in,
    30–31
  Terrio in, 136
  Tony Mannino kidnapping,
    31–33, 35
Brooklyn Bridge, 9, 68, 69
Brooklyn Eagle, 36, 163, 223
Brooklyn Italian Squad, 141–42,
  162, 175, 205–6, 221, 223

Brooklyn Superbas, 145–46
Burke, Susan, 266n106

Calabria (ship), 198
Calabria and Calabrians
  courtship rituals, 107
  earthquake in, 206
  immigrants from, 57, 82, 146,
    176
  Irish and, 10
  "Michele," 230
  monetary value of lives of, 82
California (steamship), 114–15, 116,
  118
Caltanissetta, Sicily, 197
Calvary Cemetery, 216, 220
Camorra, 115, 117, 118, 119, 120–21
Campania and Campanians, 2, 5,
  8–9, 13, 94, 111, 146. *See also*
  Naples and Neapolitans
Campisi (kidnapping suspect), 180
Campisi, Mr. (grocer), 128, 130, 131
Candela, Gioacchino, 190
Candler, Asa G., 87
Capone, Al, 136–37
Cappiello, Nicolo, 30–31
Caputo, Pietro, 135
carabinieri, 118, 188
Carbone, Angelo, 19–22
Carbone Limestone Company, 93
Carhipolo, Detective (on Italian
  Squad), 119
Carlino, Giuseppe, 111

Carnegie, Andrew, 207
Caruso, Angelo, 195
Caruso, Enrico, 98–99, 205, 210
Cascio Ferro, Vito
  after Petrosino's assassination,
    243–44
  Barrel Murder and, 26, 27–28
  in Sicily, 178–82, 195, 196, 197,
    219, 229, 230
Cassidi, Ugo, 45–46
Castellano, Paolo, 55
Catholic Church in Sicily, 182
Catholic Protective Society, 147
Catholic Times, 211
Cavone, Rocco
  Bananno arrest and injury of,
    138–39
  Francesco Longo kidnapping
    and, 237, 238, 239–40
  Petrosino's death and, 202
  Petrosino's recruitment of, 62–63
Cecala (counterfeiter), 230
Ceola, Baldassare, 191–93,
    199–200, 219, 224
Ceramello, Salvatore, 20–22
Chadwick, Father (NYPD
  chaplain), 220
Chance, Frank, 145
Chicago, Illinois
  assassination plans in, 196
  Benteregna in, 90
  Black Hand victims in, 48, 98
  Colosimo and, 135–37

Chicago, Illinois (*cont.*)
  concerned citizens' group in, 143
  fear in, 83
  Italian immigrants in, 3, 81
  Italians depicted on stage in, 42
  Longobardi as "Petrosino" of, 196, 233
  newspapers in, 32 (*See also specific newspaper names*)
  Rockefeller's granddaughter in, 158–59
  Sineni and, 17–18
  White Hand Society in, 146–47, 156
Chicago Cubs, 145
Chicago Outfit, 135–36
Chicago Police Department, 147
Chick Triggers (gang), 234
Children's Aid Society, 213
Christina, Mr. (cobbler), 128, 130, 131
Cianfarra (Petrosino family friend), 185–86
Cincinnati Enquirer, 88
Cincinnati Reds, 146
Cito (counterfeiter), 229
Clearwater, John, 51–52
Cleveland Plain Dealer, 84
Clinton, Illinois, 158
Cohan, George M., 210, 221–22
Collier's, 93
Colombo crime syndicate, 172–73, 179

Colosimo, Big Jim, 135–37
Columbia University, 205, 232, 233
Columbus, Christopher, 111
Columbus Italian Hospital, 111
Comito, Antonio, 176–77, 229–30, 238
Connery, Simon J., 85
Connors, Frances, 25–26
contadini, 9, 11–12, 50
Corrao, Charly, 113
Corrao, Francis, 113, 162, 219
counterfeiting operation, 176–77, 229–30, 238
Cozussi, Giovanni, 153
Crimean War, 106
Crowley, Joseph, 224–26
Cucozza, Angelo, 31–32
Cuocola, Gennaro, 117
Curci, Ernest, 34
Cutinelli, Maria, 117
Cuvillier, Louis, 205
Czolgosz, Leon, 75

Daily Tribune, 156
D'Antonio, John, 196, 233
Dash, Mike, 9
de Felix (Black Hand member), 89
de Giacono, Carmello, 68–69
de Gilda, Benjamin, 88–89
Delaware, 82, 86
de Martini, Felix, 145
Detroit, Michigan, 83, 146, 159
Detroit Free Press, 161

di Fiore, Felippo, 235, 236–37
Dike, Judge, 215
Dimaio, Frank, 148, 171–72
"Di Provenza il mar" (Verdi), xix
Domingo, Fransisco, 1
Dondero, Peter, 45
Dopey Benny's gang, 234
Duca di Genova (steamship), 174, 175, 178, 182–83, 212

Eighteenth Amendment, 277n243
electric chair, 18, 19–20, 21, 22
Ellamore, West Virginia, 157–58
Ellis Island, 9, 19, 81, 113, 114, 148, 172, 192, 196
Enea, Pasquale, 197
Enright, Richard, 220–21
Europa (ship), 202–3
Evening Herald, 162
Evening Sun, 103, 151, 166, 205
Evening World, 23, 31, 46, 63, 119, 133

Fairview, New Jersey, 153
Farraday, William, 13, 210
Fascietta, Mr. (barber), 128, 130
Fazia, Anthony, 50–51
Ferrantelli, Domenico De Michele, 196
Ferrari, Ludovico, 111
Fiandini, Mr. and Mrs. (Black Hand victims), 89–90
Fiaschetti, Michael, 24

Five Families of the American Mafia, 172–73, 179
Flynn, William, 57–58
Fotti, Antonio, 135
freggio, 141, 160
Frugone, Frank, 217–18
fruit peddler story, 69–70
Funston, Sergeant, 69

Gambino, Richard, 6, 206
Garibaldi, Giuseppe, 2
Gaynor, William, 228
Georgia, 160
Giamio (suspect), 123–24
Gimavalvo brothers, 67, 69–70, 77
Gould, Jay, 8–9
government corruption, xiii, 93–95
Graffi, Joseph, 36
Grant, Ulysses S., 212
Greensburg, Pennsylvania, 155–56
Griscom, Lloyd, 184

Hartford Courant, 92
Harvard, 23, 102, 103, 129, 233
Hearst, William Randolph, 37, 41, 69, 167–68, 187, 205, 246
Herod's revenge, story of, 214
Hess, Henner, 115, 179
Highland, New York, 176–77
Hillsville ("Helltown") Pennsylvania, 88, 93–95, 148–49
Hoboken, New Jersey, 206
Horowitz, Adolf, 60

How the Other Half Lives (Riis), 15
Hudson, Henry, 245
Hudson Dusters (gang), 234
hunchback story, 58–59

Illinois, 158–59. *See also* Chicago,
    Illinois
Illinois Central Railroad, 158
Il Pungolo (newspaper), 187
Immigration Act of 1907, 149
Industrial Revolution, 81, 155
Inquisition, 197
Irish gangs, 91
Irish immigrants, 3–4, 5, 14, 38–39,
    245
Italian-American Civic League,
    228
Italian immigrants
   Americanization of, 243
   arrival in United States, 81–83
   backlash against, 205–6
   Black Hand Society and, xiii,
      xv, xviii, 29, 47–48, 52–53,
      146–49
   courage of, 137
   criminals among, 18, 47, 49, 72,
      76, 118, 142, 149, 154–55,
      172–73, 175, 191, 206–7,
      226
   numbers of, 47
   Petrosino's assassination and,
      202–3, 204, 205–6, 245–46
   Petrosino's persecution by,
      10–13

Petrosino's struggle for,
    xvii–xviii, 22–23, 42–43, 112,
    121, 132
prejudice and animosity toward,
    xvi, xvii, xviii, 3–4, 17, 19,
    22, 25, 33, 36–37, 38, 40, 42,
    109, 111, 112–13, 146, 160–61,
    245–46
Sellaro's struggle for, 110–12
Tammany Hall and, 39
White Hand Society, 146–48
Italian Legion, 106
Italian Squad
   Bananno arrest and, 138–40
   Bingham's action against,
      145
   in Brooklyn, 141–42, 162, 175
   Cavone and, 62–63
   Charly Corrao on, 113
   criticism of, 161–62, 163
   disbanding of, 229
   easier cases of, 54–55
   expansion of, 62–63, 96, 105
   formation and establishment,
      44–53
   inadequacy of, 137
   McAdoo and, 38–41, 42, 44–45,
      47, 62, 102
   methods of, 121–26, 241
   NYPD's treatment of,
      63–66
   office changes, 143
   Petrosino's assassination and,
      202, 205–6, 218, 221

Petrosino's mission and, 173
Petrosino's proposal for, 38–41,
    42
at Petrosino's wedding, 151
Society decoding by, 140–42
Society schemes discovered by,
    56–58
Society's evolution in response
    to, 58–62
Waverly Place headquarters, 48,
    50, 53, 64–65
Woods and, 103
See also Petrosino, Joseph
Italian Vigilance Protective
    Association, 149, 157
Italian War of Independence,
    veterans of, 215
Italy
    Alfano's reputation in, 115
    Cascio Ferro's return to,
        27–28
    criminals in, 72, 122, 154–55,
        172–73, 175, 191, 206–7
    lives of immigrants in, 111–12
    Petrosino's assassination and,
        206
    Petrosino's early life in, 1–3
    Petrosino's mission in, 172–73
    police in, 11
    reaction to Black Hand in,
        36–37
    return of immigrants to, 91
    Vincenzo Saulino's military
        service for, 105–6

See also specific city and region
    names

Jotti, John, 94

Kansas City, Missouri, 82,
    233–34
Kelly, Gene, 223
Kelly, Paul, 136
Kenilworth, New Jersey, xv,
    xviii–xix
Kenmare Square, 245
Kenna, Michael "Hinky Dink," 136
Kennedy, John F., 220
Kentucky, 158
Kidnapped in New York (play), 92
Kingsland, New Jersey, 138
Knox, Philander Chase, 218
Ku Klux Klan, 160–61

Labarbera, William and Caterina,
    xii, xiii–xiv, xv, 97
Labarbera, Willie, xi–xv, xv–xvi,
    xviii–xix, 96–97, 98
Laduca, Vito, 52
Lagomarsini, John, 45
LaGumina, Salvatore, 228
La Questione Sociale, 74
Lavelle, Michael J., 151
Lawson Mine explosion, 82
Lebanon, Pennsylvania, 87
Leonardi, Francesco, 184–85, 197
Levi, Carlo, 182
Lincoln, Abraham, 158

Lloyds of London, 159
Lodge, Henry Cabot, xiii
Longo, Francesco (kidnapped
    child), 235–41
Longo, Mr. and Mrs. Francesco,
    235–40
Longobardi, Gabriele, 196, 233
Los Angeles, California, 32, 83,
    90–91, 120, 132
Los Angeles Herald, 45
Los Angeles Times, 90–91, 99–100,
    102
Lovecraft, H. P., xviii
Lupo, Ignazio "the Wolf," 57–58,
    124–25, 177, 229–30, 238

Macaluso, Francesco, 238, 240, 241
Mafia
    Cascio Ferro and, 179, 180, 181,
        229
    Ceola and, 191
    decline of, 244
    fear of, 93
    Five Families, 179
    Italian immigration and, 160
    Italian police and, 180, 182,
        218–19
    in 1950s, 243
    Palermo Mafia, 27–28, 179, 191,
        219–20
    Palizzolo as "King" of, 125
    Petrosino warned about, 173
    prosecutions, 121

Secret Service and, 78
    Sicily's rise against, 206, 244
Malato, Stephen, 146–47
Manhattoes (tribe), 245
Mannino, Antonio, 31–34, 36
Mannino, Vincenzo, 32, 33–34
Manzella, Salvatore, 58
Marasco, Rocco, 209
Marcello, Carlos, 243
Marendino, Tony, 52
Marria, Anthony, 4, 5, 6–7
Marvin, Horace, 86
Marx, Joel M., 76–77, 78
Marzullo, Antonio, 111
Masons, 111
Massachusetts, 147
Massage Squad, 242
Masterson, Bat, 92–93
Mayor des Planches, Baron
    Edmondo, 36, 251n*xiii*
McAdoo, William
    Bingham as replacement for, 99,
        102
    conservatism of, 242
    Italian Squad authorized by,
        44–45, 47, 62
    Italian Squad opposed by, 38–41,
        42
    racism of, 13
McCafferty, James, 210, 213
McClellan, George, Jr.
    accusation from *New Outlook,*
        227

benefit for Adelina and, 222
Bingham and, 99, 204, 221, 225, 228
Petrosino's funeral and, 211
McCormick, Edith, 158–59
McKinley, William, 73, 74–76, 100, 210, 212
Meyers, Harry "Pussy," 45
Mezzogiorno, 2, 3, 6, 9, 12–13
A Midnight Escape (play), 92
Milan and Milanese, 72, 112, 146, 191
Militano, Ernesto, 194–95
Milone, Pasquale, 241
Milone brothers, 238–39
Mississippi, 160–61
Mitchel, John Purroy, 228, 231
Molly Maguires, 91
Monte, Matthew, 243
Montesano, Valentino di, 188
Morelli (Black Hand member), 88–89
Morello, Giuseppe "Clutch Hand" or "Old Fox," 26, 27, 57, 124, 229–30, 238
Moresco, Victoria, 136
Moretti, Pietro, 73–74
Morgan, J. Pierpont, 206
Mori, Cesare, 244
Mule, Pellegrino, 154
Mullin, Paddy, 225

Murtha, Captain, 70
Mussolini, Benito, 244

Naples and Neapolitans
Alfano and, 115, 116–18
Camorra, 115, 117, 118, 119, 120–21
immigrants from, 30, 81, 111, 112, 202–3
language of, 13
Petrosino and, 11
Napoli, Gioacchino, 54–55
Nashville, Tennessee, 168
Nashville American, 37, 160
Native Americans, 245
Neapolitans. *See* Naples and Neapolitans
Nelli, Humbert, 18
New Jersey, 159, 243. *See also specific city names*
New Orleans, Louisiana
Cascio Ferro and, 27, 28
first Black Hand victim near, 1
Italian society in, 147
lynchings in, 36
Mafia in, 243
newspaper cartoons, 3
plots against law enforcement in, 196, 233
New Outlook, 73, 227
New York, 155, 159, 176–77, 205. *See also* New York City; Westchester County, New York

New York American, 205, 246

New York Board of Police
    Commissioners, 16

New York City
  assassination plans in, 196
  Black Hand victims in, 48
  Board of Aldermen, 41, 104, 167,
    168–70, 171, 204–5
  bombings in 1908, 152–55
  Broadway, 9, 42, 210
  Car Barn District, 233
  crime outbreaks in 1907, 142–43
  gang problem in, 233, 234
  gun control measures in, 204–5
  Italian colonies and immigrants
    in, xvi, xviii, 3–4, 41, 47, 58,
    63, 81, 119, 127, 145, 243
  Italian Vigilance Protective
    Association, 149
  Labarberas' neighborhood in,
    xi–xii, xiii–xiv
  Petrosino family's emigration to,
    2, 3, 25
  Petrosino Square in, 244–45
  poverty in, 15–16
  power in, 41
  rapid growth and transformation
    of, 9–10
  Tenderloin (Manhattan red-light
    district), 7, 13, 54
  White Hand Society in, 157
  See also Brooklyn, New York
New York Evening Journal, 37, 41;
    167–68, 171

New York Giants, 145

New York Globe, 206

New York Herald, 203, 234

New York Herald Tribune, 31

New York Journal, 69, 217

New York Mail, 37

New York Police Department
    (NYPD)
  Adelina protected by, 223
  Bingham appointed as
    commissioner of, 99–102,
    104–5
  Bingham fired from, 225
  Bingham's roof tree at, 152
  Bomb Squad, 153–55
  Carbone case and, 20
  Caruso and, 98
  Clubber Williams of, 7–8, 10,
    14, 41
  criticism of, 162–63
  distrust of, 34
  headquarters at 300 Mulberry,
    4, 16, 18, 22, 34, 38, 42,
    46–47, 48, 64, 73, 97, 104,
    105, 151, 152, 166, 203, 221
  indifference to Black Hand
    crime, 37, 71, 157
  McKinley's assassination and,
    75–76
  Petrosino's absence and, 175
  Petrosino's assassination and,
    200, 202, 203, 208, 214, 217,
    220–21
  Petrosino's joining of, 10–14

Petrosino's treatment by, 63–66, 70

police brutality, 123

"Psychopathic Library," 232

secret service of, 166–75, 183, 185

Society indifference to, 168

Sullivans and, 103, 104–5, 171

telegram received by, 200

Theodore Roosevelt's reform of, 16

Vachris and Crowley and, 224, 226–27

Woods as commissioner of, 231–33, 234–35, 237–43

See also Italian Squad

New York Post, 163–64

New York State Supreme Court, 205

New York Sun, xiv, 24, 203–4

New York Times, xiv, xvii–xviii, 13, 33, 36, 41–42, 47, 48–50, 60, 61, 67–68, 70, 71, 78, 79, 83, 93, 104, 121, 124, 130, 132, 137, 159, 167, 170, 204, 215, 219

New York Tribune, 77, 87, 115, 144, 149, 155, 157, 171

New York World, 16, 41, 204, 233

nfami, xiv–xv, 12, 21, 50, 71, 119

night stick cure, 122

Nizzarri, Serrino, 50–51

Nono, Francesco, 194–95

North American Review, 167

Norton, Elliot, 42

NYPD. *See* New York Police Department (NYPD)

O'Brien, John "Ginger Jack," 65–66

Ochs, Adolph, 41

Ohio, 243

Order of the Sons of Italy, 111–12, 176, 215–16

ordine della famiglia, 3, 12

organized resistance, 137

Padua, Italy, 245

Paducah, Kentucky, 120

Paladino, Nunzio, 239

Palazzotto, Domenico, 219–20

Palazzotto, Paolo, 122–23, 194, 219

Palermo, Giuseppe "Uncle Vincent," 176–77, 229–30

Palermo, Sicily

Café Oreto, 191, 194, 197–98

Cascio Ferro in, 179–82

criminals from, 122, 172–73

Lupo and, 57

Palizzolo and, 125

Petrosino in, 185–86, 187–88, 189–90

Petrosino's death and, 207, 209, 219, 220, 246

Piazza Marina in, 197–98, 224, 230, 244

Palermo, Sicily (*cont.*)
    police in, 182, 218–19
    Sellaro and, 109–12
    Taxae cancellariae et
        penitentiarieae romanae, 11
Palermo Mafia, 27–28, 179, 191
Palizzolo, Raffaele, 125–26
Paterson, New Jersey, 72–74, 87,
    148, 171
Patriotic Garibaldi, 216
Pattison, John M., 95
Pay or Die (film), 223
pazienza, 5–6, 70, 114
Peano (minister of the interior,
    Italy), 185
Peconi, Salvatore, 52
Pecoraro, Giovanni, 26–27, 195
Pecorini, Alberto, 47, 48
Pennsylvania, xvii, 83, 89, 147–49,
    158. *See also specific city and*
    town names
Pennypacker, Samuel W., 83, 95
Petrosino, Adelina Bianca
    Giuseppina, 165, 173, 174,
    175, 184, 190, 199
Petrosino, Joseph
    Alfano and, 119–21
    "arrival" of, 65–66
    assassination of, 198–99,
        229–30
    Bingham and, 102, 105, 166,
        168–70, 171–73, 185,
        190–91
    Bomb Squad and, 153–55

Caruso and, 98–99
Cascio Ferro and, 26, 27–28,
    178–79, 182, 243–44
child abductions and, xiv–xvi,
    xviii–xix, 32, 33, 34–35,
    96–97, 98, 163
conspiracy theories about death
    of, 217–18
criticism of, 161–62
danger to, 143–44
daughter of (*see* Petrosino,
    Adelina Bianca Giuseppina)
disguises of, xiv, 16–17, 20–21, 65,
    73–74, 99, 122, 252n*xiv*
early information on Black
    Hand, 29–30
early life and family of, 1–3,
    4–10
eyes of, xiv, 252n*xiv*
fake identities of, 174–75, 189,
    191, 193
as first Italian detective, 16–19
frustration of, 42–43
funeral of, 211–16, 246
gangster disappearances and,
    124–25
insights into Black Hand
    Society, 142
introduction to, xiii–xiv
Italian immigrants and,
    xvii–xviii, 10–13, 22–23,
    42–43, 80–81, 118, 132, 149,
    245–46
Italian police and, 184–85

Italian Squad and (*see* Italian Squad)

legacy of, 244–46

Mannino case and, 32, 33, 34

mission of, xvii–xviii

mourners for, 208–11, 220–21

music and opera loved by, xiv, xix, 24, 165–66, 252n*xiv*, 253n*xix*

niece of, 174

NYPD joined by, 10–14

NYPD's indifference and, 37, 237

NYPD's treatment of, 63–66, 70

organized resistance promoted by, 137

photographic memory of, xiv, 252n*xiv*

press and, 41–42

reputation and legend of, 23–25

secret mission to Italy, 172–73, 174–75, 177, 178–79, 182–88, 219

Secret Service and (*see under* Secret Service, U.S.)

in Sicily, 189–200

Society's warnings against contacting, 110, 130

Theodore Roosevelt and, 16, 18, 201–2

wife of (*see* Saulino, Adelina)

Petrosino, Prospero, 2, 5

Petrosino, Vincent, 5

Petrosino, Vincenzo, 5, 186–87, 188

Pettaco, Arrigo, 40–41, 229

Petto, Tomasso "the Ox," 26

Philadelphia, Pennsylvania, 88, 89, 158

Phillips, David Graham, 167

picciotto, 140

Pinkerton Detective Agency, 87, 148–49, 171–72

Pittsburgh, Pennsylvania, 148

Pittsburgh Post, 160

Pizano, Paulina, 233–34

Pocantico Hills, New York, 159

Poli, Lieutenant (Italian police officer), 192–93

Pozzuoli prison, 244

Profaci, Giuseppe, 172–73

Prohibition, 243, 277n*243*

prostitution rings, 122

Pulitzer, Joseph, 16, 37, 41

Quarnstrom, Oscar, 17–18

racism, 4, 13, 14, 17, 160–61

Raimo, Joseph, 233–34

Rea, Phillip, 148

Redmond, Commissioner, 169

Reeds Station, Kentucky, 158

Regina d'Italia (steamship), 225

Reid, Sidney, 69

Republican League headquarters, 209–10, 212

Riis, Jacob, 15–16

Rockefeller, John D., 158–59,
167–68, 207
Rockland County, New York,
155
Rome, Italy
Alfano and, 118
corruption in, 111–12
government in, 37, 73, 74
leaders in, 191
Petrosino in, 183–84, 185
police in, 47
Trivisonno brought from, 156
Roosevelt, Franklin Delano,
102–3
Roosevelt, Theodore
assassination plans, 193–94
Bingham compared to, 101–2
missing child and, 86
NYPD reform and, 15–16
Petrosino's assassination and,
201–2
Petrosino's reputation and, 18
police brutality and, 123
in White House, xvii, 41, 73, 75,
100
Rotolo, Nicolo, 237, 238
Rucker, George Napoleon "Nap,"
145–46

Sacco, Nicola, 245
San Francisco Call, 161
Santoro, Salvatore, 221
Sartorio, Enrico, 82

Saulino, Adelina
Joseph's death and, 203, 205,
208, 209–10, 211, 212, 213–14,
216, 221–23
Joseph's falling in love with,
106–8
Joseph's marriage to, 150–52
Joseph's trip to Italy and, 173,
174, 175, 178, 184, 190, 192,
199
Saulino, Vincenzo, 105–6, 107, 108,
150
Saulino's (restaurant), 105–8
Schiff, Jacob Henry, 205
Sirocco, Jack (gang of), 234
Scranton, Pennsylvania, 157
Seaman, Arthur and Grace, 155
Searcy, C. D., 168
Sebastian, Saint, 216
secret service (Bingham's),
166–75, 204
Secret Service, U.S.
Bresci investigation, 73
Petrosino's appeal to, 72, 77–79,
85–86, 137
Petrosino's assassination and,
204, 230
Petrosino's history with, 72, 75,
76–77
Petrosino's trip to Italy and,
193
selective protection by, 85–86,
87, 157

suggestion to investigate
Sullivans, 170
Sellaro, Vincenzo, 109–12, 114,
215–16
Seminara, Salvatore, 194–95
sequestrazione, 141
Sherman, William Tecumseh, 212
Sibiria (steamship), 52
Sicily and Sicilians
Alfano and, 115–16
Black Hand recruitment and, 71
Cascio Ferro in, 178–82, 195, 196,
197, 219, 229, 230
Catholic Church in, 182
earthquake in, 206
immigrants from, 36, 57, 82, 146
Irish and, 10
language of, 13, 45
Mafia and, 206, 219–20, 244
monetary value of lives of, 82
murder rate in, 179
Muslims in, 179
northern Italians vs., 115, 146
Operation Husky (World War
II), 244
Palizzolo and, 125
Petrosino disguised as, 17
Petrosino in, 189–200
Petrosino's assassination and,
206
Petrosino's detective work and,
26, 27, 28
police and, 11–12, 40

Sellaro and, 110–11
Sibiria crew, 52
Vachris and Crowley in, 224–25
in White Hand Society, 146
See also Palermo, Sicily
Silva, George, 45
Simonetti, Agent (in Naples),
116–17
Sineni (murderer), 17–18
Sing Sing, 18, 19–20, 22, 233
Siragossa, Antonio, 238–40, 241
Slavonia (steamship), 207–8
smallpox, 2, 21
socialism, 179
Society for the Protection of
Italian Immigrants, 42,
112–13, 204
Society of the Black Hand
Abate and, 132–34
about, xii–xiii
advertising, 121
aldermen and, 170
backlash inspired by, 36–37,
157–64
believed to be myth, xiii, 37,
251n*xiii*
Bingham's appointment and,
102, 105
bombings in 1908, 152–55
Bozzuffi and, 128–32
child abductions, xiii–xv, 31–35,
234, 235–41
Corrao and, 113

Society of the Black Hand (*cont.*)
  courts and, 41
  early members of, 19
  early reports on, 29–30
  evolution of, 58–62
  "Executive Committee," 71
  as fad, 51
  fighting back by citizens, 134–35
  government control by, xiii,
    93–95
  indifference to NYPD, 168
  initiation ceremony, 140
  Italian immigrants and, xiii, xv,
    xviii, 29, 47–48, 83, 146–49
  Italian police and, 218–19
  Italian Squad's battle against (*see*
    Italian Squad)
  lingering of, 243
  locations of, xvi
  mobsters targeted by, 135–37
  in 1915, 233–35
  numbers in New York, 47
  NYPD indifference to, 37, 71, 157
  NYPD secret mission and, 173,
    187
  out in the open, 30–31
  Palizzolo and, 125
  Petrosino's assassination and
    war against, 203–5, 211, 213,
    221, 225–26, 227, 228
  Petrosino's battle against,
    xvii–xviii, 28, 37–38, 40, 41,
    43, 49, 114, 121–22, 124–25,
    127, 152, 155

  in popular culture, 92–93
  schemes of, 56–58
  Secret Service and, 76–79
  Sellaro and, 109–10, 112, 114
  Theodore Roosevelt and,
    193–94
  as terror franchise, 140
  victims of, xvi–xvii, 1, 42–43, 48,
    84–91
  White, Frank Marshall, on, 219
  White Hand Society and,
    146–48
  Woods's approach to, 235,
    237–43
Sons of Italy. *See* Order of the Sons
  of Italy
Speranza, Gino, 112–13, 204
Spinella, Salvatore, 67–68,
    253n*xvi*
Springfield, Massachusetts, 84
Stevenson, Robert Louis, 140
St. Joseph's Italian Society, 157
St. Louis, Missouri, 48, 82, 83, 90,
    132
St. Louis Dispatch, 32
stokers on steamships, 114–15
St. Patrick's Cathedral, 151, 165,
    173, 213, 216
St. Peter's, Rome, 184
Straus, Oscar, 170
Strong Arm Squad, 242
subway tunnel deaths, 112
Sullivan, Big Tim, 103–5, 167, 170,
    225, 245

Sullivan, Little Tim
  Bingham and, 168–69, 170
  NYPD and, 103, 104, 105, 171
  Petrosino's assassination and,
    204, 205
  Tammany Hall and, 103, 104,
    167

Taft, William Howard, 201, 208
Tammany Hall
  Baker and, 226
  Bingham and, 99, 225
  Hearst and, 187
  Italian immigrants and, 10, 39
  judge in Carbone case, 19
  McAdoo and, 39, 99
  Petrosino and, 5
  Society and, 242
  Sullivans and, 103–4, 167
Tassarelli, James, 157
Taxae cancellariae et
    penitentiarieae romanae,
    11
Terrio, John "the Immune,"
    136–37
Times-Union (Jacksonville, FL),
    164
Tisza, István, 87
Tombs (detention center), 51,
    122
Tomoso, Nicolo, 35
Train, Arthur, 22, 252n*xiv*,
    253n2
Trivisonno, Godfrey, 156

troppa bircca, 141
Truglio, Frank, 215
Trunk Murder, 210, 257n30

Umberto I, King, 72, 74, 95,
    191
United Bootblack Protective
    League, 215
United States government
  House of Representatives,
    84
  Petrosino's request for help
    from, 72, 77–79
  See also McKinley, William;
    Roosevelt, Theodore; Taft,
    William Howard
uomo di rispetto, 115–16, 181
U.S. Steel Corporation, 148

Vachris, Anthony, 96, 162, 173, 175,
    223–28
Valentino, Rudolph, 212
Valpetroso, Baroness Clorinda
    Peritelli di, 180
Vanzetti, Bartolomeo, 245
Vazanini, Giuseppe, 83
Verdi, Giuseppe, xix, 214–15
Vetere, Giacento, 209
Victor Emmanuel III, King,
    xvii, 37, 117–18, 206–7,
    222–23
Vigilance League, 42, 137
Virginia, 160
Volini, Carlo, 156

Volpe (police informant in
  Palermo), 194–95

Walston, Pennsylvania, 83
War of Italian Unification (1859),
  106
Washington Post, 37, 54, 60–61, 62,
  64, 73, 85, 91, 142–43, 204,
  206–7, 218–19, 242
Washington Square Association,
  170–71
Washington Times, 36
watch of death, 141
Weisbard, Meyer, 210
Wellsville, Ohio, 243
Wenzler, Ignace, 87
Wesson, Daniel B., 85–86
Westchester County, New York,
  60–61, 83, 89, 134–35, 140,
  159
West Virginia, 81, 113, 147, 156,
  157–58, 159
White, Frank Marshall, 41, 47–48,
  76, 219, 234, 241

White Hand Society, 146–48,
  156–57, 161
white wingers, 7, 8
Williams, Aleck "Clubber," 7–8,
  10, 14, 41, 123, 174
Woods, Arthur
  Italian Squad and, 103
  Mule and, 154
  as NYPD commissioner,
    231–33, 234–35, 237–43
  Petrosino's assassination and,
    218
  Petrosino's letter to Bingham
    and, 185
  Petrosino's wedding and,
    151
  Progressive movement and,
    102–3
  Vachris and, 227
World War I, 233, 245
World War II, 244

Zarcone brothers, 237
Zarillo, Donato, 140